Praise for *No One Sees God*

"Michael Novak boldly—yet winsomely—invites believers and the radical atheists of our day to sit down at table for an honest dialogue, one that will, no doubt, challenge the atheists' blind faith in No-God; and one that will compel believers to re-examine their unexamined views of the Almighty. While some of Novak's views (about the Fall of man, for example) differ from my own and even from those held by many evangelicals and Catholics, Novak's book will inspire a lively debate from which we will all profit."

—Chuck Colson, founder of Prison Fellowship

" 'Why is human weakness slow to believe that men will one day live with God?' once asked St. Augustine. Why *is* this? In this deeply personal book, Michael Novak ponders this question, sustaining throughout a sympathetic dialogue with the so-called "new atheism" of Dawkins, Dennett, Harris, and Hitchens. Along the way, Novak advances many reasons to believe, with Augustine, that in the end our darkness yields only to the blazing light of the promise of divine friendship: 'Our hearts are restless until they rest in Thee.' "

—J. Augustine Di Noia, O.P., undersecretary of the
Congregation for the Doctrine of the Faith

"To rebut the flood of atheist propaganda pouring out of major publishing houses, Michael Novak has crafted a response that is at once a masterpiece of theological reasoning and a declaration of faith."

—Robert D. Novak, syndicated columnist of the *Chicago Sun-Times*

"Michael Novak's new book counts as both significant and moving. He deploys logic and love, emotion and erudition, to address the most enduring questions of our existence."

—Michael Medved, nationally syndicated talk-radio host,
and author of *Right Turns*

"Why should you read Michael Novak? Let me illustrate with a personal example. Novak is a devout and faithful Catholic—and reading one of his earlier books helped put me on the path to embracing Protestant Christianity. This is the sort of thing that happens when you read a writer of Novak's brilliance and intellectual honesty—you find yourself asking better questions, and you end up in unexpected places. His new book is especially helpful, coming as it does in a time when shallow triumphalisms dominate religious discourse—in the puerile vilifications of religion by the 'new atheists' as well as the tired, chest-thumping apologetics of too many who write in the name of Christianity. *No One Sees God* is the work of a man of faith and a genuine humanist, who calls us all to discuss these ultimate questions in a manner truly worthy of our nature as human persons."

—Michael Potemra, literary editor of *National Review*

"One does not have to agree with Michael Novak to find this book well worth reading. In his critique of atheism, he rightly says that no one has enough proof that there is no God. But isn't the same true of those who believe that there *is* a God? That goes a long way toward explaining why I am an agnostic. Moreover, Novak would agree that ethical behavior—living by the Golden Rule—doesn't depend on a belief in God. But I nonetheless found the force and eloquence of his argument a most helpful test for my own beliefs."

—Larry Harrison, author of *The Central Liberal Truth*

"Michael Novak, a firm theist, takes on a formidable host of clever atheists in one absorbing encounter after another. Novak holds his ground throughout without a trace of contentiousness—and with a depth of learning that should move believers, doubters, and unbelievers alike. The arguments are fascinating. The company is delightful. I have never seen the subject treated with such sympathy, urbanity, and generosity of spirit."

—Christina Hoff Sommers, resident scholar of the American Enterprise Institute

"*No One Sees God* is a lightning flash of illumination about our post-secular age—proving, as everything that Michael Novak writes does, that faith and reason can work together. Engaging on the highest level (and with intellectual charity) with today's 'new atheist' writers, and showing what they've missed or misunderstood about religion, Novak has written a book for the ages that anyone interested in the big questions, believer or unbeliever, will profit from."

—Brian C. Anderson, editor of *City Journal*

"With learning and humor, Michael Novak calls for respectful dialogue between believers and skeptics. This book could not have come at a better time."

—Glen Harlan Reynolds, professor of law at the University of Tennessee, creator of *Instapundit.com*

"Some have tried to defeat the new atheists with an equally dogmatic new fundamentalism. There is neither truth nor kindness in this approach. Finally, Michael Novak has written from his mind and his heart a rejoinder to the materialists among us. He succeeds where others have failed by honestly appreciating their critique of simple-minded faith, while also clearly demonstrating their insufficient response to the mystery of God. Only Michael Novak could have written this book because of the scope of his intellect, the depth of his faith, and his deep humility that is his greatest gift to us all."

—Rabbi Marc Gellman, syndicated columnist and host of "The God Squad"

"Even those of us who believe and trust in God know the difficulties and questions through which the Lord takes us. In *No One Sees God*, Michael Novak expresses the thoughts of both believers and atheists in a nonjudgmental and most helpful manner."

—Joanne Kemp, board member of Prison Fellowship Ministries

"*No One Sees God*, the latest contribution of Michael Novak to secular theology, is, as are all his previous works, a very persuasive book. All believers in freedom, whether Catholics or nonbelievers, have an enormous debt of gratitude to Michael. He has shed light on very important and complex issues and has done so from the perspective of those who consider liberty as the fundamental organizing principle of an open society."

—Antonio Martino, former Italian Minister of Defense

No One Sees God

MICHAEL NOVAK

No One Sees God

THE DARK NIGHT OF ATHEISTS AND BELIEVERS

DOUBLEDAY

NEW YORK LONDON TORONTO

SYDNEY AUCKLAND

CD
DOUBLEDAY

Published in the United States by Doubleday, an imprint
of The Doubleday Publishing Group, a division
of Random House, Inc., New York.
www.doubleday.com

DOUBLEDAY is a registered trademark and the DD colophon is
a trademark of Random House, Inc.

LIBRARY OF CONGRESS CATALOGING-IN-PUBLICATION DATA
Novak, Michael.
No one sees God / by Michael Novak.
p.   cm.
Includes bibliographical references and index.
1. Christianity and atheism. 2. Apologetics. I. Title.
BT1212.N68 2008
261.2'1—dc22
2007050554

ISBN 978-0-385-52610-4

PRINTED IN THE UNITED STATES OF AMERICA

5 7 9 10 8 6 4

DEDICATED TO

ELIZABETH LURIE AND W. H. BRADY

AND

JOSEPH AND BRENDA CALIHAN

WITH GRATITUDE

WORDS BY FATHER RICHARD (1962)

I AM NO LAZY LOVER

I am no lazy lover
With sweeping grandeurs
of small talk. Words, you discover,
are passing; love endures.

Proffered is no measured length
of the potential soul.
Rather, influence of strength,
corner-stone, cemented whole.

The senses know the form
and smile and eyes
of love, but the lover's norm
is to pierce through this disguise

to spirit which in all things
does love intensify
to ripened being. Each day that sings
our love is more July.

Sand below and stars above
give instancy of me.
Mine is no lazy love;
come taste my love and see.

No One Sees God

Believer and nonbeliever are both voyagers. In the
darkness in which the secret courses of human lives lie
hidden, men are sometimes closer together, sometimes
farther apart, than appearances indicate. For this rea-
son, many men look searchingly into the eyes of others,
seeking a brother, a sister, who could be anywhere.
Among us thrives a brotherhood of inquiry and con-
cern, even of those who disagree in interpreting the
meaning of inquiry—the meaning of human spirit—
in the darkness in which we live.

—Belief and Unbelief, 1965

Contents

PART FOUR | The New Conversation

No One Sees God

I was born in the year that Adolf Hitler was elected chancellor of Germany, 1933. When I was eleven I saw the weekly horrors in the news clips at the movies, when the barbed fences at concentration camps were being breached by Allied columns. Gaunt, emaciated figures in torn and dirty striped uniforms. Captured film of dead bodies heaped in stacks and pitched into trucks like sacks of sand. Young as I was, I worried that we all might yet be lumped among them.

For me, no view of life that does not account for the horrors of World War II, especially of those heaps of dead bodies, can ever be trusted. My father told me to educate myself on Nazism and Communism, and he encouraged my habit of clipping stories from papers and magazines.

It was crystal clear to me even at age twelve that life is far more horrible than anybody had heretofore suggested. Unbelief, atheism, and cursing the darkness might for me and for all turn out to be the more honest way.

I feel today no less the voyager, no less aware that however firm my duly considered judgments, I may be mistaken, while those who roar with laughter at the things I hold to be true may in the end prove to be correct.

All others are in the same predicament. We are all in the same darkness. It is not so hard, of course, to evade the rain on the windowpanes, the tapping of the night on the doors and shutters, the darkness, the mist, and the fear. Not so hard to hide from it in the protected circles lit by comforting scientific reason.

I have met people who, when you ask them how they account for the unexplainedness of life, the puzzle of it, the pain of it, smile and say: "When someone raises questions like that, I turn away, sit down, and enjoy a good lunch." Afterward, they think of it no more.

Some people live in a protected circle of light. I notice this especially about two classes of people: first, the unquestioning Christian minds, full of light and sweetness, never doubting a doctrine, seeing in the cross and resurrection of Jesus Christ the answer to all things. Second, the more scientifically minded, the people of reason, the pragmatists who see no reason to wonder about where it all came from, or where it is going, or how mad it may be. Serenely, both classes race through life—each at times fearing the other.

Yet maybe individual persons in both groups, in their lonely darkness, sometimes feel the emptiness, look in the desperate shadows for the key to the dark gate, have nightmares about seeking, seeking, seeking, and never finding . . .

When I was in graduate school, one of my favorite filmmakers was Ingmar Bergman, especially for his films of seeking: *The Seventh Seal* and *Wild Strawberries*.

I sat in dark theaters wrapped in inner resonance during *Waiting for Godot* and *Who's Afraid of Virginia Woolf?* and Eugène Ionesco's *Rhinoceros*.

The one contemporary whose life I most carefully tracked, from the beginning to at least *The Fall*, was Albert Camus. "A single sentence will suffice for modern man," he wrote in 1956: "They fornicated, and they read the papers." Well, that's a way to avoid the nothingness.

Camus articulated more clearly than anybody the challenge of being on earth during a time when more than a hundred million breathing persons, in Europe alone, had their lives violently torn from them, at a time they did not choose, and in a manner they did not foresee. He, too, saw the stacks of human bodies. And foresaw that the bodies might yet keep being stacked up, on out as far as the eye could see, generation after generation.

In fact, bodies would continue to be slung around if from the nothingness in which we then found ourselves, we did not find a way out. Did not discover a way to make something *honest*, drenched by the real suffering of our time, yet truly, humanly creative. We needed to find an honest way to imagine a new civilization, worthy of human beings, right here on the ruins of the old. Such an effort *must* begin in the nothingness left by the ruins of the old, Camus wrote. It must take nihilism as its starting point.

But how to escape from nihilism, once we are in it? It is like the darkness of descending quicksand, down and down, and down again. Nothing solid from which a foot might thrust up.

I do not mean to repeat in this book the arduous climbing over ruins and stones, the blinded exploring of the night, that I undertook in my youth, particularly in my early books *Belief and Unbelief* and *The Experience of Nothingness*. Any who care may open those little books on their own and walk along in the darkness with me to see where and how their own voyage has parted company from mine. These were books of my youth, recounting steps of my youth. I cannot disown them now—in a way, I love them, full of fault as they may be. By those steps I came toward where I am today. But I do not intend to re-walk them here.

This book is for people who, like me, have spent long years in the dark and windswept open spaces between unbelief and belief. It is about a fairly common voyage through the dark, not only in our age, but in every age.

That is why this particular book must of necessity roll in upon the reader in three separate murmurings, in the long, low roar of incoming tides. The tides come in and out, the contours of the sand shift, the moonlit sea glimmers in the dark forever.

First, I must at least briefly describe the darkness, the emptiness that I have found at the heart of my own mind, the infinite and unquenchable desire to raise questions, the restless, ever-unsatisfied, devouring *eros,* the burning drive of inquiry.

Next, in reviewing writings of certain of my favorite contemporary atheists, I must try to explain what reason has led me to discover about the presence of God and His nature (darkly, by the *via negativa*, by way of what He *cannot* be). This part of my voyage may help others to understand why I have found unpersuasive, much as I respect them, the argumentative byways happily taken by my atheist friends. I must allow that they may prove to be correct. But I do not judge that the evidence is on their side. On the contrary, I have found that they misconstrue a great many things about themselves.

Gathering force over many years, one discovery has hit me with the force of a law: *If you make mistakes about your own nature, you will make as many mistakes about God, and quite properly then, reject what your inquiries put before you.* The god you fantasize will appear to you not very great, a delusion, a snare from which others ought to be freed. You will despise this god.

Or, at least, some of you will. I have met a few others who cannot invest even that much passion in God. They are rather indifferent about the "God thing." These are, especially, the people who put higher value on a good lunch than on inquiring after God. They certainly are not standing among the passionate atheists, no more than with the proselytizing believers. They look down upon enthusiasm.

So we must inquire awhile about God, within the bounds of our intellect alone, before looking behind the veils that Judaism and then Christianity pull back before our straining eyes.

This looking behind the veils of reason is what many in North America and in Western Europe today passionately resist. They do not so much despise "God" as they despise the *Jewish* and *Christian* God. (Not for the reason Nietzsche did—because Judaism and Christianity are "slave religions," Judaism first and in its wake Christianity—but on the contrary, because these faiths assign to humans too much liberty, and judge them too exactly for their use of it.) Passionate secularists heap ridicule on the Bible. They tear to shreds Christian doctrine—the whole garment—or with some effort rip out the seams that hold its parts together.

Thus, I will need to show how out in the dark, and without

ever wholly coming in from the dark, I have come to understand that what the Jewish Testament and the Christian Testament teach us about God, about human beings, and about ourselves is a truer account of reality than any other I have encountered.

Much as my atheist friends will loathe it and mock it, I have tested this judgment in living and found it to ring true. It better meets the facts of my own reality, and the urgent inquiries of my own mind, and better turns aside thrusts intended to wound it and to destroy it, than any other account I have discovered. My reasoned judgment on this matter cannot really be discounted as "merely subjective," for it is shared under great stress by hundreds of millions of others. About one of every three human beings on this planet is Christian, over two billion in all. And in no age has the persecution of Christians reached such horrific numbers with so much cruelty. The even more barbaric assault upon our Jewish "older brothers," no matter what they believe, awakens amazement and full contempt.

My underlying thesis is a simple one: that unbelievers and believers need to learn a new habit of reasoned and mutually respectful conversation.

The conversation among Western atheists and Christian/Jewish believers is particularly important. An excellent model was offered in January 2004 between one of Europe's most prominent public philosophers, Jürgen Habermas, and the Vatican's Joseph Cardinal Ratzinger, prefect at the time of the Congregation for the Doctrine of the Faith. They discussed moral relativism, Islam, and the problematic but fruitful tension between atheism and Jewish/Christian belief. In chapter ten, I try to extend and deepen their argument. Before coming to that, however, I want to listen to and engage with some of the vocal atheists for whom I have admiration.

These conversations lead me to questions about the Absurd. The shocking events of September 11, 2001, moreover, emboldened a number of atheists to lump all religious people with those hatred-spreading fascists who claimed they exploded themselves in the Twin Towers out of fidelity to Islam. Face-to-face with "radical" Islam (more exactly, a faction enflamed with political lust), many atheists insist that the only solution for the world is to become "secularist" like them—and to precipitate as speedy an end to religion as possible. "Secular" is a good term, an invention of Catholic thinkers, initially a positive term. But that term does not mean the same as "secularist." To make such distinctions clear is the task of chapter nine.

During the nights of comparing notes on this voyage, I do not expect all to agree. At different points, some will part company with me, and I from them. The world today nourishes six billion personal stories.

Still, I will be surprised if there are not some glimpses of mutual recognition. We are not so different from one another that we have nothing to learn from every human we chance upon.

Michael Novak
Lewes, Delaware
August 22, 2007

The Darkling Plain

Ah, love, let us be true
To one another! for the world, which seems
To lie before us like a land of dreams,
So various, so beautiful, so new,
Hath really neither joy, nor love, nor light,
Nor certitude, nor peace, nor help for pain;
And we are here as on a darkling plain . . .

—Matthew Arnold, "Dover Beach"

Just as I was writing this book, Christians and non-Christians alike wrote to question me about the meaning of Mother Teresa's forty-five years of inner emptiness, feeling "neither joy, nor love, nor light . . . and on a darkling plain." The experience of this darkness is common to all, believer and unbeliever. The fact that Mother Teresa experienced it surprised many people, friend and foe. It should not have. But it did.

In a way that has startled many readers today, Mother Teresa revealed her own darkness in confidential letters written to her spiritual directors during the long time that she suffered from it. Since these letters necessarily became part of the inquiry required for the process of canonization, and since this process would become public fairly soon, an editor was charged with putting them together in a book for the general public. The point of picking out an outstanding Christian in a public way as a "saint" is to shed light on one unique way in which the gospel of Jesus Christ was realized in history. We learn a great deal from the lives of others. There is a "community of spirit," which is also a community of those who have experienced the common darkness.

Many of my correspondents had not recognized Mother Teresa's inability to sense the presence of God, and the inner agony in which this left her. All they had seen was her amazing smile, as if she felt God's love in her heart (when in fact her heart felt empty) during long days and nights when she brought tenderness to abandoned persons dying in the streets of Calcutta. If she couldn't find God, why did she go on believing in Him? Why did she go on bringing tender care to the abandoned, when she herself felt so abandoned?

Some atheists, such as my friend Christopher Hitchens, now gloat that Mother Teresa was just an unbeliever like the rest of "us." But few atheists—and, alas, not many believers—understand the depths of the interior life of Jewish and Christian faith. They don't understand that it is a never-ending struggle. In the Talmud, Moses points to the vision God has shown him of the great Rabbi Akiba viciously tortured to death by the Romans. Moses says to God, "Master of the Universe": "This is Torah and *this* is the reward?" And God can only say, "Quiet! This too has occurred to me." Biblical faith demands putting childhood behind, and adolescence, and the busy-ness of young adulthood. It requires an appetite for bravery for going into unknown territories alone to wrestle against inner demons, and a willingness to experience darkness, if darkness comes. Faith is not for those who seek only man-made pleasures.

I had one tiny reason for feeling especially close to Mother Teresa from the first time I heard of her. My younger brother Richard was also a missionary to Bengali speakers, as Mother Teresa was. But Richard did his work across the ocean from Calcutta, in Dhaka, then part of east Pakistan. Two years after he arrived there, as he was setting out by bicycle on a mission of mercy during the cruel Hindu-Muslim riots of January 1964, Dick was knifed to death by a group of young men who seized his bicycle and his wristwatch. He was twenty-seven years old. They threw his body into a river already thick with corpses.

Dick's favorite saint was Saint Thérèse of Lisieux (1873–1897), a frail Carmelite nun, the most beloved of all Catholic saints second only to Saint Francis of Assisi. (I have only once in years of traveling around the world found a Catholic church without some depiction of her.) Saint Thérèse lived for most of her adult life in utter darkness and dryness and abandonment by her divine Lover. She wrote an autobiography about her experience, and how it led her to interpret the inner heart of Christianity. So powerfully and clearly did she write that Pope John Paul II inscribed her name among the historic handful of "Doctors of the Church"—teachers so profound and so sweeping in their wisdom that they instruct the whole Catholic people.

The canonization of Saint Thérèse in 1925 was at that time one of the swiftest on record. Miracles attributed to her care and her attention to the needy—which she promised she would "shower down" from heaven—were too many to count. As early as the war of 1914, Thérèse was the favorite saint of French soldiers in the trenches, held by them coequal with Saint Jeanne d'Arc. And so she remains today, this twenty-four-year-old victim of consumption, who after the age of fifteen never set foot outside her cloistered contemplative convent—with Jeanne d'Arc copatroness of France.

The kernel of Saint Thérèse's teaching is often called "the little way," meaning that no Christian is too humble or too insignificant to follow it and no thought or action too negligible to infuse with love. In other words, God cherishes not only great actions of love, but also minor, childlike ones. No matter what spiritual darkness you find yourself in, choose as your North Star a tender love of the persons that life's contingencies have put next to you. Do not go looking around for more fascinating neighbors to love. Love those right nearest you.

You cannot see God, even if you try. But you can see your neighbor, the tedious one, who grinds on you: Love him, love her. As Jesus loves them. Give them the tender smile of Jesus, even though your own feelings be like the bottom of a birdcage. Do not ask to see Jesus, or to feel Him. That is for children. Love him in the dark. Love for the invisible divine, not for warm and comforting human consolation. Love for the sake of love, not in order to feel loved in return.

It happens that Agnes Bojaxhiu of Albania eventually became a missionary nun in Ireland, and chose for her religious name Therese, in the footsteps of her patron saint of darkness from Lisieux. In Spanish, the same name is Teresa, and Saint Teresa of Avila (1515–1582) was also an experienced traveler in inner darkness. She came to be a Doctor of the Church, builder of scores of convents of Carmelite nuns all over Europe—administrator and guide extraordinaire, and a canny operator in bureaucracies, running rings around most of the male hierarchy of her time. Saint Thérèse of Lisieux took the name Teresa in her honor, and followed her teaching as inscribed in Teresa's books and in the traditions of the Carmelites. (Pope John Paul II was a close follower of the Carmelites.)

For those who love God, that way is excruciating. They would like to feel close to God, but they find—nothing! Like Saint John of the Cross (1542–1591), the Carmelite priest who was her spiritual guide, Teresa gradually came to see that if God were a human invention, a human contrivance, then warm human feelings would be quite enough. But God is far greater than that. He is beyond any human frequency. He is outside our range, divine. One must follow Him without any human prop whatever, even warm and comfortable inner feelings. That may be why Jesus loved the desert as a place for prayer.

The Jewish scholar David Gelernter has written:

This exactly (or very nearly) underlies Judaism's ubiquitous image of the veil, & God beyond or behind it. In its simplest form this veil is embodied in the *tallit* or prayer-shawl men wear at morning prayer. A more substantial instance: in the First Temple destroyed by Babylonians, worship centered on the Holy of Holies, which contained the ark of the covenant. In the Second Temple destroyed by Rome, worship centered on the Holy of Holies—which was an absolutely empty space. After that—today—the holiest site in Judaism is a blank wall (the Western Wall) with nothing behind or beyond it. This sequence is no accident. It's part of the Jewish people's coming of age and being weaned from what you properly call the child's view to the adult's understanding of God.

That is to say, our senses cannot touch God. Neither sight nor sound, scent nor taste, nor touch, either. Our imagination cannot encompass Him, nor even bring Him into focus. How can we count on our memory? Our minds can form no adequate conception of Him; anything the mind imagines is easily ridiculed. The God who made us and out of His infinite love redeemed us and called us to His bosom is divine, not human. As such, He cannot be found using human perceptual equipment.

This is not a new idea. Serious and devout believers from the time of Elijah and Job have known about the darkness in which the true God necessarily dwells. In order for one's soul to be ready to go far beyond any human contrivance, one must be willing to go out into the desert and the night. Thus we read of the prophet Elijah:

And he came thither unto a cave, and lodged there; and, behold, the word of the LORD came to him, and he said unto him:

"What doest thou here, Elijah? Go forth, and stand upon the mount before the LORD." And, behold, the LORD passed by, and a great and strong wind rent the mountains, and

brake in pieces the rocks before the LORD; but the LORD
was not in the wind: and after the wind an earthquake; but
the LORD was not in the earthquake:

And after the earthquake a fire; but the LORD was not in the
fire: and after the fire a still small voice.

And it was so, when Elijah heard it, that he wrapped his
face in his mantle, and went out, and stood in the entering
in the cave. And, behold, there came a voice unto him, and
said, What doest thou here, Elijah? (1 KINGS 19:9–13, KJV)

Thus, also, Job, after he had been stricken with painful boils all
over his body, and sat outside where others might mock him,
scraping off the scabs, and unable, now, to find the Lord in whom
he had placed such utter trust:

But if I go to the east, he is not there; or to the west, I cannot perceive him; Where the north enfolds him, I behold
him not; by the south he is veiled, and I see him not. Yet
he knows my way; if he proved me, I should come forth as
gold. My foot has always walked in his steps; his way I have
kept and have not turned aside. From the commands of his
lips I have not departed; the words of his mouth I have
treasured in my heart . . . Therefore am I dismayed before
him; when I take thought, I fear him. Indeed God has made
my courage fail; the Almighty has put me in dismay. Yes,
would that I had vanished in darkness, and that thick gloom
were before me to conceal me. (JOB 23:8–12, 15–17, NAB)

The teachings of Elijah and Job were not so different from
those of the teacher of Saint Teresa, Saint John of the Cross, the
other great Spaniard who founded the male order of Carmelites,
expert practitioners of the way to God in the darkness.

In more than one book, but especially in *Dark Night of the Soul,*

Saint John of the Cross proceeded lesson by patient lesson to mark
out for the novice at prayer the terrors yet to be faced in the
desert, while human expectations were shed for those seeking to
receive the divine. He vividly described the aridity and emptiness
that the lover of God ought to expect, as he traded a child's faith
for that of an adult, as he was weaned away from the sweet milk
of infancy and obliged to live on hard, dry bread for long stretches
of time. And what the North Stars are. And the dangers to watch
for. And the characteristic temptations of every stage of the journey.

Beginners prone to "spiritual gluttony," St. John writes,

> are, in fact, like children, who are not influenced by reason,
> and who act, not from rational motives, but from inclina-
> tion. Such persons expend all their effort in seeking spiritual
> pleasure and consolation; they never tire, therefore, of read-
> ing books; and they begin, now one meditation, now an-
> other, in their pursuit of this pleasure which they desire
> to experience in the things of God. But God, very justly,
> wisely, and lovingly, denies it to them, for otherwise this
> spiritual gluttony and inordinate appetite would breed innu-
> merable evils. It is, therefore, very fitting that they should
> enter into the dark night, whereof we shall speak, that they
> may be purged from this childishness. (CHAPTER 5)

> There is thus a great difference between aridity and luke-
> warmness, for lukewarmness consists in great weakness and
> remissness in the will and in the spirit, without solicitude
> as to serving God; whereas purgative aridity is ordinarily
> accompanied by solicitude, with care and grief as I say,
> because the soul is not serving God. (CHAPTER 9)

Dark Night of the Soul is not an easy book to read. For one
thing, it relies heavily upon the experience of the reader. It is intended to show the voyager of the spirit the ways through the
night and the desert. How can anyone who has not known the

night and desert recognize the symptoms and the signs? This is not a book for reading, but for experiencing.

Perhaps its main point may be expressed thus: Go, seek with love your Beloved, follow wherever He leads. Yet even when you come up to Him you must anticipate that there will be no one to be seen. Your faculties are simply inadequate. Were you actually to see, you would be destroyed. It is too much. Your bulbs would short out. Be prepared, therefore, to walk in darkness. Not at all in doubt; on the contrary, for the first time ever, aware that you are not now following illusions, but only the true darkling light of the true God, beyond human range. Anything else is human contrivance and illusion.

Saint John of the Cross imagines his soul as the bride, the spouse, eagerly seeking her Beloved for just one sight of Him. This is his great classic song to the *Dark Night of the Soul,* in eight brief stanzas, of which the following four are the most telling.

1. On a dark night, Kindled in love with yearnings—oh, happy chance!—
I went forth without being observed, My house being now at rest.

2. In darkness and secure, By the secret ladder, disguised—oh, happy chance!—
In darkness and in concealment, My house being now at rest.

3. In the happy night, In secret, when none saw me,
Nor I beheld aught, Without light or guide, save that which burned in my heart.

4. This light guided me More surely than the light of noonday
To the place where he (well I knew who!) was awaiting me—A place where none appeared.

It would be easy here to multiply texts from Saint Teresa of Avila, the distant mother and guide of her young follower of three centuries later, Saint Thérèse of Lisieux, meditating on this dryness, even as she, too, was surprised at how acute was its pain. Instead, let us take up only a few samples:

The memoirs of Saint Teresa of Avila recount years of spiritual aridity and torment:

> I may say that it was the most painful life that can be imagined, because I had no sweetness in God, and no pleasure in the world.

> I believe that it is our Lord's good pleasure frequently in the beginning, and at times in the end, to send these torments, and many other incidental temptations, to try those who love Him, and to ascertain if they will drink the chalice, and help Him to carry the Cross, before He entrusts them with His great treasures. I believe it to be for our good that His Majesty should lead us by this way, so that we may perfectly understand how worthless we are . . .

> It is certain that the love of God does not consist in tears, nor in this sweetness and tenderness which we for the most part desire, and with which we console ourselves; but rather in serving Him in justice, fortitude, and humility. That seems to me to be a receiving rather than a giving of anything on our part.

Recently, a Jewish friend wrote me as follows:

> Yom Kippur was a few weeks ago; the day-long prayers end in the *N'eilah* service, in which the fasting congregation, which stands throughout this hour-and-a-half-long concluding ritual, repeats in Hebrew with increasing fervor, or desperation, the verses spoken to Moses—"The Lord, the Lord God merciful and gracious, long-suffering and full of goodness and truth"—and it all concludes with the mournful

blast of the shofar. But it sometimes happens, as it did this year at my synagogue, that after all this, the exhausted congregation breaks out spontaneously in what you'd call a joyous song, and dances together round the Torah-table at the center. Jews know the dark and accept the dark, but are obligated nonetheless to rejoice. I wonder whether this might not be a fundamental distinction between Jewish & Christian worldviews.

Yet Saint John of the Cross, Saint Teresa, and Saint Thérèse all break out in joy in an analogous way. Dante saw the Christian story as a happy one (*commedia*), not a tragic or crestfallen one—as Easter follows Good Friday.

For example, of her own spiritual aridity, Saint Thérèse of Lisieux wrote:

> But during the Paschal days, so full of light, our Lord . . . allowed my soul to be overwhelmed with darkness, and the thought of Heaven, which had consoled me from my earliest childhood now became a subject of conflict and torture. This trial did not last merely for days or weeks—I have been suffering for months, and I still await deliverance . . . I wish I could express what I feel, but it is beyond me. One must have passed through this dark tunnel to understand its blackness.
>
> Sometimes, I confess, a little ray of sunshine illumines my dark night, and I enjoy peace for an instant, but later, remembrance of this ray of light, instead of consoling me, makes the blackness thicker still . . . And yet never have I felt so deeply how sweet and merciful is the Lord.

This is the context in which *Come Be My Light* by Mother Teresa of Calcutta must be grasped. Teresa of Avila and Thérèse of Lisieux are her two "mothers" in spiritual growth and authentic

Christian faith, in the light of the passion and death of Jesus Christ. The forty-five years of emptiness, darkness, and inner pain experienced by Mother Teresa, and honestly set forth in her private letters to her spiritual director, follow in a long tradition. They are not really signs of doubt, although the black darkness feels like that. They are in fact signs of Christian adulthood, following in the only way in which illusions of human contrivance can be scraped away, as Job tried to scrape away the dry boils on his arms and ribs. And in which the truly faithful, like Job and Elijah, can find Him whom they love in the darkness. "Then his wife said to him, 'Are you still holding to your innocence? Curse God and die.' But he said to her, 'Are even you going to speak as senseless women do? We accept good things from God; and should we not accept evil?' Through all this, Job said nothing sinful" (Job 2:9–10, NAB).

It is from "human fabrication" that the darkness and the desert free us. When God subtracts His gifts, as He subtracted Job's, Job does not take this withdrawal as punishment. Job knows his innocence, he knows his fidelity, even in the darkness and in utter suffering. He utters not one denial of his Lord. His soul stands firm beneath the pain.

So also Mother Teresa of Calcutta stood darkly in the presence of her Beloved, confident that even unseen, He was best found where love for her nearest dying neighbor presented Him.

To the place where he (well she knew who!) was awaiting her—A place where none appeared.

Turning Now to More Secular Lessons

In the glory days of ancient paganism, even while others may have believed their nation's gods hovered close, watchfully and efficaciously, many learned men did not believe in those multiple gods. In the most robust eras of Judaism and Christianity, similarly, there were always those who mocked the faith around them. In the so-imagined "Age of Faith" of the Middle Ages, a great many did not believe, and many others believed only weakly. Cynics have abounded in every age, in the dialogues of Plato, in biblical narratives, in all times.

In our time, many scholars have held that for some generations now, day by day, the world is becoming less religious. One day, they hold, the secular conscience will prevail, and the religions of the past will slip away, like pink sand from an almost empty hourglass. That will be a happy day, their theory has predicted.

Almost as long ago as I can remember, the atheist position seemed to me credible, attractive, real. I was born into a strongly Catholic family, a family also built upon the Harvard Classics, the first joint purchase of my mother and father, poor as they were, when they were married in 1932. On this basic library, my father wanted to build his family. From about the age of twelve I was becoming fairly certain that I must test a vocation to become a Catholic priest. Therefore, it was important to me whether or not there is a God. That was a question I needed to confront for myself. For I did not want to be surprised later in life by encountering realities I had not faced internally before the fact. To me, atheism was not so much a temptation as a real possibility. The important question was, But is it true?

I also thought non-Catholic versions of the Christian religion were real possibilities. After all, most people in the larger world— as I began to become aware of it—manifestly think that Catholicism is false. The Protestants and the Enlightened have both named themselves for their opposition to the Catholic faith. Many in the West define themselves still today against the Catholic ascendancy, aka the "Dark" Ages. Compared to the "Bright Ages"?

All this did not mean that I was blown off course. I kept plowing ahead, yet quite aware that life is long, and evidence flies thick around like a winter blizzard. There was plenty of time to make up my mind.

As a consequence, I used to study carefully articles on apologetics (why Catholics believe this or that; the advantages of belief over atheism) and also articles by Protestant writers and atheists

(why they thought the Catholic faith was wrong and even dangerous), as well as articles portraying the satisfactions of alternative
ways of life.

By the time I was fourteen, I had entered a minor seminary on
the quiet shores of St. Mary's Lake—catty-corner from the can-
dlelit grotto of Our Lady—on the campus of the University of
Notre Dame. But I kept my eyes open.

Down through the years, we in the seminary used to devote
nearly four hours a day to formal prayer, beginning with a half-
hour meditation before six-thirty in the morning, followed by the
Holy Mass. Of course, we tried to keep in prayer all day long, too,
as we went about our work or energetic play on the basketball
court, baseball diamond, or football field. Prayer, we were taught,
is minute-by-minute conversation with God.

Many, many times our prayer (mine at least) seemed empty, a
constant round of temptations to think of other things or simply
to doze off. Many times there seemed to be no God present to talk
to, no God who knew my necessities. At such times, I wondered
if I were an atheist—or, more exactly, what made me any different from an atheist. For the atheist, too, I imagined, the term
"God" conjured up an emptiness, an absence. A nothingness. And
I empathized.

Somehow I early learned that the important move in prayer is
to direct an inner, quiet, steady will toward God's love, to be
united with that love, even in dryness and aridity. Prayer, essentially, is saying "Yes" to the will of God. Not knowing exactly what
that will is now, or yet will be, saying "Yes," in any case—and in
whatever tranquility one can bring to one's disorderly, discordant
self.

From about fifteen I had come in contact with the example,
and eventually the writings, of that little Carmelite nun from
France, Thérèse of Lisieux. That is probably where I learned to
pray. And not to be overly distressed by kneeling (or sitting)
silently in nothingness.

As my studies in philosophy and the history of the spirit proceeded, I came to learn that, while one can come to know that God is present, our minds are unable to form an adequate conception of Him, or to grasp Him with any of our five senses, or to imagine Him. His mode of drawing us into His presence is necessarily by way of absence, silence, nothingness. I remember an image fixed in my mind by the poetry of Saint John of the Cross, mentioned earlier: "The place where he . . . was awaiting me—A place where none appeared."

It must necessarily be so. The true God is beyond human concepts, senses, imagination, memory. On those frequencies He is not reachable. Mother Teresa of Calcutta acknowledged her inability to reach God on human wavelengths in a 1979 letter to one of her spiritual directors, the Reverend Michael Van Der Peet: "Jesus has a very special love for you. [But] as for me—the silence and the emptiness is so great—that I look and do not see,—listen and do not hear."

If a Christian has not yet known this darkness and aridity, it is a sign that the Lord is still treating him like a child at the breast, too unformed for the adult darkness in which alone the true God is found. Any who think they can make idols, or images, or pictures, or concepts of God remain underdeveloped in their faith. Darkness is not a sign of unbelief, or even of doubt, but a sign of the true relation between the Creator and the creature. God is not on our frequency, and when we get beyond our usual range, which in prayer we must, we reach only darkness. This is painful. In a way, it does make one doubt; in another way, experience shows us that when one is no longer a child, one leaves childish ways behind.

Our intellects, our will—these can reach out to God, like arrows of inquiry shot up into the infinite night. These are not shot in vain. They mark out a direction. Waiting in silence, in abandonment, even in the dry sands of the desert, one comes to know His presence. *Not* believe in it. *Know* it. In a 1959 interview with the BBC, C. G. Jung once made the same point. Asked whether he believed in God, Jung replied, "I don't believe—I *know*."

This is a dark knowledge. One cannot expect anyone else to know it, unless they have also walked the rocky and darkling path—or somehow by God's grace been brought to it by a different journey, along a different route. *Ascent of the Mountain, Flight of the Dove,* I called another book of mine. Some of us labor sweatily, others are borne on eagle's wings.

I do not mean that this knowledge consists of warm sentiments, feelings of devotion, uplift, and "faith." I mean a certain quiet emptiness. A dark resonance of wills. Echo to echo.

Mother Teresa wrote of her own emptiness in 1961: "I accept not in my feelings—but with my will, the Will of God—I accept His will."

This is not a "will" characterized by effort, unrelenting desire, unshakable determination. I mean something almost the opposite: the quiet of abandonment, and trust. This is another mode of will, quite different from the striving will. It is the willingness to forgo any other reinforcement except the blind and dark love we direct toward that infinite Light, on which we cannot set our eyes.

Nor do I mean a turning away from intellect or rationality. On the contrary, I mean taking these with utter seriousness "all the way down" to the very roots of the universe. I mean trusting our own rationality, our own intellect. I mean serene confidence in infinite Light, even when our senses go quite dark. Trust the light, the evidence-demanding *eros* of inquiry, within us.

I mean the suffering love in which that Light issues forth among us. Not to remove us from suffering. But to transfigure us by means of it.

ALL THIS, I KNOW, is senseless to the atheist, even a repulsive childishness. In this, too, there is a kind of necessity. The conditions of the two states of mind are such that the one cannot help regarding the other (at times) with dismay.

Nonetheless, those who share the one state of mind and those who share the other are doomed to everlasting conversation, forever. In every age there have been atheists. In every age there have been believers. Sometimes I think that the proportion of each hardly ever changes. True enough, within a given civilization the relative prominence of one may favor it far beyond the other. Furthermore, many people at any one time may take neither choice with much seriousness. Swirling along the streets, the fallen leaves of autumn. Too passive to act, one way or the other.

In my own life, I have tried to keep the conversation up between the two sides of my own intellect. The line of belief and unbelief is not drawn between one person and another, normally, but rather down the inner souls of all of us. That is why the very question stirs so much passion. I have known people who declaim so passionately and argumentatively that they do not believe in God that I am driven to wonderment: Why are they so agitated, if, as they insist, God does not exist? Why, then, do they pay so much attention? Some of the greatest converts, in either direction, are those who wrestled strenuously for many years to maintain the other side.

I want to add here, before I go back to an earlier theme, that I left the seminary after twelve years, but not out of lack of faith. On the contrary, I was much deepened in its darkness, convinced only that I could not be a good priest and also experiment and write as by then I knew was my true vocation. Maybe others could do it. I could not. Besides, the attraction of women was more than I thought that, over the long run, I could bear. For a long time, yes. But forever? It seemed to me that life as a layman would be far better for my soul. So I returned to my philosophical studies, experiments in fiction, and close attention to Albert Camus.

What particularly struck me in Albert Camus was his insistence that we begin *within* nihilism. Only by finding our way out from nihilism could any new civilization rest on solid ground. He meant: finding our way out by intellect, the kind of intellect that can engage with the Absurd. Now some fifty years after my first book, much of the spiritual terrain has changed—on a massive scale, and more than once.

My aim at the present moment is to give one more report from that no-man's-land, at the crossroads where atheist and believer meet in the darkness of the night.

What is it that keeps us from getting through to each other? What is it that needs to be looked at from a fresh perspective, or disentangled in one's own mind, before true disagreement can occur? What goes through the minds of some when they use a name like "God" is very different from what goes through the minds of others.

Naturally, coming face-to-face with God is to be feared (*Mysterium tremehdum et fascinans*, "The Mystery fascinating, attracting, and to be feared," in Rudolf Otto's phrase). Happily for some, this encounter within the self is fairly easy to avoid. There are many ways to avoid inwardness and to "kill time" simply by keeping busy; frequenting rooms throbbing with the strong beat of certain kinds of music; picking up the car keys to search somewhere else for something to do.

It is not at all hard for a believer to become an unbeliever. A great many do. The seed has often been thrown on dry ground, or on thin soil over rocky shale, and cannot bear the heat of the afternoon. Often enough, faith leads one to feel abandoned to darkness, isolated in inner dryness, undermined by a fear of having been seduced into an illusion. For a believer, it does not take a prolonged thought experiment to imagine oneself an unbeliever.

Yet atheists may actually find it harder to imagine themselves coming by way of reason to know God than believers to imagine the opposite. I hypothesize that unbelievers, especially those who have never known religion in their personal lives, or who have had bad experiences with it, experience a revulsion against reasoned knowledge of God, and even more so against a Jewish and/or Christian faith. Indeed, they find it harder to imagine themselves as believers than believers to imagine themselves as unbelievers. Am I wrong?

INTO THE DARK

We had a secularist woman living next to us in one of the homes in which I grew up. She had lost her husband and was herself intermittently ill. Yet it was not her illnesses that bothered her, rather, now in her seventies, it was her relative health. Without youth, without children, without any work to do, without enough strength in her bones for volunteering, she felt useless. An energy-sapping pointlessness pursued her every minute and followed her into every room she entered. She lived in anguish. She told me so herself. She did not believe in God, and her sand was flowing out. The question "why?" no longer had an answer.

My neighbor thought she would be better off dead. Yet she was afraid of death's finality. I could hardly bear to look into her mournful eyes, feeling totally inadequate to help. She was a very proud and independent woman. She was utterly isolated. She would have resented any attempt to suggest a different outlook.

When he was asked, What is nihilism? the answer Nietzsche gave was my neighbor's: "The aim is lacking; 'why?' finds no answer." Later he approached the definition another way: "Something is to be *achieved* through the process—and now one realizes that becoming aims at *nothing* and achieves *nothing*."

In our age and in our kind of society—mobile, fast, free—the experience of "nihilism" is common even among fourteen-year-old "valley girls." Boredom today is the first taste of nothingness. "Waddya want to do tonight, Beth?" Beth, chewing gum: "I dunno, what do you wanna do?" Nowadays, one of them is likely to have a cell phone to her ear. The interest of the other runs to shopping malls, movie theaters, boys in cars. . . .

The experience of nothingness is, therefore, practically universal. Yet some in the two groups mentioned earlier seem blessedly to have been spared it. Trying to understand it, however, I prefer to speak of this experience without the *-ism,* prior to any ideology about it, as "the *experience* of nothingness." How we are to understand that experience, in Nietzsche's way or in any other, is a different matter.

It is an experience I well know in my own life. Everybody does.

Without being tedious, but to make certain that the point is as clear as examples can make it, let me mention Joan, who married for the first and only time when she was forty-three. Not immediately but some three years later and much to her surprise and joy, Joan conceived a child. Months of happy expectation followed. On the day after the child's exhilarating birth, however, she learned that the dear little boy was afflicted with a rare disease that meant her son would probably live only until nine or ten, and would for all the years until then need extraordinary care. The question "Why?" arose inside her with much anguish.

A couple I know of had a handsome, athletic, extremely smart, and warmly popular son who excelled in almost everything in high school. It was only at the end of his first year in college that his health faltered, and then slowly it became apparent that he was afflicted with an incapacitating case of schizophrenia and would have to be hospitalized. His adoring parents were crushed. He was an only child. Their world fell apart.

A student I once had in class had been acing all her classes at Stanford, a perky and happy and optimistic young woman determined to get into medical school, in the tradition of her family. She had not a doubt in her mind. Her sailing was exceptionally clear. Until one day. One day it suddenly hit her very hard that she did not really want to become a doctor. Her grandmother had years ago, seeing the child care for a wounded robin, been the first to say that Janette would make a great doctor. Janette's life dream had been implanted in her imagination from that day on.

Now suddenly, as a sophomore, some inner tunnel collapsed and all her dreams came tumbling down. The irrepressible thought had overpowered her: that she had been *thrown* into this project, it was not her project, she had never given it any real thought. She was just so darn good at it, and her record had gotten her into the university of her dreams, and everything looked far too rosy to endure. And it didn't. She began to show the symptoms of the experience of nothingness that many sophomores come down with: She began to sleep a lot. She could hardly get out of bed. She could no longer see any point to it. With her friends she was, as never before, short and cynical. They knew she wasn't well. But she wasn't sick, either, except with the disease of autonomy and inner freedom.

Granted that I am overcome with the experience of nothingness, how should I live? The alternatives come down to two: some form of suicide (drugs, drink, fast living, killing time will do) such as Albert Camus contemplated in the *Myth of Sisyphus*. Or this: *creatio ex nihilo,* reaching down into nothingness to create a new being. But by what light? Following which stars?

Woody Allen found his: "The heart wants what it wants." Even the U.S. Supreme Court has abandoned the Constitution to dabble in its own philosophy of life in *Casey*: "At the heart of liberty is the right to define one's own concept of existence, of meaning, of the universe, and the mystery of human life." This is not the American legal and moral tradition, but contemporary postmodernism.

Another man I met along the way figured out in his twenties that life is a game. The only trick is to think up a game that will last for a lifetime without ever being finished, but with the satisfaction of reaching certain marks along the way. He chose to visit every town on this planet with a population greater than 25,000. He had the kind of job that allowed him to make quite a lot of money as an independent contractor, enough money to work at most two years and then take a year off to begin visiting the towns carefully highlighted on his regional map. Visiting one, he would put an X through it on his map, and head for the next. He thoroughly enjoyed himself, and found that in a single year, with good planning, he could fulfill his objective on almost one entire continent, except Asia and Africa. In many places, transportation was unreliable and rather primitive. The beauty of his life plan, he once told me, was that the population of cities kept expanding. So he would always have reason to return to one continent after another to cross new towns off his list. His seemed to me an empty project, but where it got its energy was from his recognition of the pointlessness of life.

In a year that was especially dark for me, I remember once hearing my infant son Richard crying out in the middle of the night. Untypically, I was the first to hear him, not my wife. His cry was like a moan, and when I got to him in the next room in his crib, his bed clothes were soaked with sweat, and he was crying out as in a fever. I lifted his hot body to my shoulder, and then I told him: "It's all right, Richard. It's Daddy. Here's your dresser, here's your Teddy." I tapped the crib, the closet door, the dresser, trying to reorient him from his fevered dream back into the world of solid things. "You'll be all right, Richie," I said to him, lightly patting his back, as his cries softened to occasional breathy sobs. "You'll be all right. Everything is all right."

Then I wondered to myself: Is this a lie? Shouldn't I be telling him how awful life can be, how much closer life actually is to his fevered dream than to these supposedly solid objects I am trying to orient him to? An image of all those bodies stacked like bags of sand came over me. Am I lying to him? Am I lying to myself?

Nothingness Inside Out

I went back to reflecting on illusions and realities in later months. Something told me that Nietzsche's mad nihilism is not the only, nor the best, theory for explaining life-crushing experiences of the sort he adverted to. I noticed that Nietzsche and Sartre, Turgenev and Dostoyevsky, and all those other early writers on nihilism did one remarkable thing at variance with their theories: They wrote books for others to read. In a world that makes no sense, why would they endure the hours and hours of sitting on their back-sides, moving old pens across resisting pieces of blank foolscap? If everything is as meaningless as they say, why would they do it?

And since some people seem oblivious to the experience of nothingness, what is it that those who have the experience do, that others don't do?

I began reflecting on what goes on *inside* the experience of nothingness, first within myself, and then among others I could talk to about it. Here a brief summary will have to do. The normal way in which Nietzsche, Sartre, and we ourselves come to an awareness of the experience of nothingness is through four activities of our own minds and wills. The one Nietzsche and the others most stress is ruthless *honesty,* forcing ourselves to see through comforting illusions and to face the emptiness. The second is *courage,* the habit that gives force and steadiness to our ability to see truly. Without courage, we would avert our eyes, as so often we have done.

Third is the ideal of *community* exemplified in reaching out to others through books—the good moves outward to diffuse itself. There is a kind of brotherhood and sisterhood among those who recognize the experience of nothingness in one another. There is a sort of honesty and cleanness in it one wants to share. One of the marks of "the good" is that, as the Latin puts it, *bonum est diffusivum sui*—the good diffuses itself. It wants others to participate in it.

Fourth is *practical wisdom,* that is, practical reason applied to action, by an adult experienced enough to take virtually everything concrete into account—or at least to avoid most of the common mistakes of the inexperienced. When the experience of nothingness hits, one cannot simply take to one's bed. Well, sometimes one does, but then one can't *stay* there. Moment by moment, in a kind of staccato, action keeps calling to us. Sooner or later, I have to start acting as an agent of my own future again. "Granted that I have the experience of nothingness, what should I do?"

Yes, there are such things as relativity and meaninglessness and pointlessness. Question is, What are we going to do even if that is true? We will not be able to escape practicing honesty, courage, community, and practical wisdom—or else withering into dry leaves for stray winds to blow about. The choice is ours, and un-avoidable.

These four virtues do not constitute a complete quiver of all the virtues needed to be a good man or a valiant woman. Still, these four do constitute quite an admirable list. They are a wonderful starting place for an ethic rooted in the experience of nothingness. Here is the point at which Albert Camus began his own ascent out of the problem of suicide (*The Myth of Sisyphus*), on the road to the heroic and clear-eyed compassion of Dr. Rieux in *The Plague*. Sartre, locked inside his own solitariness, writing that "hell is other people," faltered on the idea of community. No, hell is not other people. Hell is total isolation within one's own puny mind. It is solitary confinement. (To step out of philosophy for a moment and into the terms of Christian faith: Hell is the solitary soul who freely and deliberately rejects friendship with God.) Hell is becoming conscious of what one has irretrievably chosen for oneself. This Hell has been deliberately chosen.

What we do with the experience of nothingness depends on our proven reserves of practical wisdom, community, courage, honesty. By the end of our lives, learning from experience, we ought to be wiser than we were in the beginning.

Interpreting Our Time

If I am right in this analysis, however abbreviated, we may observe how the generation that fell into the nihilism of the 1930s at last stumbled onto the way out (see Appendix I). In the concentration camps and prisons, many a poor wretch unexpectedly felt himself morally bound not to become complicit in the lies his torturers demanded him to sign. But why? Why, if before they had thought they were nihilists, why couldn't they manage to be cynics and nihilists and liars here at the end, under torture and torment and soft blandishment ("You can go free, you can have drinks with your friends again")? Is not a lie a small price to pay in a world without truth? What would a lie mean anyway? "No one will ever know. No one will ever care."

But the liar himself would know, his soul would know; in his own mind's eye, his integrity would forever lie in the dust, humiliated. And his torturer would use this petty surrender to weaken the will of his next victim. "If *he* did as he was told, why can't you?" The aim of these torturers was to destroy every last vestige of the moral sense, every fiber of integrity of soul *within everyone.* For those in prison, the torturers could use the harshest methods and take all the time they needed to break a man. The integrity of the entire public could be assaulted by incessant intimidation and occasional, unpredictable terror. After seducing almost everyone to spy on their associates, the slave masters could easily blackmail them forever. These poor sinners could never forget their own treason to loved ones.

Even with their almost unlimited power and ferocity of will, it proved impossible for totalitarian regimes to instill nihilism into everyone. Nihilism turned out to be antihuman. However powerfully nihilism is enforced, the human spirit is sometimes able to triumph over it by honesty, courage, community, and practical wisdom.

Those who have doubts about the power of this argument should read the biographies of Anatoly Sharansky, to whose stirring memoir we will turn our attention in chapter one; as well as the stories of Václav Havel, Mihailo Mihailov, Armando Valladares, Pavel Bratinka, Irina Ratushinskaya, Maximilian Kolbe, and hundreds of others. From the ashes of nihilism, the human spirit rose stronger and truer.

I have tested this moral principle and have found it fortifying: *Accept the experience of nothingness as a gift, search deep into it, live by its living streams.* One thing I particularly appreciate about this moral principle is that it requires no illusions. Far from shutting one's eyes to the nothingness and the meaninglessness, one keeps the cellar door open in order to feel, at all times, its cool, stale draft. In that way, one is never allowed to forget. And from these four moral virtues, one forges creative strength. Creation out of nothingness.

Freedom means choosing every moment who I am, and what exactly I must do this minute. Self-government—yes, precisely that.

Yet not exactly without community, community down through time, community around the planet. Not exactly isolated. One's ancestors continue to live in one's own consciousness. One's universal brothers also do.

All together, on a darkling plain.

In "Dover Beach," Matthew Arnold wrote of an ebbing Sea of Faith:

But now I only hear
Its melancholy, long, withdrawing roar,
Retreating, to the breath
Of the night-wind, down the vast edges drear
And naked shingles of the world.

But today there is a difference. The melancholy roar of a receding sea belongs to atheism.

PART ONE

False Starts

Critical thinking might be to secularism what faith is to devout religious believers. Thinking rationally, questioning assumptions, embracing complexity and eschewing the black-and-white—these habits of mind are, to the champions of non-belief, a keystone of the secular worldview and a crucial part of what separates them from religious people.

So why, when it comes to matters of religion, do secularists so frequently leave their critical thinking at the door?

—Tom Krattenmaker, "Secularists,
What Happened
to the Open Mind?"
USA Today, August 20, 2007

Not the Way to Invite a Conversation:
Dawkins, Dennett, and Harris

ATHEISTS SPEAK OUT

A recent shower of books by atheists—among them *Letter to a Christian Nation* by Sam Harris, *Breaking the Spell* by Daniel C. Dennett, and *The God Delusion* by Richard Dawkins—has fallen on the parched lips of lonely American atheists. These books have three purposes: to speed up the disappearance of biblical faith in America; to proselytize for rational atheism; and to boost morale among atheists, in part by calling attention to support groups to console them. Their overriding purpose is the first one: in Harris's words, "to demolish the intellectual and moral pretensions of Christianity." But the third one—to raise the morale of atheists—is not far behind.

All three books evince considerable disdain for Judaism, too. Dawkins calls it "a tribal cult of a single fiercely unpleasant God, morbidly obsessed with sexual restrictions, with the smell of charred flesh, with his own superiority over rival gods, and with the exclusiveness of his chosen desert tribe." And the God of the Old Testament, Dawkins calls a "psychotic delinquent."

It is not as if these authors admire Islam; rather, they use Islam as a weapon for bashing Christianity and Judaism. Harris says to Christians, "Nonbelievers like myself stand beside you, dumbstruck by the Muslim hordes who chant death to whole nations of the living. But we stand dumbstruck by you as well—by your denial of tangible reality, by the suffering you create in service to your religious myths, and by your attachment to an imaginary God." In truth, though, the main intention of all three authors is to praise the superiority of atheism, at least the rational atheism of professors such as themselves.

IN PRAISE OF ATHEISTS

In fact, there is much in atheism to praise. With the evidence of the admirable moral code laid out in Aristotle's *Nicomachean Ethics* in his hands, Saint Thomas Aquinas wrote that in order to be good, in at least one important sense, it is not necessary to share in biblical faith. Aristotle showed a path toward human flourishing, both for an entire polity and for noble individuals. (To be "good" in another important sense, "being born again" or "saved," requires a bit more than Aristotle could provide, or even imagine.) Atheists—or, at least, nonbiblical pagans—were able to build such magnificent buildings as the Parthenon, the pyramids of Egypt, the palaces of Babylon; and to produce great literature and the beginnings of several key sciences in varied fields such as astronomy, arithmetic, medicine, and agriculture. Finally, atheists—or, at least, nonbelievers—have always been a spur to biblical self-understanding, by raising questions, doubting, or throwing down insulting or respectful intellectual challenges. It was from the pagan intellectual class that many of the early Fathers of the Church (Origen, Clement of Alexandria, and Saint Augustine himself) came to biblical faith, and they usually remained in close dialogue with their unbelieving peers, much to the benefit of their own understanding of their faith.

To come down the ladder a great distance, my own early work was centered on the dialogue between believers and unbelievers, the intellectual horizon of the Absurd (as Camus, Sartre, and so many others called it) and that of biblical faith—in such books as *Belief and Unbelief* and *The Experience of Nothingness,* for instance. For that reason, I really wanted to like these new books of atheism. I have learned a lot about atheists and believers from Jürgen Habermas, possibly the best-known atheist in Europe. Habermas writes of believers with respect and as equal partners in an important dialogue. A respectful regard for mutual dignity is, Habermas holds, essential to the practice of rationality among human beings; we shall have reason to return to his views on religion further on in this book. A very smart American atheist, Heather Mac Donald, agreed to engage me in conversations that were a pleasure to conduct, showing on her side patience, respect even in spirited disagreement, and candor. Heather's precise, incisive contributions to this happy discussion also warrant a closer look; we shall reflect on her arguments in chapters three and four.

DIALOGUE OR DISMISSAL?

Alas, it is extremely difficult to engage on the same level with Harris, Dennett, and Dawkins (and, as we shall see in the next chapter, Christopher Hitchens). All of them think that religion is so great a menace that they do not show much disposition for dialogue. The battle flags they put into the wind are Voltaire's "Wipe out the infamous thing": *Écrasez l'infâme!* Meanwhile, all three pretend that atheists "question everything" and "submit to relentless, almost tedious, self-criticism." Yet in these books there is not a shred of evidence that their authors have ever had any doubts whatever about the rightness of their own atheism. Self-questioning about their own scholarly indifference to their subject; about the horrific brutalities committed in the name of "scientific atheism" during the twentieth century; about the restless and mercurial dissatisfactions in atheist and secular movements during the past hundred years (at times wearily nihilistic and bored in Parisian cafés; at times passionately marching toward murderous utopias; often full of free-floating dreads of "nuclear winter," then "global warming"). All such questions are notable by their absence. Despite the fact that an atheist Zeitgeist dominates university campuses in

America, it has not proved persuasive to huge numbers of students, who hold their noses and put up with it. Why does atheism persuade so few? Our authors never ask.

I particularly wanted to like the book by Richard Dawkins. I had heard that his is a well-furnished and well-rounded mind, and that he writes with the music and wit of an elegant literary stylist. His fans present him as the very model of a reasonable man. Dawkins, too, expressly presents himself and other atheists as "brights," distinguished by their "healthy" and "vigorous" minds. Poor believers—he openly complains—are (by contrast with him) trapped in delusion, unquestioning, mentally dead. He makes not a gesture of seeking to learn from them.

Actually, Dawkins's public record is worse than that. He led a two-part show on religion for the BBC, called *The Root of All Evil?* While writing now that he disagrees with the title the producers gave it, he freely appeared under it. This is what he asks of religious people: "Imagine, with John Lennon, a world with no religion." Wouldn't most of the violence and distortion introduced into human life disappear? Now it would be rather original of Dawkins to make such a point, except that in Britain this view is quite conventional. Propagated by pop star and scientist alike, it is according to a recent poll shared by 82 percent of the British population.

REASON AND MORAL COURAGE

Throughout the West, it appears that neither scientist nor pop star takes time to consider contemporary religious experience in the light of some of its most sophisticated and heroic practitioners. For instance, never before our own time have so many millions of persons of biblical faith been thrown into concentration camps, tortured, and murdered as they have been under recent self-described atheist regimes. It would have been wonderful if any of our three authors had measured their vision of religion against the hard-won biblical faith of the originally atheist scientist Anatoly Sharansky, who served nine years in the Soviet Gulag simply for vindicating the rights of Soviet citizens who were Jews. Sharansky has written the record of his suffering in a brilliant autobiography, *Fear No Evil*. I think I have never read of a braver moral man, determined to live as a free man, courageously showing nothing but moral contempt for the morals of KGB officials, under whose total power he had to live. Sharansky went on courageously day by dreary day, deprived of sufficient food, deprived of sight of the sky and sun. He was punished in innumerable ways under a kind of scientific Skinnerian conditioning designed to "correct" his behavior, and this regimen went on year after year, attempting to wear down his resistance, to hold out for him trivial blandishments, tormenting his soul by isolating him and depriving him of human support.

Ironically, however, his prison experiences led Sharansky to dimensions of *reason* that far exceeded anything he had encountered in his earlier scientific practice. To survive, he needed to open himself to learning far more than science had taught him. He was asked to sign his name to certain untruths: "Who will ever know? What difference will it make? It is such a small thing, and it will make things go much better for you and for us, it will be for the common good." One of Sharansky's colleagues, a noble soul, nonetheless deceived himself into thinking that it would be better to lie about a few small things so that he would soon be freed to carry the message of human rights outside the camps. Sharansky watched still other men try to keep their spirits up by hope—hoping for better treatment, hoping for earlier liberation—and then suddenly find themselves so weakened by false hopes that they could no longer resist complicity. Sharansky found that he needed a source of discernment deeper than any he had previously known.

In those days, the love of his beloved and brave wife, and friends and other dissidents, came to his cell in rarely received letters or messages. But such messages could also have weakened and betrayed him. In his torments of soul, he found enormous companionship with King David of many centuries earlier, when a ragged old Hebrew edition of the Psalms was allowed to fall into his hands with the mail. The realism of David went right to his heart, and heavily bolstered his defenses. He learned the strength to be found in community—his community—in partaking of traditional rituals, drawing sustenance from the earlier sufferings, strivings, and hard-earned wisdom of his ancestors. Unwittingly, one cellmate (who might have been working with the KGB) gave Sharansky another lesson in "the interconnection of souls." One of Sharansky's greatest scientific heroes had long been Galileo. In telling Sharansky of how other prisoners had made "life easier for everybody" simply by signing "harmless" papers that no one outside would ever see, his cellmate mentioned that even Galileo had been persuaded to sign certain statements about his own errors, just to put the whole mess behind him. Like a thunderbolt, these words of his cellmate flooded Sharansky's mind with the interconnectedness of all souls in history—those who remain faithful to the truth, and those who betray it. Galileo's betrayal four hundred years earlier was now being used to seduce Sharansky, just as every spiritual surrender of another individual in the Gulag was used to pound home to him that long-term resistance was useless. In that lightning flash, Sharansky saw the power of inner truthfulness down the ages, that electronic belt of fidelity that ties all regions and all times together, in however many hearts that remain faithful to the truth. Sharansky wanted to be reborn as a member of that community, and he changed his name to Natan, signifying the biblical community with which he wanted to be identified through all time.

Sharansky became, even in the Gulag, more and more an observant Jew, in one comic scene forcing even his camp supervisor to participate—just the two of them—in a lighting of the menorah. Sharansky writes very little directly about God, but it is certain beyond a doubt that he came to see something profoundly deficient in his earlier scientific habits of mind. These were noble as far as they went, and he has never renounced them, but in his extreme circumstances they proved too limited. He came also to be ashamed of his earlier agnosticism and cavalier attitude toward "organized religion." The community that had preserved the Psalms of King David down so many centuries offered him companionship of soul, and recharged his will to resist at a crucial point in his long imprisonment.

Unquestioning Faith?

It was, then, a huge disappointment to me to find that Dennett, Harris, and especially Dawkins paid no attention to the actual conversion experiences and narratives of fidelity, which are so common in the prison literature of our time. Moreover, none of them ever put his weak, confused, and unplumbed ideas about God under scrutiny. Their natural habit of mind is anthropomorphic. They tend to think of God as if He were a human being, bound to human limitations. They are almost as literal in their readings of the Bible as the least educated, most literal-minded fundamentalist in Flannery O'Connor's rural Georgia. They regale themselves with finding contradictions and impossibilities in these literal readings of theirs, but the full force of their ridicule depends on misreading the literary form of the biblical passages at stake, whether they be allegorical, metaphorical, poetic, or resonant with many meanings, for the nourishment of a soul under stress. The Bible almost never pretends to be science (even in the ancient sense), or strictly literal history.

Our three authors pride themselves on how science advances in understanding over time, and also on how moral thinking becomes in some ways deeper and more demanding. They do not give any attention to the ways in which religious understanding also grows, develops, and evolves. They seem utterly ignorant of John Henry Newman's brilliant *Essay on the Development of Christian Doctrine.* It hardly dawns on them that the biblical faiths have been, from the very beginning, in constant—and mutually enriching—dialogue with skeptical and secular intelligence. One can see progress in religious understanding from one part of the biblical era to another, and the authors of Scripture themselves call attention to it.

Our three authors, it does seem, are a bit blinded by their own repugnance toward religion. Even his good friends, Dawkins writes, ask him why he is driven to be so "hostile" to religious people. Why not, they say, as intelligent as you are, quietly lay out your devastating arguments against believers, in a calm and unruffled manner? Dawkins's answer to his friends is forthright: "I am hostile to fundamentalist religion because it actively debauches the scientific enterprise . . . Fundamentalist religion is hell-bent on ruining the scientific education of countless thousands of innocent, well-meaning, eager young minds. Non-fundamentalist, 'sensible' religion may not be doing that. But it is making the world safe for fundamentalism by teaching children, from their earliest years, that unquestioning faith is a virtue." Dawkins refuses to be part of the public "conspiracy" to pay religion respect, when it deserves contempt.

Yet his complaint about "unquestioning" faith seems a bit odd. Some of us have thought that the origin of religion lies in the unlimited drive in human beings to ask questions—which is our primary experience of the infinite. Anything finite that we encounter can be questioned, and seems ultimately unsatisfying. That hunger to question is the experience that keeps driving the mind and soul on and on, and is its first foretaste of that which is beyond time and space. "Our hearts are restless, Lord," Saint Augustine recorded, "until they rest in Thee." These words have had clearly echoing resonance in millions upon millions of inquiring minds down through human history ever since. "Unquestioning faith?" The writings of the medieval thinkers record question after question, disputation after disputation, and real results in history hinged upon the resolution of each. Many of the questions arose from skeptical, unbelieving lawyers, philosophers, and others in the medieval universities; still others from the Arab scholars whose works had recently burst upon the Western universities; still others from

Maimonides and other Jewish scholars; and a great many from the greatest pagan thinkers of every preceding century. Questions have been the heart and soul of Judaism and Christianity for millennia.

To be sure, Dawkins at least does think there are some religious people who can be converted to atheism by his arguments. He describes them as the "open-minded people whose childhood indoctrination was not too insidious, or for other reasons didn't 'take,' or whose native intelligence is strong enough to overcome it." Dawkins presents such believers with an ultimatum: Either join him in "breaking free of the vice of religion altogether" or remain among the close-minded types who are unable to overcome "the god delusion."

On the fifth page of his book, Dawkins describes his hopes: "If this book works as I intend, religious readers who open it will be atheists when they put it down." It surprised me that Dawkins would turn out to be such a proselytizer. Most of all what surprised me is that, while all three authors write as if science is the be-all and end-all of rational discourse, these three books of theirs are by no means scientific. On the contrary, they are examples of *dialectic*—arguments from within one point of view, or horizon, addressed to human beings who share a different point of view. Surely, one of the noblest works of reason is to enter into respectful argument with others, whose vision of reality is dramatically different from one's own, in order that both parties may learn from this exchange, and come to an ever deeper mutual respect. Our authors engage in dialectic, not science, but they can scarcely be said to do so with respect for those they address. Thus, Dawkins: "Of course, dyed-in-the-wool faith-heads are immune to argument, their resistance built up over years of childhood indoctrination . . . Among the more effective immunological devices is a dire warning to avoid even opening a book like this, which is surely a work of Satan." Here, of course, Dawkins flatters himself. "Screwtape" would have been far more insidious.

What most surprised me in the Dawkins book, however, is

its defensiveness. He describes atheists, particularly in America, as suffering from loneliness, public disrespect, spiritual isolation, and low self-esteem. In one passage he recounts a letter from a young American medical student recently turning from Christianity to atheism. A medical student? Surely at least some of the doctors and scientists working near her are atheists. Nonetheless, the student writes: "I don't particularly want to share my belief with other people who are close to me because I fear the . . . reaction of distaste . . . I only write to you because I hoped you'd sympathize and share in my frustration." In an appendix, which Dawkins kindly adds for such unsupported souls, he offers lists of organizations in which lonely atheists may find community and solace. He devotes not a few pages to boosting his community's morale—how large their numbers are, how smart they are, how comparatively disgusting their antagonists are.

Building a Culture of Reason

I have no doubt that Christians have committed many evils, and written some disgraceful pages in human history. Yet on a fair ledger of what Judaism and Christianity added to pagan Greece, Rome, the Arab nations (before Mohammed), the German, Frankish, and Celtic tribes, the Vikings and the Anglo-Saxons, one is puzzled not to find Dawkins giving thanks for many innovations: hospitals, orphanages, cathedral schools in early centuries, universities not much later, some of the most beautiful works of art—in music, architecture, painting, and poetry—in the human patrimony.

And why does he overlook the hard intellectual work on concepts such as "person," "community," *"civitas,"* "consent," "tyranny," and "limited government" ("Give to Caesar what is Caesar's . . .") that framed the conceptual background of such great documents as the Magna Carta? His few pages on the founding and nourishing of his own beloved Oxford by its early Catholic patrons are mockingly ungrateful. And if Oxford disappoints him, has he no gratitude for the building of virtually every other old and famous university of Europe (and the Americas)?

Dawkins writes nothing about the great religious communities founded for the express purpose of building schools for the free education of the poor. Nothing about the thousands of monastic lives dedicated to the delicate and exhausting labor of copying by hand the great manuscripts of the past—often with the lavish love manifested in illuminations—during long centuries in which there were no printing presses. Nothing about the founding of the Vatican Library and its importance for the genesis of nearly a dozen modern sciences. Nothing about the learned priests and faithful who have made so many crucial discoveries in science, medicine, and technology. Yet on these matters a word or two of praise from Dawkins might have made his tiresome lists of accusations seem less unfair.

I don't wish to overdo it. There have been and are toxic elements in religion that always need restraint by the Logos—the inner word, the insight, the light of intelligence—to which Christianity from the very first married the biblical tradition: "In the beginning was the Logos"—the inner word, the light, in Whom, and by Whom, and with Whom all things have been made (John 1:1 NAB). Still, any fair measuring of the impact of Judaism and Christianity on world history has an awful lot of positives to add to the ledger. Among my favorite texts for many years, in fact, are certain passages of Alfred North Whitehead—in *Science and the Modern World* and *Adventures of Ideas,* for instance. In these passages, Whitehead points out that the practices of modern science are inconceivable apart from thousands of years of tutelage under the Jewish and Christian conviction that the Creator of all things understood all things, in their general laws and in their particular, contingent dispositions. This conviction, Whitehead writes, made long, disciplined efforts to apply reason to the sustained Herculean task of understanding all things seem reasonable. If all things are intelligible to their Creator, they ought to be intelligible to those made in His image, who in imitation of Him, press onward in the human vocation to try to understand all that He has made.

In addition, Judaism and Christianity have inculcated in entire cultures specific intellectual and moral habits, synthesizing them with the teachings of ancient classical traditions, without which the development of modern sciences would lack the requisite moral disciplines—honesty, hard work, perseverance in the face of difficulties, a respect for serendipity and sudden insight, a determination to test any hypotheses asserted. What would modern science be without belief in the intelligibility of all things, even contingent, unique, and unrepeatable events, and without culturewide habits of honesty, intellectual rigor, and persevering inquiry? Whitehead pointed to this marvelous indebtedness many times, much more generously than Dawkins. In *Science and the Modern World* (1925), he wrote: "My explanation is that the faith in the possibility of science, generated antecedently to the development of modern scientific theory, is an unconscious derivation from medieval theology."

The path of modern science was made straight, and smoothed, by deep convictions that every stray element in the world of human experience—from the number of hairs on one's head to the lonely lily in the meadow—is thoroughly known to its Creator and, therefore, lies within a field of intelligibility, mutual connection, and multiple logics. All these odd and angular levels of reality, given arduous, disciplined, and cooperative effort, are in principle penetrable by the human mind. If human beings are made in the image of the Creator, as the first chapters of the book of Genesis insist that they are, surely it is in their capacities to question, gain insight, and advance in understanding of the works of God. In the great image portrayed by Michelangelo on the Sistine ceiling—the touch from finger to finger between the Creator and Adam—the mauve cloud behind the Creator's head is painted in the shape of the human brain. *Imago Dei,* yes indeed.

Had Professor Dawkins made even a semiserious pretense of

fairness, I would have thought much more carefully about his criticisms of Christian peoples. Yet some of his criticisms of particular Christian deeds and ways of thinking have real bite. Christianity did not come to remove from human beings all capacity to sin, and simply being Christian gives no exemption from awful human sinfulness, of which in history there are sickening examples. Sin, unreason, betrayal—to Jews and Christians nothing human is alien.

I wish I could write that Daniel Dennett and Sam Harris were more open and respectful than Dawkins, but their books, too, were disappointments. The letter that Harris claims is intended for a Christian nation is, in fact, wholly uninterested in Christianity on any level, is tremendously ignorant, and represents in its essence a love letter to himself, on account of his superiority to the stupid citizens among whom he lives. Dennett's concept of reason and science is so narrow that he seems trapped in something like early-period A. J. Ayer. Let us hope that some brave and caring soul can one day lead him by the hand, out of his sheltered cave. His main thesis, that religion is a "natural phenomenon," was already hoary by the time Saint Augustine was discerning what novelties Christianity introduced to classical Roman religion. But, of course, Dennett's idea of "natural" is not large enough to comprehend either the heroic fidelity of Natan Sharansky, or the timeless, liberating power of King David's poignant Psalms.

All this taken into account, it strikes me that the only way to proceed is to lay out, on one side, the way in which young questioning minds in American universities are repelled by the atheism that is the lingua franca of nearly all classrooms and academic discussions, and, on the other side, a very brief confession of what exactly about Christianity Dennett, Harris, and Dawkins find distasteful, evil, dangerous, and disgusting. Despite their disrespect, Christianity manages somehow to be highly attractive to approximately one-third of the world's people, and is still today the fastest growing of all religions. It is important to explain that attraction before addressing their specific objections.

MY AGNO-THEISTIC DAUGHTER

A few years back, our daughter revealed to us that she was "an agno-theist." (Every well-ordered Catholic family should have one.) When she went off to Duke, she thought she was an atheist. She certainly found plenty of atheism in the air there. Not that everybody was atheist; far from it. Only that the working assumption in practically all public discourse was that every *serious* person is an atheist. Thoughtful religious people kept quiet about their beliefs.

Yet it didn't take my daughter long to see through the pretenses of atheism. In the first place, the fundamental doctrine seemed to be that everything that is, came to be through chance and natural selection. In other words, at bottom, everything is irrational, chancy, without purpose or ultimate intelligibility. What got to her most was the affectation of professors pretending that everything is ultimately absurd, while in more proximate matters putting all their trust in science, rationality, and mathematical calculation. She decided that atheists could not accept the implications of their own metaphysical commitments. While denying the principle of rationality "all the way down," they wished to cling to all the rationalities on the surface of things. My daughter found this unconvincing.

She decided that atheism cannot be true, because it is self-contradictory. Moreover, this self-contradiction is willful, and its latent purpose is pathetically transparent. Atheists want all the comforts of the rationality that emanates from rational theism, but without personal indebtedness to any Creator, Governor, Judge. That is why they allow themselves to be rationalists only part of the way down. The alternative makes them very nervous.

My daughter concluded that it was more reasonable to believe that there is a God, who made all things. But she couldn't figure out how this made any difference to her personally. Why did such a God care about her, or anything else? What practical difference did such a God make in the world? Besides, she wasn't at all sure how even to think of such a God. What image works? What concept? About all these matters she found herself agnostic. That's why she called herself an "agno-theist."

It seemed odd to my daughter that there can be so much reason in the world, while there is no reason *for* the world, even with its manifest irrationalities. (She herself painfully experienced many irrational tragedies among her so-promising, intelligent, gifted friends, at least one of whom was prematurely struck down in his youth.) Our daughter is no Pollyanna. She has always perceived the dark, irrational side of life. What surprises her is the degree of rationality in all things, not the presence of absurdities. What surprised her in her professors was the self-contradiction at the root of their lives.

REAL CHRISTIANITY?

In an inn in the little village of Bressanone (Brixen) in northern Italy, there is a fresco painted many centuries ago, whose main subject is an elephant, by a painter who had obviously never seen an elephant. Clearly, he was trying to represent on the wall what someone had tried to tell him about elephants. He painted a large, heavy horse, with unusually floppy ears, and a nose considerably longer than that of an average horse—but still a horse's long nose.

We used to smile at that fresco, and similarly the Christian reader will smile at the primitive fresco of Christianity painted by Dawkins, Dennett, and Harris. These atheists miss the real thing by a country mile.

One does not experience the real thing simply by being born into a Christian home, either. It is far from sufficient to have performed certain boring rituals, and attended "Sunday school" with an inattentive and unquestioning mind. As Cardinal Newman laid out in some detail in his *Grammar of Assent,* a broad and shimmering gulf separates "notional" from "real" assent. For the first, vague, insignificant ideas will do. For the latter, one has to think about one's faith, question it from all sides, study its dimensions, implications, and relations with other modes of knowing. One has to "make it one's own." One cannot just be "thrown" into it by birth and early instruction. Faith that is not nurtured under trial and severe questioning is a little like grass in thin soil, which is fresh in the morning, wilts in the afternoon, and dies before twilight. Our authors, it seems, want to rake up the most shallowly rooted grass.

Thus it seems useful—and necessary—to sketch out some of the facets of Christian faith to which our atheist threesome seem inattentive. Each Christian (each Catholic) sees this differently, of course, but right off the bat I notice four questions on which Christian faith offers arresting reflections.

1. A Theology of the Absurd. Begin with the bloody cross of Calvary. On this gibbet dies the Son of God? The cross is the very symbol of contradiction, and the absurd. When Christians speak of the act of Creation, we do not think of a perfectionist artificer making Lladró dolls, but rather of God creating flesh and blood in all its angularity, deformations, imperfections, and concrete limitations, and in the midst of myriad evils and abominations. The world of His creation is riven through with absurdities and contradictions, species that die out, and the teeming, blooming, buzzing confusion of contingencies and chance. When God singles out a chosen people, He picks a small and difficult tribe in a poor, backward, and underdeveloped part of the world. His chosen ones are overrun by enemies again and again, and carted off into slavery and exile for long, long years. Then, when the Creator sends His Son to become flesh, the Son also roots his new community mainly among the poor, the uneducated, the humble, the forgotten.

But then, blasphemy is added to blasphemy, and this Son of God is condemned to death as a common criminal, and forced into the most disgraceful sort of death known to men of that time: public mockery, a scourging virtually unto death, and then put out to hang on a cross where the public can shout insults, until the vultures come to pick at his eyes and his wounded flesh.

This is not a Pollyanna, this Creator. But what He does do is assure those who suffer and who groan under the weight of the absurd that, though at times they feel icy fear, they do not in the end need to be afraid. God is a good God and has His own purposes, and it is no mistake to trust His kindness, ever. The Creator did not make us to face a reasonable world in a rational, calm, and dispassionate way—like a New York banker after a splendid lunch at his Club, sunk into his favorite soft chair in the Library where a fragrant cigar is still permitted, as he comfortably reads his morning papers. Instead, there is war, exile, torture, injustice. Life is to be understood as a trial, and a time of suffering. A vale of tears. A valley of death. Even in the bosom of wealth, and luxury, and plenty—even there, cancer and failure and radical loneliness strike; but even more often still, simple boredom.

Not at all a land of happy talk, not at all the perfect world of *Candide.* Atheism is in the main suitable for comfortable men, in a reasonable world. For those in agony and distress, Christianity has seemed to serve much better and for a longer time, not because it offers "consolation" but precisely because it does not. For Christians, the cross is inescapable, and one ought always be prepared to take it up. I myself have watched three deeply religious people die without consolation, bereft, empty of feeling for God. To be empty of consolation, however, is not to be empty of faith. Faith is essentially a quiet act of love, even in misery: "Be it done to me according to thy will."

Like Stephen Jay Gould, our three authors think they are destroying the argument from design by showing how poorly designed are so many parts of human anatomy, how many species have perished since the beginning of time (something like 90 percent), how chancily and seemingly without reason so many steps in natural selection are taken. They want to show that if there is a Designer, he is an incompetent one; or, more exactly, there is too much evidence of lack of design. What kind of Lladró doll do they think God is? Our God is the God of the Absurd, of night, of suffering, and silent peace.

2. The Burden of Sin. It took me some years, but I have come to understand that, just as some people have no ear for music, so others (as Friedrich Hayek put it) "have no ear for God." Still others say they have no "need" for God. They sense in themselves no round hole into which God fits. One of the blessings of atheism seems to be that it takes away any sense of Judgment, any sense that by one's actions one may be offending a Friend, any awareness of sin. "Sin" seems, indeed, to be a leftover from a bygone age. *Beati voi!* I want to cry out to atheists. Lucky you.

"At the heart of Christianity is the sinner," a very great Christian, Charles Péguy, once wrote. Some of us are aware of doing things that we know we ought not to have done, and of not doing things that we know we ought to have done. We are aware of sinning against our own conscience—deliberately doing what we know to be wrong, whether from weakness or from a powerful desire that is still out of control. Afterward, sometimes, we feel a remorse so keen that it hurts—and yet what has been done is done, and nothing we now do can take that fault away. And at times the fault is shamefully grave, at that.

It is to this common, virtually universal experience that Jesus, like John the Baptist before him, first addressed his auditors. "Be sorry! Do penance. Resolve not to sin again." (Even though the probabilities of sinning again are high, just as a man with a bad knee, though his knee has healed, knows that it will too easily go out on him.)

Christianity is not about moral arrogance. It is about moral realism, and moral humility. Wherever you see self-righteous persons condemning others and unaware of their own sins, you are not in the presence of an alert Christian but of a priggish pretender. It was in fact a great revolution in human history when the Jewish and Christian God revealed Himself as one who sees directly into consciences, and is not misled merely by external acts. (This God would be unpersuaded by the external *pietas* of the numerous Greek and Roman pagan philosophers who—unconcerned about conscience—were sure to be present at religious rites, whether they took the gods seriously or not.)

The biblical respect for conscience greatly dignified and honored inner acts of reflection, commitment, and choice. It turned a powerful beam of attention away from the external act to the inner act of conscience. It greatly honored truthfulness and simple humility. Eventually, the inner duty of conscience toward the Creator became the ground of religious liberty—no other power dares intervene in this primal duty to God, which is antecedent to civil society, state, family, and any other institution. (See James Madison's *Memorial and Remonstrance,* 1785.)

3. The Bright Golden Thread of Human History. Emphasized in the liberation of the Jews from the Seleucid Empire (celebrated at Hanukkah), from Egypt (celebrated at the Passover), and from Babylon (celebrated in the poetry of Israel's prophets), a pilgrimage toward liberty and truth is the defining theme of the Torah. Every story in that testament has at its axis the arena of the human will, and the decisions made there (whether hidden or external). Thus, for biblical religion, liberty is the golden thread of human history. This conception of liberty is realized internally in the recesses of the soul and also institutionally in whole societies or polities.

No other world religions except Christianity and Judaism have put liberty of conscience so close to the center of religious life. For instance, Islam tends to think of God in terms of divine will, quite apart from nature or logic. Independently of reason, whatever Allah *wills,* does occur. Judaism and Christianity tend to think of God as *Logos* (reason), light, the source of all law and the intelligibility of all things. This difference in the fundamental conception of God alters, as well, the fundamental disposition of the human being proper to each religion: inquiry, versus submission.

4. The Point of the Cosmos Is Friendship. If it has ever occurred to you to ask, even if you are an atheist, why did God create this vast, silent, virtually infinite cosmos, you might find your best answer in the single word "friendship." According to the Scriptures, intelligently read, the Creator made man a little less than the angels, a little more complex than the other animals. He made human beings conscious enough, and reflective enough, that they might marvel at what He had wrought, and give Him thanks. Even more than that, He made human beings in order to offer to them, in their freedom, His friendship and companionship.

Friendship is not only the biblical way of thinking about the relationship between God and man; it is also a good way to imagine the future of our nation and of the world toward which we should work. From this vision, Judaism and Christianity imparted to the world a way of measuring progress and decline. William Penn called his capital city "Philadelphia" (brotherly love), and made freedom of religion its first principle. If there is no liberty, there can be no friendship. Even the atheists of the French Revolution named their fundamental principles "Liberty, Fraternity, Equality"—each of them a term that, as we will see in chapter two, derives not from the Greeks or the Romans, but from biblical religion.

A worldwide civilization of mutual friendship is a powerful magnet, and a realistic measure. Friendship does not require uniformity. On the contrary, its fundamental demand is mutual respect, willing the good of the other as other. It births a desire to converse in a reasonable way about fundamental differences in viewpoint, hope, and a sense of practical responsibility.

DIFFERENCES BETWEEN CHRISTIANITY AND ATHEISM

I recognize that the Christian horizon as it has been sketched in broad strokes in the preceding paragraphs may seem preposterous to such atheists as Dawkins, Dennett, and Harris, not to mention Mac Donald and Hitchens. They may look in vain for empirical evidence, of the sort they are able to recognize as evidence, that this sketch of God and man can even in a minimal way be in touch

with reality as they know it. On the other hand, it is not so difficult for a serious Christian to stand in the moccasins of an atheist,
and to see the world as atheists see it.

The four principles of the paradigm sketched above—friendship, liberty, the forgiveness of sin, the acceptance of absurdity—
do not exclude the viewpoint of the atheist. In fact, one learns a
great deal about some of these principles from the writings of
atheists, including Sartre, Camus, Silone, Moravia, Dewey, Seneca,
and thousands of others in between. It seems that any educated
Christian is better able to account for, and to sympathize with, the
contemporary atheist than the latter is able to sympathize with the
Christian.

If nothing else, the three authors who are now part of this conversation show how hard it is for the contemporary atheist (of the
scientific school) to show much sympathy for a Christian way of
seeing reality. Since just over two billion persons on our planet today are Christians, the inability of the contemporary atheist to
summon up fellow feeling for so many companions on the brief
voyage of a single human life seems to be a severe human han-
dicap.

Again, it is not difficult for the serious Christian to put on the
viewpoint, methods, and disciplines of evolutionary biology. Thousands of religious graduate students do so each year. One simply
has to limit one's attention and understanding to what that discipline counts as evidence and methodological rigor. One has to
master its concepts and important axioms. One has to limit one's
point of view and the sorts of questions one asks (no use asking
questions that go beyond the strict limits imposed by the discipline
itself). If you can live within these limits, all the easier.

The art of doing so is not altogether different from learning to
think as an ancient Greek, or for Catholics to learn how to look
at things as a Baptist, a Lutheran, or a Presbyterian, and for the last
named to stand provisionally in the moccasins of a Catholic. The
odd way in which Dawkins, Dennett, and Harris understand human life is something the sensitive believer must necessarily learn

along the way. I cannot imagine getting through graduate studies at Harvard, teaching at Stanford and other universities, without learning how to think, and speak, and work within the horizon, viewpoints, methods, and disciplines of the atheist.

Nor is this art solely the product of our modern pluralistic age. The young Thomas Aquinas, in his late twenties, was one of the first men in the West to have in his hands an authentic translation of several key books of Aristotle. As his extended line-by-line commentaries on several of the most important of these books show, Aquinas mastered a viewpoint quite foreign to his own. Not many years after, he had to do the same in reading al-Fārābi, Avicenna, Averroës, and other major Arab philosophers.

And so, when a Christian reader comes across Professor Dawkins's argument that God cannot exist, because all complex and more intelligent things come only at the end of the evolutionary process, not at the beginning, the Christian's first reflex may be to burst out laughing—but as an attentive student, he is also obliged to observe that, yes, from the viewpoint of evolutionary biology, that must in fact be so. The argument may be intellectually or philosophically satisfying, yet when its practical implications are compared with those of the Christian viewpoint, evolutionary biology may not be attractive as a guide to life. If one wants to be an evolutionary biologist, however, one must learn to confine oneself within the disciplines imposed by that field.

From a Roman Catholic point of view, at least, there is no difficulty in accepting all the findings of evolutionary biology, understood to be an empirical science—that is to say, *not* as a philosophy of existence, a metaphysics, a full vision of human life. It is easier for Christianity to absorb many, many findings of the contemporary world—from science to technology, politics, economics, and art—than for those whose viewpoint is confined to the contemporary era to absorb Christianity. That is just one reason that we may expect the latter to outlive the former.

It is obvious that Dawkins, at least, is quite aware of the conventional limitations of the scientific atheist's point of view. He writes that "a quasi-mystical response to nature and the universe is common among scientists and rationalists. It has no connection with supernatural belief." A few pages of his book, in almost every section, are given over to showing how an atheistic point of view can satisfy what have hitherto been taken to be religious longings. Atheism, too, he shows, has its consolations, its sources of inspiration, its awareness of beauty, its sense of wonder. For such satisfactions, there is no need to turn to religion. Dawkins does good work in restoring human subjectivity, emotion, longing, and an awed response to beauty to the life of scientific atheism. For Dawkins, scientific atheism is humanistic, a significant step forward from the sterile logical positivism of two or three generations ago.

EVERYTHING IS PERMITTED?

But atheism has a more severe limitation, one that shows itself in the actions of its proponents. One of my favorite parts of the Sam Harris book is his attempt to explain away the horrors of the self-declared atheist regimes in modern history: Fascist in Italy, Nazi in Germany, and Communist in the Soviet Union and Asia. Never in history have so many Christians been killed, tortured, driven to their deaths in forced marches, and imprisoned in concentration camps. An even higher proportion of Jews suffered still more horrifically under the same regimes, particularly the Nazi regime, than at any other time in Jewish history. The excuse Harris offers is quite lame. First he directs attention away from the ideological character of the *regime,* toward the odd *personalities* of Hitler, Mussolini, and Stalin. No, the problem is the ideology, the regime, the millions of believers in atheism. Harris ignores the essential atheism of the *ideologies* of the regime, "scientific secularism" and "dialectical materialism." Yet it is these ideologies, not just a few demented leaders, that bred a furious war on God, religion, and clergy. The nature of a regime and its ideology matter more than mad leaders. Yet here is Harris, limping: "While it is true that such men are sometimes enemies of organized religion, they are never especially rational. In fact, their public pronouncements are often delusional . . . The problem with such tyrants is not that they reject the dogma of religion, but that they embrace other life-destroying myths." In other words, delusional atheists are not really atheists.

Would Harris accept a claim by Christians that Christian evildoers are not really Christians? The real problem is not that tyrants reject the "dogma" of religion, but that they derive their furors from a dogmatic atheism that brooks no rival. They build a punitive totalitarian regime far more sweeping than their own personal madness.

Enthusiasts such as Harris may dismiss the argument that atheism is associated with relativism. Sometimes it isn't. Some atheists are rationalists of a most sober, moral kind. Nonetheless, the most common argument against placing trust in atheists is Dostoyevsky's: "If there is no God, everything is permitted." There will be no Judge of deeds and consciences; in the end, it is each man for himself. Widespread public atheism may not show its full effects right away, but only after three or four generations. For individual atheists "of a peculiar character," brought up in habits inculcated by the religious cultures of the past, can go on for two or three generations living in ways hard to distinguish from those of unassuming Christians and Jews. These individuals continue to be honest, compassionate, committed to the equality of all, firm believers in "progress" and "brotherhood," long after they have repudiated the original religious justification for this particular list of virtues. But sooner or later a generation may come along that takes the metaphysics of atheism with deadly seriousness. This was the fate of a highly cultivated nation in the Europe of our time, Germany, before it voted its way into Nazism.

George Washington considered this risk in his Farewell Address: "Let us with caution indulge the supposition that morality can be maintained without religion. Whatever may be conceded to the influence of refined education on minds of peculiar structure, reason and experience both forbid us to expect that national morality can prevail in exclusion of religious principle." If morality were left to reason alone, common agreement would never be reached, since philosophers vehemently—and endlessly—disagree, and large majorities would waver without clear moral signals. Adds Alexis de Tocqueville:

> There is almost no human action, however particular one supposes it, that does not arise from a very general idea that men have conceived of God, of his relations with the human race, of the nature of their souls, and of their duties toward those like them. One cannot keep these ideas from being the common source from which all the rest flow.
>
> Men therefore have an immense interest in making very fixed ideas for themselves about God, their souls, their general duties toward their Creator and those like them; for doubt about these first points would deliver all their actions to chance and condemn them to a sort of disorder and impotence. . . .
>
> The first object and one of the principal advantages of religions is to furnish a solution for each of these primordial questions that is clear, precise, intelligible to the crowd, and very lasting.

This extremely practical contribution is one reason Tocqueville saw religion as essential to a free people, and unbelief as tending toward tyranny.

Moreover, in times of stress distinguished intellectuals such as Heidegger and various precursors of postmodernism (including deconstructionist Paul de Man) displayed a shameless adaptation either to Nazi or to Communist imperatives—or to any other anti-Hebraic relativism. Even the elites may lose their moral compass.

Dawkins attempts to get around this flaw in (what he calls) the neo-Darwinian view of chance and blind natural selection by counting out four reasons for altruism rooted in evolutionary biology: "First, there is the special case of genetic kinship. Second, there is reciprocation: the repayment of favours given, and the giving of favours in 'anticipation' of payback. Third, the Darwinian benefit of acquiring a reputation for generosity and kindness. And fourth, there is the particular additional benefit of conspicuous generosity as a way of buying authentic advertising."

To these reasons based upon nature's egotism (which furnishes little motivation to be kind or virtuous when no one is looking), Jews and Christians would add four or five others. To begin with, altruism is morally good, rooted in natural law, and most highly commended among the "laws" of God. Second, not to love one another is to disappoint the Creator who wishes us to be His friends. Next, not to love one another is a failure to imitate the Lord Jesus, who asked us to imitate Him. Fourth, experience confirms that loving others is in tune with a communal dimension of our nature, beginning in the family, but radiating outward through the polity and the economy. (Adam Smith referred to this highest law as "sympathy.") Last, as Tocqueville pointed out, every Mosaic commandment has a foundation in nature, but tends to stretch nature's outer limits. Maimonides, Aquinas, and many others discussed this in great detail centuries ago.

As Thomas Jefferson recognized, it is self-evident that any creature owes his Creator certain duties in conscience; that much is clear by nature itself. But the commandment "Remember the Sabbath" is more specific than the natural law of reason; it stretches nature by adding to it a specifically Hebraic duty. Meanwhile, Christianity specifies this duty in terms of Sunday, rather than the Jewish Sabbath. Thus, nature alone reaches the fundamental principle, but this Third Commandment, at least, specifies more than nature alone does. Jewish and Christian faiths do not reject, but build upon nature, add to it, bring it to a more concrete expression.

Finally, our three authors fail to think carefully about what Jews and Christians actually have to say about God. Their own atheistic concept of God is a caricature, an ugly godhead that anybody might feel duty-bound to reject. Dawkins makes fun of an omniscient God who would also be free. If an omniscient God knows now what future actions He will take, how will that leave room for Him to change His mind—and how does that leave Him omnipotent? Isn't He caught in a kind of vise?

But, of course, this is to imagine God being in time as Dawkins is in time. Dawkins fails to grasp the difference between a viewpoint from eternity, outside time, and his own viewpoint from within time. He also fails to grasp the freedom that the primary cause allows to secondary causes, to contingencies, and to particulars. God's will is not *before* human decisions are made. Rather, it is simultaneous with them, and thus empowers their coming into existence. Ancient philosophers proved able to grasp this point. Surely our contemporary atheists can become equally as learned?

When Catholics celebrate the sacrifice of the Mass, for example, we imagine that our moment of participation in that particular Mass is—as it is for every other Mass we attend in our lives—in God's eyes simultaneous with the bloody death of His Son on Calvary. In our eyes, it is experienced as a "reenactment," but in God's eyes both moments are as one. No doubt, for some minds this is all too mystical, and its underlying philosophy is a bit too sophisticated, especially to those of literal and purely empirical tastes. Our three authors, in any case, present a quite primitive idea of God. If the rest of us had such a view, we, too, would almost certainly be atheists.

The whole inner world of aware and self-questioning religious persons seems to our atheist authors unexplored territory. All around them are millions who spend many moments each day (and hours each week) in communion with God. Yet of the silent and inward parts of these lives—and why these inner silences ring so true to those who share them, and seem more grounded in reality than anything else in life—our writers seem unaware. Surely, if our atheist friends were to reconsider their methods, and deepen their understanding of such terms as "experience" and "the empirical," they might come closer to walking for a tentative while in the moccasins of so many of their more religious companions in life, who find theism more intellectually satisfying—less self-contradictory, less alienating from their own nature—than atheism.

The only way human beings can come to understand each other is by learning, out of mutual respect, how to stand in one another's shoes. If that maxim of Habermas is true (see chapter ten), we might wish our three authors had done more, from their side, to close the great divide between belief and unbelief in the human spirit of our time. Still, we can be grateful that our authors have opened a window into the souls of atheists, so that the rest of us might better understand what the world looks like from their point of view—and even to see ourselves for a while as they see us.

Christopher Hitchens, in some ways a national treasure for the United States, an unusually well-read, graceful, and delightful writer, often witty and even comedic, has opened his soul to an unusual degree. He predicts that his believer friends will be surprised by how harshly antireligious his true views actually are. Well, he has let fling poisonous invective against one of the most gentle, self-sacrificing, loving souls most of us have ever met, Mother Teresa. He has even called her a "whore." That is about as gross as the jihadist expectation of seventy-two blue-eyed harlots in the martyr's Paradise. And he now avows his hatred and enmity against "all that is called God." I was sorry to see this. But it would be patronizing and unfair to Hitchens to take him at less than his word. Let us look into it more closely.

TWO

Nor Is This the Way: Hitchens   *

A few atheists, as we shall see in chapters three and four, want to converse with believers; many want merely to dismiss them. For instance, to his book *God Is Not Great* Christopher Hitchens appends the dismissive subtitle *How Religion Poisons Everything.* Yet in real life, as opposed to his fiery denunciations, Hitchens does love to talk with religious people. He occasionally does so with such biting satire that, embarrassed for him, the recipient observes a courteous silence. But often in real life Hitchens is very kind.

"The first hope I had for the book," Hitchens told *The Atlantic* in July 2007, during his book tour, "was that it would put some hope into the growing atheist secular movement." Thus with Hitchens, as with his colleagues, one stumbles upon a surprising defensiveness, as though his book is less a sign of victory than of loneliness. Everywhere on earth except Western Europe, religion is surging. Each of the authors admits that most people, especially in America, do not agree with him. Each pictures himself as a man who is fighting against heavy odds. Each rehearses his arguments for atheism, perhaps to convince himself.

Certainly, these authors are not convincing many others. According to a 2007 Princeton Survey poll for *Newsweek,* 91 percent of Americans believe in God. Only 3 percent say they are atheists. Another 7 percent report that they are of no religion or are agnostic. (A tiny group responds "believe in God" and also "no religion.") The whole group of nonbelievers accounts for 10 percent, at best, of all Americans. Worse for the new atheists, a full 87 percent of Americans identify with a specific religion: 82 percent are

Christian, 2 percent Jewish, and 1 percent Muslim, Buddhist, or other. Similarly, Gallup's May 2007 poll found that only 6 percent of respondents did not believe in God. On the other hand, in fairness, we must note that many who call themselves Christians belong to no local church, are "unchurched." Further, the vast extent of religious illiteracy among Americans is appalling.

Christopher Hitchens writes that several of his favorite conversation partners are religious people—as they would pretty much have to be, given the percentages. He becomes angry, he says, when these friends describe him as a "seeker." I agree that he is not a seeker—but he must be almost out of breath from being sought. He hates God so much one wonders how he can *not* believe in Him. He believes in the tormenting light of conscience and the human drive of honest inquiry too much not to be fueled (at least by a little) with the spirit of God. That spirit, after all, dwells in pagans as well as in believers; it dwells in Plato, Aristotle, Cicero, and legions of others. Maybe also in Hitchens, despite himself.

Seeker or sought, Christopher Hitchens is one of the writers whose courage and polemical force I highly admire. He gives frequent proof of a passionate honesty, which sometimes has obliged him to criticize ideological soul mates when he thinks they are wrong on some important matter—the acute threat from Islamofascism, for example. Many of our colleagues today, out of a panicky fear that they might "help the wrong people" on the evil Right, pretend publicly to have no enemies on the Left. Though always a man of the Left, Hitchens will have none of that. Being on the Left is dear to him; honesty, more dear.

Another thing: Hitchens does his homework and he thinks clearly. If you go to debate him, you had better think things through rather carefully and well, for his is a well-stocked, quick, and merciless mind. Trained in the British university school of arguing by way of ridicule (and even over-the-top accusations), Hitchens gets audiences at debates laughing at his foes and cheering his every thrust. He credits Socrates as the source of two maxims in his method of arguing: "The first is that conscience is innate," that is, not limited to people of faith. No argument from me about that. "The second is that the dogmatic faithful can easily be outpointed and satirized by one who pretends to take their teachings at face value." With much enthusiasm, Hitchens seeks to outpoint his dialogue partner and satirize him. In doing this, he is not above a bit of bullying. Withal, he is an excellent man (so others tell me) to have a drink with.

Four "Irreducible Objections"

Something peculiar happens to Hitchens when he wrestles against God, even with murderous intent: Hitchens always loses (and he may secretly suspect that). Preposterous as this seems, he may fear that one day he will wake up and see it all plainly, right before his eyes. Otherwise, why year after year keep striking another stake into the heart of God?

Ever since he was thirteen years old, apparently, Hitchens has cherished "four irreducible objections to religious faith." He was then, he writes, one of those precocious students who by force of a native skepticism just drifted away from the fairly pallid religious views of his father (Calvinist) and mother (nonreligious Jewish).

The first irreducible objection he announces is that religious faith "wholly misrepresents the origins of man and the cosmos." At the age of thirteen, Hitchens might well have thought that. But nowadays Hitchens excuses naïve scientific errors and missteps (the phlogiston theory) of great scientists such as Newton, Priestley, and Franklin, by kindly covering their nakedness: "Remember that we are examining the childhood of our species." Is not religion also entitled to its childhood? Christians have also learned from earlier errors.

Hitchens is much too smart to mistake the book of Genesis for a contemporary account of string theory in an advanced text of physics. The largest of all Christian churches, the Roman Catholic Church, leaves to science the task of figuring out descriptions and theories of the material "origins of man and the cosmos." In the Jewish tradition, Rav Joseph Soloveitchik (1903–1993), among the most eminent Orthodox Talmudists of the twentieth century, taught that *imitatio Dei* requires believers to imitate God's creativity, particularly through intellectual inquiry and scientific practice. Rav Soloveitchik was among the key founders of Yeshiva University, which has as its motto *"Torah U'Madah,"* in modern Hebrew "Torah and science." The succinct story of the book of Genesis, and the theological affirmations that draw out its main lessons, emphasizes three points:

- All creation is suffused with intelligence, as a unified whole.
- All creation is, on the whole, good and worthy to be affirmed and loved.
- Its Creator is separate from creation, so that the latter is to be neither idolized nor perceived as under taboo; humans are intended to investigate it and come to understand it thoroughly, naming all things.

None of these three affirmations seems contrary to Hitchens's own way of proceeding in regard to man and the cosmos. To refer to the natural world as "creation," though, might cause him gastric pain.

His second irreducible objection to religious faith: "Because of this original error it manages to combine the maximum of servility with the maximum of solipsism." Really? The reader is likely to imagine that something important must be meant by "servility" and "solipsism." But what have these to do with Dante, Shakespeare, Lord Nelson, Abraham Lincoln, John F. Kennedy, Ronald Reagan, and the millions of other Christians who stand in their shadow and imitate from afar their boldness, capaciousness of character, wide range of vices and virtues, and zest for building a better world?

Hitchens's third irreducible objection to religious faith: "That it is both the result and the cause of dangerous sexual repression."

I would have thought that the history of England gave witness to a great many lusty Christians; the tales of Chaucer and the plays of Shakespeare ought to be enough on which to rest the case. Graham Greene and Evelyn Waugh were not exactly prudes.

Personally, I am rather glad about the Jewish and Christian emphasis upon honoring the human body as sacred, a temple of the Creator. I am glad that this vision instructs Christians, in self-control, to channel their sexual acts within the bonds of marriage. These are, I would have thought, great civilizing and liberating injunctions. As Tocqueville shrewdly observes, where fidelity establishes trust in the bosom of the family, trust among citizens of the Republic is more natural.

> In Europe, almost all the disorders of society are born around the domestic hearth, not far from the nuptial bed. It is there that men conceive their scorn for natural bonds and permitted pleasures, their taste for disorder, the restiveness of heart, their instability of desires. Agitated by the tumultuous passions that have often troubled his own dwelling, the European submits only with difficulty to the legislative power of the state. When, on leaving the agitations of the political world, the American returns to the bosom of his family, he immediately meets the image of order and peace. There all his pleasures are simple and natural, his joys innocent and tranquil; and as he arrives at happiness through regularity of life, he becomes habituated to regulating his opinions as well as his tastes without difficulty.

For tiny Jerusalem, too, neighboring kingdoms to the east and north and south—the Persians, the Babylonians, the Africans—did not have such channeling for sexual polymorphism, and in their own excess fell civilizationally behind Jewish and later, Christian cultures. Even science and enlightenment depend on a certain self-control, even asceticism.

I can see how atheists might wish to experiment further afield and live under fewer sexual restraints than those just stated. God knows, I have sometimes wished I could. Moreover, the many stories of love triangles invented by and for Christian civilization during the past twelve hundred years (since the troubadours) dramatize the tensions that monogamy sets up in the human heart. How could they not? These are the fantasies that arise from sexual self-control. I find it unlikely that Hitchens believes self-control to be morally equivalent to repression.

In the same vein, Sam Harris also makes a crack about how ignoble it is of the so-called God to care "about something people do while naked." As for gorillas and chimpanzees in the zoo, which Hitchens brings up in his opening pages, it is plain that the Creator does not care when they openly rub their genitals, or whether out in the open they mount a female or are mounted. Of human beings, it appears, he expects a little more self-control, romance, restraint, and mutual respect. As a matter of human dignity.

Actually, come to think of it, surveys of sexual behavior regularly show that secularists enjoy sex rather less than devout Christians do. It may be like the difference between relieving a biological urge and knowing that marital love is in harmony with "the Love that moves the Sun and all the Stars." The feminist writer Naomi Wolf published a fascinating essay several years ago noting the bruises that casual sex with multiple partners leaves upon the psyche; and the absence of a sense that a faithful love can last forever. The inherent symbol of two bodies coupling is unity of heart and soul, in which two become one. A great many sexual acts, in that light, are lies.

The enormous weight that a secularist culture places on sexual fulfillment is insupportable for one simple reason. Sexual intercourse is an organic expression of entire psyches, not a mechanical plugging in. Among the young, the weakening of cultural forms supporting sexual rituals and restraints deprives sexual intercourse of sustenance for the imagination and the spirit. It comes too cheaply: its intimacy is mainly fake; its symbolic power is reduced to the huddling of kittens in the darkness—not to be despised, but open as a raw wound to the experience of nothingness. Close your eyes and plummet through the empty space where a lover ought to be.

Hitchens's fourth irreducible objection: "That religion is ultimately grounded on wish-thinking." Of course, it may be, but perhaps it is atheism that is based on wishful thinking. For some, atheism may be a defiant thrill and self-glorying attraction. With virtually no effort, one becomes a hero in one's own eyes. And think of the burdens that slide off one's shoulders just by becoming an atheist. It's a helluva temptation.

There is one thing profoundly irritating about the atheist pose, however. Some atheists are among the most satirical, dismissive dogmatists one encounters anywhere in life, constantly ridiculing others, setting these others up for logical traps and hoots of laughter. And yet these dogmatists routinely boast, as Hitchens does:

> And here is the point, about myself and my co-thinkers. Our belief is not a belief. Our principles are not a faith. We do not rely solely upon science and reason, because these are necessary rather than sufficient factors, but we distrust anything that contradicts science or outrages reason. We may differ on many things, but what we respect is free inquiry, openmindedness, and the pursuit of ideas for their own sake.

I am certain, having in admiration watched Hitchens in print for many years, that Hitchens does not really wish to be a dogmatist—he hates the breed—and does not think he is a dogmatist. Still, I would have thought that all men who in argument routinely ridicule their opponents extend the secret handshake of all dogmatists everywhere: Opponents are for mocking.

Dear, dear Mr. Hitchens. We have all experienced the dogmatism of those who claim to have none. And close-mindedness in regard to God does no honor to those who claim to live by free inquiry, open minds, constant questioning, and ceaseless searching.

In a word, Hitchens's "four irreducible objections" don't amount to much.

DESIGN AS FORMAL LOGIC

Like many antireligious polemicists, Hitchens suggests that believers in God imagine God as a Designer, whereas experience shows that this world is of inferior design. Indeed, he writes:

> Thomas Jefferson in old age was fond of the analogy of the timepiece in his own case, and would write to friends who inquired after his health that the odd spring was breaking and the occasional wheel wearing out. This of course raises the uncomfortable (for believers) idea of the built-in fault that no repairman can fix. Should this be counted as part of the "design" as well? (As usual, those who take the credit for the one will fall silent and start shuffling when it comes to the other side of the ledger.)

Hitchens seems to hold that believers think of the Creator as a simple-minded Geometer, a Rationalist Extraordinaire, a two-times-two-equals-four kind of god, a flawless Watchmaker, a bit of a Goody-goody, a cosmic Boy Scout. If that is so—Hitchens leaps for the believer's throat—then evidence is overwhelming that this Creator botched things up, like a rank amateur. In short, evidence all around us shows there is no such god.

Let's be honest. The God who made this world is certainly no Rationalist, Utopian, or Perfectionist. We can see for ourselves that most acorns fall without generating a single oak tree. Some species die away—perhaps as many as 90 percent of all that have ever lived upon this earth have already perished. Infants are still-born, others born deformed. Children are orphaned and little girls, terrified, sob at night in their beds. Human sex seems almost a cosmic trick played upon us, a joke, a game that angels laugh at. 'Tis a most imperfect world that *this* Designer has designed.

But suppose God is not like the Hitchens model. Suppose that God is not a Rationalist, a Logician, a straight-line Geometer-of-the-skies. Suppose that the Creator God—like a great novelist, and long before man arrived on earth—created a world of probability schemes and redundancies, of waste and profusion, of heavy buffeting and hardship. Blossoms fell to earth, turned to dust. Stars for millions of light-years brilliant in the far firmament suddenly burn out. Suppose that this God loved untended forests as well as architectural design, statistical schemes of order as much as classical logic. Suppose that this God loved the idea of a slowly developing, incomplete, imperfect history, most good things emerging from suffering. Such a world might be stunningly beautiful. The cross might fit its door like a key.

Suppose He desired a world of indetermination, with all its crisscrossing confusion, so that within it freedom could spread out its wings, experiment, and find its own way:

> *Glory be to God for dappled things—*
> *For skies of couple-colour as a brinded cow;*
> *For rose-moles all in stipple upon trout that swim;*
> *Fresh-firecoal chestnut-falls; finches' wings . . .*
>
> *All things counter, original, spare, strange;*
> *Whatever is fickle, freckled (who knows how?)*
> *With swift, slow; sweet, sour; adazzle, dim;*
> *He fathers-forth whose beauty is past change:*
> *Praise him.*
>
> —"Pied Beauty," Gerard Manley Hopkins

What Jewish/Christian Insight Adds
to British Enlightenment

At one point, Hitchens proposes a thought experiment that goes like this. Practically everything in civilization is wiped out. The human race has to start all over again. "If we lost all our hard-won knowledge and all our archives, and all our ethics and all our morals . . . and had to reconstruct everything essential from scratch, it is difficult to imagine at what point we would need to remind or reassure ourselves that Jesus was born of a virgin."

But is this actually the way things have worked out? If there were no Annunciation of the angel to Mary of Nazareth, if there were no birth of the Son of God in a decrepit stable, if there were no passion, death, and resurrection—or even if all memory and record of such events had been erased—would the world have lost anything of permanent human value? There are, in fact, a number of points of great significance for human conscience and politics, and even science, that the human race might never have come to. As Jürgen Habermas points out, nearly all the basic ideals of the Enlightenment—*fraternity* clearly so, but also *liberty* and *equality*—derive from Jewish Christianity, not from Greece or Rome. In his own words:

> For the normative self-understanding of modernity, Christianity has functioned as more than just a precursor or a catalyst. Universalistic egalitarianism, from which sprang the ideals of freedom and a collective life in solidarity, the autonomous conduct of life and emancipation, the individual morality of conscience, human rights, and democracy, is the direct legacy of the Judaic ethic of justice and the Christian ethic of love.

Set aside any religious significance to the birth and death of Jesus Christ. Set aside any hint of redemption and eternal life. Consider only the implications of Christian faith for politics and science. Only in the Jewish and Christian conception of God is God "Spirit and Truth," and more concerned about what goes on in individual conscience than in outward gesture. From this conception derives the argument for liberty of conscience in George Mason, James Madison, and Thomas Jefferson. Theirs is a Jewish/Christian conception of God; not quite like that of Newton or other rationalists. In his 1785 *Memorial and Remonstrance Against Religious Assessments*, James Madison writes:

> [W]e hold it for a fundamental and undeniable truth, "that Religion or the duty which we owe to our Creator and the manner of discharging it, can be directed only by reason and conviction, not by force or violence." The Religion then of every man must be left to the conviction and conscience of every man; and it is the right of every man to exercise it as these may dictate. [SEC. I, PARA. I]

The American God peers into inner conscience, not merely outward behavior; and this biblical God asks conscience to bow only to evidence. In the draft of his 1779 *Bill for Establishing Religious Freedom* (later pushed through the legislature by Madison in 1785), Thomas Jefferson affirmed, "Well aware that the opinions and belief of men depend not on their own will, but *follow involuntarily the evidence proposed to their minds,* that Almighty God hath created the mind free, and manifested his Supreme will that free it shall remain, by making it altogether insusceptible of restraint" (emphasis added).

Judaism and Christianity considerably deepened their own resources with the moderating habits that they partly learned from pagan ethical systems, from Socrates, Aristotle, and the Stoics. In return, Judaism and Christianity infused into young and inexperienced Northern Europe a spark of the asceticism, self-denial, discipline, dedication to long years of study, and habits of honesty and limpid transparency that are necessary for sustained scientific work. Here was powerfully reinforced the conviction that everything in the universe, being the fruit of a single intelligence, is in principle understandable and worth all the arduous labor to try to grasp it. Here recent scholars such as Daniel Boorstin (*The Creators*) and David Landes (*The Wealth and Poverty of Nations*) have uncovered the Western conviction that it is the human vocation to be inventive and to help complete the evolving work of creation.

In this vein, Hitchens praises the efforts of two Princeton professors, Peter and Rosemary Grant, who for thirty years have traveled between campus and "the arduous conditions of the tiny island of Daphne Major" in the Galapagos Islands. "Their lives were harsh," Hitchens notes, "but who could wish that they had mortified themselves in a holy cave or on top of a sacred pillar instead?" With this quip, Hitchens dismisses a more central question. Who could wish that there had been no Jewish and Christian ascetics to inspire the Grants with two incandescent lessons? First, that there is intelligibility in all things, waiting to be discovered. That is, there is a fit between the universe created by God and the human mind created by God—they were made for each other. Second, the vocation of the inquiring mind requires patience, discipline, precise observation, honest reporting, and careful thinking that can withstand the objections of others and persuade even the dubious. The first of these lessons assures researchers in advance that their pain and suffering will be rewarded with new light into our world, and perhaps also into ourselves.

In our generation, Jürgen Habermas has called for a greater tolerance on the part of atheists toward religious believers, and a kind of mutual human respect, which will demand from atheists an attempt to state honestly all their debts to the religious civilization of the West. By contrast Hitchens is quite a bit over-the-top in his hatred of Judaism/Christianity.

GOD KNOWN BY REASON

Yet, in a more limited sense, of course, Hitchens is correct. If all we had to depend upon were science, empiricism, and our own inquiring minds, we could still have discovered the existence of God (but not the God of Judaism and Christianity)—as did the ancient Greeks and Romans. Reason might well have shown us—did, in fact, show us—that there is living intelligence flashing out from everything on earth and in the skies above. All earthly things are alive with reasons, connections, and also with oddities yet to become better understood, puzzles yet to be solved. We learn by experiment that if we apply our minds to trying to understand how things truly are, how they work, how they are best used, there seems always to be some intelligible light within them that yields up precious satisfactions to the hungry mind. Everything, that is, seems understandable—in principle, if not just yet. This is the outer limit to his sense of the divine that Einstein confesses (as quoted by Hitchens):

> It was, of course, a lie what you read about my religious convictions, a lie which is being systematically repeated. I do not believe in a personal God and I have never denied this but expressed it clearly. If something is in me which can be called religious, then it is the unbounded admiration for the structure of the world so far as our science can reveal it.

Hitchens may have been too quick in misinterpreting Einstein. In *Einstein: His Life and Universe,* Walter Isaacson uncovers Einstein's objections to aggressive atheism.

> But throughout his life, Einstein was consistent in rejecting the charge that he was an atheist. "There are people who say there is no God," he told a friend. "But what makes me really angry is that they quote me for support of such views." And unlike Sigmund Freud or Bertrand Russell or George Bernard Shaw, Einstein never felt the urge to denigrate those who believed in God; instead, he tended to denigrate atheists. "What separates me from most so-called atheists is a feeling of utter humility toward the unattainable

secrets of the harmony of the cosmos," he explained. In fact, Einstein tended to be more critical of debunkers, who seemed to lack humility or a sense of awe, than of the faithful. "The fanatical atheists," he wrote in a letter, "are like slaves who are still feeling the weight of their chains which they have thrown off after hard struggle. They are creatures who—in their grudge against traditional religion as the 'opium of the masses'—cannot hear the music of the spheres."

Engaged in polemics, many atheists like to do two things, which certainly Hitchens does. The first is to make fun of believers on every matter possible, even when that requires outrageous misstatements of fact and employs such clumsy logic as atheists would mock in others. The second is to generate as many incoherencies in the faith of believers as their fertile minds can make up. Hitchens is in our time one of the great masters of mockery and satire. He out-Paines Tom Paine, yet that same Thomas Paine, mocker of the Bible-toting, endured imprisonment in France after 1789 for forewarning the Jacobins that their atheism would cut the ground out from under their declared human rights. In moral heroism, standing up against angry mobs, Hitchens is often Paine's equal. Like Paine, Hitchens also seems quite annoyed by Him in Whom he does not believe. (Paine was no atheist, but he accepted only the basics about the biblical God—creation, the vocation to love all humans universally—he called it "theophilanthropy"—and final judgment.)

One of the favorite objects of Hitchens's mockery is the Jewish and Christian belief in the omnipotence and omniscience of God, proud fortresses that once protected the claim that God is good, against the maelstrom of evils that descend like rain upon the just and the unjust alike. Hitchens makes one think of the rather amusing quatrain debunking omnipotence and omniscience summoned up by Richard Dawkins:

Can omniscient God, who
Knows the future, find
The omnipotence to
Change His future mind?

A cute little quatrain.

Yet it does have the defect of putting God in time as though He were just an ordinary Joe like the rest of us. In the classic formulation, "omniscience" and "omnipotence" characterize a being outside of time, unchanging, unchanged. Thus, God has no "future" mind, but only a present mind, in which all Time is present as if in simultaneity. The god presented us by atheists, by contrast, is awfully anthropomorphic and fundamentalist. Unnecessarily so. The eternalness of the mind and will of God, in the Judeo-Christian view, does not forbid His creation from taking a wild, unpredictable, highly contingent adventure through history. The Creator's relation to His creation may not be at all what Dawkins and Hitchens project. It may be that of the Artist, or Novelist, who does not infringe upon the liberty of His living creations, even while testing them with difficulties, setbacks, and self-revealing choices.

For the atheist—for Hitchens—the problem of goodness, which his passionate conscience well exemplifies, may create an intellectual problem. If everything is by chance and merely relative, why is it natural for so many to be good—if not all the time, at least often enough to be quite striking? Why is conscience innate?

Put another way: Isn't it unlikely that random chance alone has arranged the world so that many human qualities—the very ones that Plato, Aristotle, the Stoics, and Jews and Christians find good on other grounds—should also work better for the survival of the human race? It would be at least mildly interesting that philosophy, revealed religion, and random natural selection lead to many of the same moral principles. Perhaps that explains why some atheists are so nobly good (the "secular saints" of Albert Camus), and why some insist on being credited with being good. Some do seem to hate it when believers suggest that in the absence of faith, moral relativism prevails. Christopher Hitchens plainly (and in his case, rightly) resents it.

Besides, atheists of conscience have often placed their trust in very human faiths, in very human causes and systems and utopian visions. Hitchens testifies to how deeply he sympathizes with this kind of atheist, as in his splendid tribute to Doris Lessing on her receiving the 2007 Nobel Prize:

> For much of her life, the battle against apartheid and colo-nialism was the determining thing in Lessing's life. She joined the Communist Party and married a German Com-munist exile (who was much later killed as the envoy of East Germany to Idi Amin's hateful regime in Uganda), and if you ever want to read how it actually felt, and I mean truly *felt*, to believe in a Communist future with all your heart, her novels from that period will make it piercingly real for you.

Communism was, of course, a "God that Failed." Generation after generation such gods do arise—and disappear into the void. One should not overlook—should marvel all the more—at that lowly faith in the God who does not fail, but generation after gen-eration, century after century, millennium after millennium, is faithful to His people. Hitchens regards all that as "poison." His choice.

AMERICAN CONCEPTIONS OF GOD AND CONSCIENCE

One point that Hitchens ought to concede is that Judaism and Christianity do add to reason insights and virtues that derive from forms of intelligence that range more broadly and deeply than a too-narrow construction of reason. It was against common sense and practical reason for the Americans in 1776, without an army and without a navy, to make war on the greatest naval and military power in the world. But their Declaration of Independence did fit with the conviction that God created the world for freedom, in order to offer His friendship to every woman and every man, with a right of refusal. As Thomas Jefferson put it, "The God who gave us life, gave us liberty at the same time." Our founders concluded that even though they prayed to the same Providence as the British, those who fight for freedom are better in tune with God's ultimate purposes than those who, though apparently stronger, fight to repress it. George Washington urged Americans to give thanks to "Almighty God" for "his kind care and protection of this country previous to their becoming a Nation . . . [and] the favorable *interpositions* of his providence, which we *experienced* in the course and conclusion of the late war" (emphasis added). The cause of liberty brought the revolutionary forces and their new Republic into line with God's purposes.

Hitchens himself is a public protagonist of compassion and solidarity. But along with conceptions of brotherhood and love of neighbor, these virtues derive, don't they, from the same Creator to whom Judaism and Christianity point? So also does the Declaration of Independence, which appeals to God four times: as the Author of nature and its laws, as Creator who endowed in us our rights, as Judge of all consciences, and as divine Providence and Governor of the affairs of men.

A book on American atheists some years back showed that well more than half of them, while calling themselves atheists, nonetheless believed in an intelligent order visible to them in the universe and/or a life force running through every living thing from the blade of grass to the newborn child. Many thought the whole universe partook of some of the central attributes the ancients attributed to God, such as its mysterious pull toward goodness, justice, and beauty—qualities that are not found in their pure state on earth, but attract us onward by their own higher levels of perfection, like mountain peak rising above mountain peak as far as the eye can see.

Reading Hitchens, one wonders if he leans a bit in that direction. There is no doubt about his passion for an ever more complete justice, or his anger against any falling off from it on the part of others. He becomes livid about Mother Teresa, because of her tender care for the dying and the poor—he thinks she should have become a socialist and helped eliminate poverty. As if socialist economics usually does. He may be even harder on himself. There is something in him he seems intent on killing.

He is conscious of and deeply pleased about his Jewish inheritance. As he told *The Atlantic* during his book tour, he enjoys holding the annual seder in his home, with the help of his mother-in-law. He expresses satisfaction in honoring the long line of Jews reaching far back in history through his family line. He appreciates the role of ritual, and the use of physical things such as vinegar, and salt, and unleavened bread, to signify memorable historical moments, and willingly participates in them. He does not want his daughter to be forced, however gently, into believing all the stuff about the Creator, the burning bush, the plagues that the Protector of Israel inflicted upon the eldest sons of every Egyptian family, and the locusts, and the blights upon the harvest. But he himself participates, willingly and with appreciation, in the moving celebration of his people's liberation from Egypt. Hitchens affects being unmoved by the beauties of this earth; even peering down into the awesome Grand Canyon he tells an interviewer that he thinks: "What the hell is that?" He tries to claim that this is a form of awe, and supplies clever assurance that he is not being conned into an inner prayer of praise. He urges believers to forget all that design and "beauties of nature" stuff, and peer instead into the Hubble telescope. There they will find beauties, he avers, that will really move them (as they move him) to awe. Somehow what he is in awe of is science, not the Artist who created the beauty science merely discovers and does not itself create. Whereas most humans in beholding such sights give glory to God, who placed the beauties out where the telescope might find them, Hitchens gives glory to science. Through Hubble, the Creator seems to hint that there are many other stunning beauties, out farther beyond, waiting for telescopes made by human hands to allow us to contemplate them—their glorious colors, their shapes, their patterns, and their movement. Hitchens's praise of science is altogether proper. It is also a tad shortsighted. It is true that except for science we never would have seen such beauties. But also, without an Artist of infinite capacity, science would never have had such beauties to discover.

R. M. Hare taught philosophers to call this trick of perception a "blik." Looking at the same scene, the unbeliever sees one view, the believer quite a different one.

Two men looked out from prison bars
One saw mud, the other stars.

Instead of arguing why choose one blik, rather than the other, Hitchens simply dumps all the mud he can upon the one he does not like and makes his own seem magical and shiny with the dawn. This is not persuasive.

In fact, his tactic makes him seem rather color-blind and tone-deaf. There are so many ordinary things he does not see or hear in the way that most people do. Or perhaps he is frightened or nervous—some things he would rather not see, some things he would rather not hear. Better to keep them away with mockery.

In another of his multiple interviews during his book tour (*The New York Post*), Hitchens claims to have laid down a dare that, so far, no believer has picked up. First, he puts believers on the defensive (his favorite opening gambit) by lifting his chest and saying he finds them highly condescending in telling him that, without faith in God, he can have no virtue and no morals. Actually, one doubts that anyone ever even thought of that, let alone said it. No one has ever said it to me, and I have lived seventy-four years in all kinds of environments. But let that pass. At that point, while his interlocutor squirms in his chair, Hitchens lays down the defiant dare: "I defy you, or anyone, to name one moral deed that I would not do, unless I . . . became a Christian." Hitchens boasts with satisfaction that he has never had a taker. Poor chaps probably had their tongues tied by fear of ridicule.

What Judaism/Christianity Adds to Open Reason

In my little study *On Two Wings: Humble Faith and Common Sense at the American Founding* (2002), leaning heavily on Tocqueville, I found at least seven advantages in morals that the Hebrew/Christian traditions offer that go beyond what Enlightenment reason provides. Let me mention only two of these. The first is the conviction that an immoral act is not so much a violation of a moral law, or a betrayal of chosen moral principles, as it is a disappointment and hurt to a Friend. This Friend is also our Creator and our Lord. This is but one of the dimensions of moral life that differentiates the two moralities.

Another lies in the Hebrew/Christian emphasis on Awakenings, on the honest confession of fault (even inward faults invisible to others), on repentance, and on a conversion of one's old life, from morally sliding downward toward a new life in God. It is this capacity that, in the First Great Awakening, enabled our founders to find a sense of dignity equal to that of the king. In it, they also found the moral strength to risk being hanged as traitors for daring to declare their country's independence. Further, our founders based their war upon protection of their own inalienable rights, whose source is not the State but the Creator of the world. Rational probabilities said that they might lose. Rational analysis pointed out that the rule of the king of England was mild compared to that of the tyrants who ruled France and other lands. Why not be reasonable and simply go on under the king? A religious vision of the way things ought to be, tamed and subdued by common sense, wise practicality, and modesty, lifted our bold forebears to reach higher than that. Religion needs reason to detoxify it. Reason needs faith to lift its aspirations.

A Direct Question Answered Directly

I will not here repeat yet more of what I wrote in *On Two Wings*. Instead, I should answer the direct question that Hitchens posed with a direct answer. Let me name just a few of the actions that a Christian would feel inspired to attempt, even though the probabilities that a secular man would find them foolish are rather high.

Does Hitchens obey the first three commandments? Does he accept that there is a Lord, his God, above whom he should hold no other gods?

Second, Hitchens may well think that he avoids taking the name of God in vain, but at that claim readers of his book might break out in laughter. Third, does Hitchens keep holy the Sabbath? Better, does he hold respect for the Sabbath to be a moral obligation? The founders of this nation did take some form of worship and thanksgiving to God to be a self-evident duty of any conscious creature. It is worthwhile to reread the Thanksgiving addresses proclaimed by the Continental Congress from 1776 on, by President Washington, and later by President Lincoln. From Lincoln:

> It is the duty of nations as well as of men to owe their dependence upon the overruling power of God; to confess their sins and transgressions in humble sorrow, yet with assured hope that genuine repentance will lead to mercy and pardon; and to recognize the sublime truth, announced in the Holy Scriptures and proven by all history, that those nations are blessed whose God is the Lord . . . It has seemed to me fit and proper that God should be solemnly, reverently, and gratefully acknowledged, as with one heart and one voice, by the whole of the American people. (October 3, 1863)

Closer to the heart of the matter, does Hitchens feel bound by "the two Great Commandments that sum up the Law and the Prophets"? That is to say, does he "love God with all his heart, and all his soul, and all his mind"? The evidence of his book and all his interviews does not suggest that Hitchens loves God.

Further, does Hitchens love his neighbor as himself?

The evidence seems very strong that in a large range of cases, Hitchens does love his neighbor. His love may be shown by rather more statist and collectivist ways than many of us have confidence in. Yet Hitchens shows that, by his own lights, solidarity with the weak and those who suffer is one of the rules by which he governs his life. On this score, Hitchens may well be more favorably judged on the Last Day than many of the baptized. This index is ranked especially high by Jews and Christians. The first epistle of Saint John insists that this is the only way by which a human can prove he loves God—if he has love for his neighbor.

Now I hate to ruin Hitchens's remaining years on earth by bringing him the bad news—that he may well end up in heaven. He claims he would be bored. He imagines heaven to be a sentence to North Korea, under the worst combination of coerced adulation and a crushingly boring authoritarian leader, with no possibility of escape. Poor Hitchens, to suffer so from a truncated imagination.

There remains only one point on which I suspect (only suspect, not knowing nearly enough) that Hitchens does not measure up: in loving himself. In the command to "love your neighbor as yourself," the most difficult part is often the "as yourself." Self-love is common. Self-love dies, Saint Bernard told his monks, fifteen minutes after the self. But a good self-love, loving yourself as God loves you, loving yourself in honesty and full truthfulness, is very rare. A great many human beings, I find, deeply underestimate how radiant with love God has created them, how good in His eyes they really are. They are much too hard on themselves, insecure, and unsatisfied. Usually, they cover this by putting others down.

In his interviews and published reflections after his book tour, Hitchens reveals a little more about the state of his own soul. He tends to imagine God in the most awful terms. He calls God many vile names, including "capricious dictator." He accuses God of meanly, arbitrarily, and spitefully throwing confused people down into everlasting punishment for breaking some silly taboo. (Like a child hopping down the sidewalk: "Step on a crack, break your mother's back.") He says that the God who created sex, of which the reader takes it Hitchens approves, walled it around with prohibitions: No, no, no, no! To abortion, homosexuality, adultery, fornication, masturbation—you name it, Hitchens avers, there is a prohibition against it.

Without the tutoring of Hitchens, a normal person might be forgiven for thinking that God's point has been to get humans thinking of some other things beyond sex. Sex is very good; one may be certain God enjoyed the humor of its creation, its zones of delight embedded in organs of waste removal, its whole execution rather clumsy, and its uneven outcomes as between males and females seemingly unfair. Nonetheless, this lopsided, comical activity preoccupies human beings, makes some *obsess* about it, and maintains a steady horniness in many more sets of breeches than one might imagine. Still, look at all the guidebooks on the subject, the "adult" movies, the "candid" photos on the Internet, the self-help manuals. Pleasure in sex must be a bit harder to find, or to maintain, than one might have thought. So much trouble to put up with on its behalf. A pretty huge business, sex.

And actually, all the evidence is that serious Jews and Christians report more satisfaction from sex than do nonbelievers.

Besides, without sex, there isn't any future for the human race. When sex is suffused with a lifetime's love, and permeated with friendship and loyalty, it is a wondrous part of human life. Indeed, of cosmic life. One imagines even the angels dancing, or howling with laughter, and with maybe a touch of envy. Every day is springtime.

A FINAL REPORT CARD

Another atheist committed to conscience and the innate good of human reason is Heather Mac Donald. In the next two chapters, we shall exchange thoughts with Heather about the nature of reason, and the persistent questions it has long driven humans to ask.

But first, a few final words about Hitchens. Hitchens tries to meet standards that come from an innately good human reason. These standards, as Hitchens pursues them, are normally quite high. He fails them most when, contrary to the sense of the American founding, he is venting his bile against God, who (Hitchens thinks) does not exist.

Still, even for believers Hitchens is useful. One can take the rake of his arguments to pull out the dead grass in one's own sloppy thinking about God.

PART TWO

The Common Darkness

But if I go to the east, he is not there—
Or to the west, I cannot perceive him—
Where the north enfolds him, I behold him not—
By the south he is veiled, and I see him not.

—Job 23:8–9, NAB

THREE

Letter to an Atheist Friend

FOUR MAIN POINTS

Let us begin now to listen to questions that have haunted all our race for centuries. My colleague Heather Mac Donald of the Manhattan Institute sparked an intense and long-running debate on these matters with one short article in *The American Conservative* (August 28, 2006). Calling attention to the many "skeptical conservatives" who "ground their ideas in rational thinking and (nonreligious) moral arguments," who are—in other words—atheists, Miss Mac Donald made four main points.

It is a mistake, first, for those conservatives who are believers to lean "too heavily on religion, to the exclusion of temperamentally compatible allies," that is, atheists. For many atheists openly support American values, including family values, precisely as atheists. Second, many atheists "find themselves mystified by the religiosity of the rhetoric that seems to define so much of" the country today. They just can't follow its logic or discern its sense.

Third come several real objections to the religious rhetoric in the American air. Heather does not pretend to have studied theology, even of the natural, nonbiblical kind. She only reports what she has observed: In the face of a tragedy averted, "believers decipher God's beneficent intervention with ease." But they seem silent about the unnecessary human suffering they encounter every day. Isn't the same God responsible for the bad as well as the good? A torrent of other such questions pours from her.

Finally, Heather holds that during recent centuries, "Western society has become more compassionate, humane, and respectful of rights as it has become more secular." There is no need to be religious in order to be good and to effect moral progress in human society.

The Internet replies to Heather, pro and con, were plentiful. Some critics cheered Heather on; others found her inexcusably ignorant of what religious people actually believe, and of their reasoned arguments for these beliefs.

It is rare in American life today to conduct public argument at the depth Heather chooses. Her arguments are crucial to our national life.

A famous Jesuit once said that to achieve real disagreement, two disputants must drink a case of brandy together. Most of what seem to be "disagreements" are the result of mutual misunderstandings. These are not so much real disagreements as false leads. What is needed, then, is a patient willingness to circle round and round together, during many long evenings, narrowing the issues. At some points, both may conclude, "Well, on this one we will just have to disagree." At least for now. After a time, we can come back and see whether each of us has learned something more in the interim. Or not.

One of the best things about friendship is lifelong disagreement on important points, cherished in affectionate argument.

WHERE WE AGREE . . . AND DISAGREE

Here are some points on which an unbeliever and a believer are probably in agreement:

- Arguments for moral values can proceed on reason alone. Other good arguments have come from Jewish and Christian teachings. Some voyagers prefer one of these routes over the others. Some travel both together.
- Religious people nowadays should more frequently express publicly their respect for those who do not believe in God. The reverse is also to be desired.

- Religious persons should approach questions about human nature and destiny, God, and the choice of their own community of "ultimate concern" with the best reasons they can present to a candid world. It is best if these reasons are not merely from subjective experience or personal faith. They very much need to be communicable through reasoned discourse, if nonbelievers and believers are to meet on the same ground, at least initially.

- Arguments about the real facts of history usually take the parties too far afield, and end inconclusively. These should be addressed by the methods of reasoned historical inquiry. Disagreement is to be expected, but a lot of mutual learning can take place. For example, the humanistic atheism of many in the Anglo-American world needs to be sharply distinguished from the bloody and coercive atheism imposed by Communism and Fascism early in the twentieth century. Then, again, Catholics (and some other scholars) tend to make an evidential case different from what one gets in the standard history course in our universities—about the Crusades, the inquisition, the "two powers" of church and state in modern European history, the French Revolution, and so forth. The real achievements of evangelical Christians like the Baptists on behalf of religious liberty in the United States have seldom been given the credit they deserve. In a word, the full stories of many particular traditions have not been adequately and fairly told in most secularist circles. Polemical habits on all sides do not die, they all too slowly fade away.

YET ALONGSIDE THESE AGREEMENTS there remain strong disagreements. Like Ludwig von Feuerbach, many atheists today assert that religions are created by human beings, to meet human needs felt by some people (but not all). Religions do not come from God but from man. It is not God who created man, but man who created God.

Within certain limits, of course, religions *are* created by human beings. When Jesus established an ordered community that he said would continue until the end of time (which then seemed more imminent than it has turned out to be), he did not specify how it should be organized, ensure its own continuity and fidelity to his word down the generations, teach, preach, educate the young, prepare its leaders. Jesus did not mention councils of the Church, popes, cardinals, or the Holy See as an independent state among states, and so on. He left an immense array of concrete details to human ingenuity and initiative. One could say he expected his church to "evolve" from age to age, learning, expanding, repenting, reforming, undergoing persecutions (never more so than in the twentieth century), rising and declining, at times barely surviving, and yet withal prevailing.

Nonetheless, if the Christian church is simply a human invention and has not really received its mission from God, then the Christian church is a fraud. If so fell the evidence, I would certainly agree with that conclusion.

As a Christian, I ask any searcher to examine the evidence for the truth of the Christian faith commonly advanced by the best Christian minds in generation after generation. From Clement of Alexandria to Augustine and Aquinas, to Paul Tillich and Reinhold Niebuhr, through writers such as John Henry Newman, C. S. Lewis, G. K. Chesterton, Arnold Lunn, and Romano Guardini in more recent times, these evidences are steadily advanced, for those who seek them. The evidence is public and accessible to all, not simply private and individual. It is the witness of a public visible community, not merely subjective.

But the main issue that stops Heather cold, she keeps reminding us, is the most difficult one for the believer—but for all that, the most frequently addressed: the problem of why a good and just God allows so much evil and injustice to metastasize in this world.

Reason and the Knowledge of God

Some of the ancient "pagan" philosophers were able to figure out that this world is too filled with intelligibility and exquisite beauty for there not to be some transhuman power of great intellectual capacity that draws men toward this deity by his beauty. Some long ago reasoned to the conviction that this unseen deity must be spirit, not matter. Some were repulsed by stone idols and did not really admire the antics of the gods of Greek and Roman myth. But most of these philosophers also showed *pietas* toward the traditions of their ancestors.

Some pagan philosophers reasoned to the notion that the deity is outside Time, existing in some kind of timelessness that they called the "realm of the unchangeable," the world of simultaneity without time, "eternity." These thinkers reasoned that it is an error to think anthropomorphically of such a remote and awesome God. From his vast power come many secondary causes more imposing than man—the Alps, the seas, the horrific storms filled with lightning and thunder and merciless winds. The deity, of whom we know so little, "transcends" not only the human world but all the stars in the sky. He (or It) dwells in a wholly other dimension, not cut to our size.

In short, reason alone figured out quite a lot about God, gathered together as settled knowledge in the "philosophy of God," or "natural theology," as it was called at the time of the American founding. (Natural theology was a required course at almost every university any of the founders attended.) Much of this knowledge was reached before Judaism or Christianity entered into human consciousness.

Thus, it is not only "moral values" that can be reached through the use of reason alone, but also knowledge about God. But there remains much that is hidden about the divinity, much that is behind veils. Is the deity benevolent or hostile, too great to be bothered with us, indifferent, or totally controlling of human fate? It hardly occurred to the philosophers of old that this deity is a judge of consciences, who invites humans into his friendship, forgives sins, offers eternal life. All this extra insight is from Jewish and Christian revelation. Yet insight is one thing; a judgment that the insight is true is another. That is why Christians have always proffered evidences for the truth of revelation, to be weighed by each seeker, and accepted or rejected.

Very few pagan philosophers during most of Western history thought that the world is absurd, random, lawless, purposeless. Only after the "death of God," which Nietzsche announced, did reason come to seem inadequate, and the world also to seem absurd, random, and purposeless. Many humans experience that moment as the death also of modernity, or at least of its hubris. As Nietzsche first saw it, the death of God meant the death of reason, and the birth of the random and the absurd. To the extent that "Reason" signified modernity, the death of reason has been called "postmodernity."

One quality that I especially cherish in a certain kind of atheist, including Heather (a type almost old-fashioned to postmodernist eyes), is that she has not given up on reason, even though the idea of God—or at least the Christian God, as she understands the term—makes no sense to her.

A Just God?

The biggest disagreement between us, in fact, arises out of our different conceptions of the Christian God. Let me just mention three assertions she and others make about the Christian God that seem to me to be wide of the bull's-eye (even though she may hear them from the lips of Christians).

- God *foresees* events such as the death-dealing accident in Los Angeles that she reports, in which a car missed a stop sign, ran head-on into a train, and two in this small family died, while two were crippled. (A human father who foresaw and did not prevent that cruel suffering would be charged with criminal passivity. Why not God, too?)

- Christians exclaim about God's providence and goodness only when good things happen to them. One does not hear them call the tragedies, absurdities, and horrors of life providential. (Isn't this a double standard?)
- Christians claim that God is just. But that is simply contrary to what we actually see. Often enough, the good suffer, while the evil are rewarded.

Heather marshals good arguments concerning why she cannot accept a God of this sort. However, I sometimes think she must have been long exposed to a very sentimental, sweet type of Christianity, and not read much for herself in the Scriptures or in the classic commentators. Because, contrary to her assertions, the Christian vision of God (and also the Jewish) is quite the reverse from the picture she draws. Let me begin with the third point.

Far from describing Himself as just, the God who parts the veils in Jewish and Christian scripture, those veils that hide the inner life of God, gives countless warnings about how unjust in the eyes of humans His justice will seem. The Psalms of David, the book of Job, and countless other texts present the opposite of a pretty picture of God; rather, He is a sovereign Governor of the universe not trimming His will or His wisdom to meet human measurements or expectations.

As David Gelernter writes, "I've always thought Abraham's to be the strongest statement of this fact, which is given with the Bible's faultless ear for human speech, and beautifully communicates a mixture of outrage and bewilderment: 'The judge of the whole earth, not to do justice?'" The full context from Genesis 18:22–25 is translated in the Revised Standard Version as

So the men turned from there, and went toward Sodom;
but Abraham still stood before the LORD. Then Abraham

drew near, and said, "Wilt thou indeed destroy the righteous with the wicked? Suppose there are fifty righteous within the city; wilt thou then destroy the place and not spare it for the fifty righteous who are in it? Far be it from thee to do such a thing, to slay the righteous with the wicked, so that the righteous fare as the wicked! Far be that from thee! Shall not the Judge of all the earth do right?

The Jewish and Christian God makes no secret of being a God who in the full view of humans acts in a manner that is cruel, unfair, and terribly tormenting. Consider Job, his seven sons and three daughters killed, his property seized and livestock dead, his body covered with painful sores, pitiful.

The Christian revelation borrows heavily from this vision. Just look at what happens to Jesus, God's own Son, in his passion and death. If this is what God does to his Son, Scripture seems to suggest, we should not expect better treatment for ourselves. We are told, in fact, to pick up our cross and get ready to bear trial and suffering, as Christ did. As Job before him did.

Moreover, there is parable after parable about how unjust God is: He warmly embraces His prodigal son while turning his back on his dutiful, hardworking, self-denying brother; He pays workers in the vineyard the same wage even though some have worked all day and others only an hour; and there are many other such parables. God is just? Not by human standards. Not in the Christian Testament.

Heather is not wrong to claim that often God seems to her, from watching the world as it is, criminally passive, callous, cruel, monstrous. God's self-descriptions in the Bible often forewarn that this is the way it will seem, even to those who know and love Him.

One other place closer to home from which to learn how Christians understand Providence is to chart George Washington's usage of the term. Contrary to what Heather thinks Christians do, Washington saw the hand of Providence in his greatest defeats, sufferings, and losses. Through these, God was teaching him, toughening him. He found God's ways inscrutable and almost impossible to bear. Yet he felt even at such times "in the hands of a kind Providence," and warned himself to keep a steady keel. He suffered more defeats than victories, sometimes through stupid blunders or character flaws of his own. For him, the presence of Providence kept him from too much elation in victory, and too much despair in defeat.

For Washington, God is sovereign. We bow our heads before Him, trusting in His ultimate kindness. He is *always* present, in all things. He is there in the most evil, senseless, and horrific moments of human life. He is there in the days of narrow escape from evil and the full enjoyment of dreams come true. He is there in bad times, as in good. He is not the plaything of our desire.

Look at what He allowed to happen to his Son. He "forsook" him.

These last two points, on God's cruel kindness and on his empirically unjust justice, are not matters of reason. We would not have such insight into God's nature if He had not pulled back the veils on it. These are, in this sense, matters of Jewish and/or Christian faith. You either accept them as rational and verifiable in lived experience, or you reject the scriptural concept of God and go elsewhere. Many of Christ's own disciples found his sayings hard, left him and went elsewhere.

The saccharine faith that some atheists encounter in Christians is a shallow, sentimental, and much too prettified version of the faith. It does not compare well when held up against the whole of the Christian intellectual tradition.

METAPHYSICAL REFLECTIONS: DISORDER BY DESIGN

What I am about to write may seem preposterous to Heather and many like her, who reject metaphysical thinking. Metaphysical methods, they say, are not congenial to American empiricism and pragmatism. But against that point there is the fact that both empiricism and pragmatism rest upon certain background assumptions about nature and history. To be sure, many American philosophers do not subject these background assumptions to critical reason (the proper task of metaphysics). Here my point is not to persuade, but to clarify. So I ask Heather just to entertain this next section for consideration, even if her good habits of mind lead her to reject it. The main point is not particularly Christian, but philosophical.

It is a category mistake to hold that God "foresees" future events. In fact, and here the conception is philosophical, not based on Christian data: God dwells in a simultaneous present. Past, present, and future are all present to Him in one vision. He sees the whole world of Time and all of this creation in one instant. He wills it all into being, and sustains it in being. Since by contrast we are in time, we must speak of past, present, and future. God is not bound by that constraint.

Why, then, did Jesus instruct us to pray to our Father for our humblest needs, as well as for grand and seemingly impossible things? If to Him everything is present instantaneously, isn't the deal already done? Yet in that one same instant, God's eternal vision sees our prayers as part of the texture of events that unfolds itself in time. For us, all events are sequential. For Him, all is simultaneous. He wills the whole all-at-once. He understands it all, and He wills it all. He sees it as good, and He loves it. Our prayers, therefore, may enter into the outcome in a way unknown to us, but known to Him. In one simultaneous act He knows the (to us) later outcome, even as He knows our (to us) prior prayers.

Many rationalists argue that this God must be a bumbler. They can imagine a far more perfect world. More perfect in what respect? We have seen that Jefferson holds in the *Virginia Statute for Religious Liberty* that the Almighty might have made the world without human liberty. But, for reasons that escape us, He did not. For reasons not known to us, He made a world of probabilities, chance, hazard, contradictory tendencies, competitions, struggle, pain as well as pleasure, many stories of frustration and failure, as well as some with happy endings. Such a metaphysical vision of the real world that God did create seems remarkably compatible with the world of evolutionary chance and competition and odd harmonies described by Darwin and other empirical discoverers.

If you hold that all the beauty, intelligence, justice, love, and truth that are found here in fragments in this actual created world of ours—if you hold that all these spring from the creative energy of the Creator, then you gain some idea of the beauty, justice, and benevolence He has within Him. Clearly, He could have created a simple paradise of goodness, mutual cooperation, and trust, and peace on earth. The story of Adam and Eve in paradise holds before our eyes just this possibility. Instead, it seems, God allowed the human story to be one of weakness, betrayal, and evil by the free choice of many, and severe trial for the good who are also tempted by evil (seeing all its rewards on this earth).

God as He reveals Himself to Jews and to Christians has somehow imagined this earth as a great stage, an immense drama, a drama of liberty, and of the misuse and noble use of power, and of love and also betrayal. It is a play worthy of an Aeschylus, a Dante, a Shakespeare, a Milton, a Goethe. It is not a prettified morality play. It is ironic and tragic—and yet, withal, a comedy.

Heather notes that the father driving the car that hit a train in Los Angeles read a sign wrong and paid for it with his life. Would she really prefer that all of us were robots who could never err on our own, never fail, never come to grief? When the Creator in fact chose to bring out of nothingness the contingencies and happenstances of this world as we see them, in its absurdities and tragedies, and if He took pleasure in the whole ("He saw it, and it was good"), then He had to allow a great deal of rope to human liberty. An open world order hospitable to freedom requires a world of wild contingencies, some ironic and some tragic.

Speaking metaphysically then, such an order God did not base on geometric logic, but on schemes of probabilities, unique occurrences, and wide-open spaces for various chains of probability to work their way out. Only in such a world could humans help to determine the course of history. They were not born robots, but free agents. God did not have to make the world this way, but He did.

DIVINE WILL AND HUMAN LIBERTY

Now a different line of thought, but bearing on the same point about human liberty. Certain Islamic writers of the time just before Aquinas saw the world as predetermined by Allah, so that there was not really liberty in which humans might act. All humans could or should do is to bow to the will of God. Humans are passive instruments of God's will. Frederick II had built (c. 1224 AD) a Muslim university in Naples, and the encroachment of this Muslim philosophy was being felt everywhere around the Mediterranean basin.

The principle that Aquinas deployed in refusing to go down that intellectual route runs like this: *If* Heather chooses to go to the store, *then* God wills that she go to the store. God does not will it "in advance." For Him, His willing is simultaneous with her willing. In one sense, Heather has the initiative; she makes the choice. In another sense, God has the initiative; He gave her life and gave her liberty at the same time. Thus when Heather uses her freedom to go the store, then God ratifies her freedom and her choice. Simultaneously.

The ratifying act of God's will does not *precede* human action. It is simultaneous with it. *If* Michael chooses X, then God permits X to be done. Thus does God make good on the scriptural promise of human liberty. For the proposition that God wills to be true, humans have to fill out the conditional—"*If Heather does* X . . ." God is not jerking Heather's strings around or forcing her to act contrary to her own will. But when she does will something, God is present to sustain her liberty in action.

It might be that the X that Heather chooses to do is to disbelieve in God. When she does that, He sustains her liberty to do so. Even though in another sense, His will is that she not do that. He has made His will clear, but He is also committed to sustaining a world of human liberty. So thought Jefferson, for instance.

The Los Angeles driver in Heather's story, alas, was permitted to be more careless than his responsibilities to those in the car with him required. He read a sign wrong. No one forced him to do so. Alas, free deeds can have awful consequences.

If Heather had reported a case in which a man with his children and mother died in a hurricane, we would not have said that he was careless when he should not have been, but that he was overpowered against his choice by the fury of the storm.

The Creator didn't promise us a rose garden.

Yes, those who love Him thank Him when they enjoy success or are spared from suffering. But even when they suffer terribly, some find His judgments just and kind. As Washington did, taking every act of Providence as meant for his own instruction. That is to say, God has in mind for all of us, not contentment, nor a state of constant pleasure, nor ease, but a time of trial. He could scarcely have been more clear about that. Everything that happens to us is for our good, even when we cannot see how that can possibly be true. Those who love God attend to every event and every new direction, in order to discern what wisdom they can glean from it. "Though he slay me, yet will I trust in him" (Job 13:15, KJV).

THE GOD OF THE PHILOSOPHERS, like the God of Judaism and Christianity, is not overprotective. He does not spoil us. He asks us to be grown-ups, with tip-top attentiveness, and with a reliable force of character. Only a few in any generation manage to do this well, under terrible trials and misfortunes.

Yet many millions suffer more than is easy to witness. They endure their pain nobly, and praise God for what they have. They know that God does not owe them anything, and has in fact given them everything they have. I repeat, there are philosophers who have written about such consolations, brought to us through philosophical reflection—for one, Boethius of the sixth century after Christ, in *Consolation of Philosophy*. One does not have to be a Christian or Jew in order to come to such wisdom.

But one does have to work out for oneself, at least in practice if not in a theoretical statement, a conception of God that allows for liberty, contingency, and all the hazards as well as the successes and triumphs of history. *"In la sua voluntade é nostra pace,"* as Dante wrote, "In his will, our peace."

There are souls whose integrity leads them to kick and bite in protest against this world, and also against its Maker. Indeed, almost everyone sometimes feels the urge to protest at ear-shattering volume: "This is not fair!" As Job did.

Nothing wrong with protesting. Nothing wrong with wrestling against God.

There are others who simply say, "Thy will be done." And find there stillness, and also strength.

Subjective Experience: What Counts as Evidence?

One further point deserves attention.

Most people are not philosophers but, rather, want to find answers in a way that comports with common sense—a way that fits with their working knowledge of how the world works, and what spoken words normally mean.

So I will close on this no doubt too simple note. The experiences of Christians are not always merely "subjective." Sometimes they *are,* and such opinions are likely to be brushed aside by others. But sometimes certain experiences awaken memories of yet others, well recognized in a long tradition. Sometimes, personal experiences meet other criteria that lift them from the merely "subjective" into what might be called the "intersubjective." They match what the tradition predicts. They meet the criteria designed over the centuries to "test their spirit."

"Ecstatic" experiences among the ordinary run of people, such as ourselves, are rare. The religious experience of most of us is more like "give us this day our daily bread," a more ordinary and plain-vanilla awareness.

Yet when even an exceptional ecstatic experience has historically been shared with innumerable others, in a way highly scrutinized by a long tradition, "subjective" is not quite the right word.

Perhaps, though, this is too Catholic a point of view. It may be that the whole point of evangelical religion is to stir in the listener a strong emotional experience of the forgiveness of God. In that case, "subjective" may be an appropriate term. However, even here the form through which the experience is brought about is by now "traditional" and the words to describe it are also "traditional." So here also, more than the *purely* "subjective" is going on.

Correlatively, when atheists insist upon "objective" evidence, one must ask, What are the criteria of "objectivity"? I have had conversations with people who call themselves atheists, and who also say that they would like to believe in God—*if only* they could find some objective evidence for His existence. At this point, I strain to see what they are looking for when they say "objective" evidence. Often the background of such persons has been the sciences, and so one can see that what they are looking for are "testable hypotheses." But this expectation supposes that God is just one other item in the universe among other items, of the same sort as those others that are subjected to testable hypotheses involving evidence available to our senses.

Most such persons have in my experience been sophisticated people and have been by no means logical positivists of the early A. J. Ayer type. They are not simple-minded materialists. For them, the gate to rationality is no longer so narrow as it was in the 1940s. So the question becomes, what sorts of "tests" would Heather count as yielding evidence? No use searching for God if she is searching in all the wrong places. Or trying to find God in all the empty categories.

Suppose that the proposition were put this way: Would you

count as evidence a proposition that listed some of the classical characteristics of what the most astute philosophers count as "knowing that God exists"? By "most astute" philosophers, I mean those who not only give you an account of their own moving viewpoint, but can also give a very good account of other moving viewpoints not their own. (By "moving viewpoint" I mean the often-experienced change of horizon brought by new experiences and better arguments. Sometimes so great are these changes of perspective that Thomas Kuhn calls them "paradigm shifts.") Further, they can show why their own viewpoint more comfortably explains a larger body of data than any known alternative, makes a greater number of helpful distinctions, predicts specific outcomes from certain courses of action or certain patterns of belief, and generates new and illuminating insights. For example, the historic shift from imagining that the sun moves around the earth to imagining the reverse did change an entire mental framework, or "paradigm."

Would you count it as evidence, that is, if someone laid out the characteristics involved in saying "I know that God exists," and you came to see that you, too, could fulfill those characteristics in your own rational mind? It is worth trying to imagine what those characteristics might be.

The evidence of our senses in the material world is not likely to help, because God is spirit, not matter, according to the philosophical traditions of ancient (and perennial) bodies of thought. But if God is not just one additional object in a universe of automobiles, cement blocks, bald eagles, and common viruses, can we get closer to a true insight by understanding "God" as a kind of insight or understanding or longing capable of indwelling within us?

The evidence for God's existing and ever-present sustaining power, in short, lies in one's own cognitional life, as this can be understood intersubjectively. Our unrelenting, inexhaustible drive to ask questions leads us gradually to catch a glimpse of the boundary line between finite and infinite. The drive to ask questions is infinite and will carry us beyond everything in creation that we know, or can ever know, if we give it free rein.

WHENCE COMES INQUIRY?

Even if we understood everything there is to know about the material world in which we live, our spirits would still raise questions. It is our endless drive to raise questions that is, generation after generation, the active fire in us that propels us beyond the immediate world of our experience. That same fire keeps breaking out in human history. It is the central dynamic of the religious quest, pushing beyond the boundary of the finite. Our own consciousness nudges us to cross that boundary.

Who are we under these stars, with the wind on our faces? What should we do? What may we hope?

The Jewish and Christian reply to these questions of the soul is that humans are created in the image of God—not in the sense of being a painting or an icon of God, but in the sense of having inner capacities (insight, judgment, love) that we share with Him.

It is in coming to understand our own identity that we come face-to-face with the God Who summoned us into being, and Who propels us onward. Socrates gave intimations of this route when he began his inquiries with the imperative *"Know thyself!"*

Who am I? One who bears the Source of all intelligibility in all things within me. To humble me.

The atheist has a very different sense of who she is.

We are talking pure philosophy here, not yet about matters of any particular revelation or church tradition. *Who are we, under these stars?*

As I see it, one sort of atheist gives up trusting in intelligence at this point and finds the whole of our material existence absurd, based upon chance, random, undirected, meaningless.

Another sort of atheist continues to trust in reason, even after giving up on God as the Light suffusing both reason and reality itself.

One sort of believer distrusts reason and trusts only a "leap of faith" in Jesus.

Another sort of believer comes to believe in God by trusting all the way down her own drive to question, which first awakened her from her slumbers, woke her into awareness, and kept sending out questions like radar into the dark. The believer does not believe that this drive is in vain. This drive is at the heart of reason itself.

The insight finally dawns upon her that to say "God" is to say the Subject that awakens the restlessness within me and fires my infinite drive to ask questions. That is the ultimate Light that we catch sight of, in a backward-glancing reflection upon our own active cognitional life. Whence does our inner light spring? Even though it is merely a taste of God, when the mind glimpses however darkly all that it was made for, that taste is very sweet.

Who am I? I am the questioning being who participates in the infinite capacity of the Source of all intellectual Light—the capacity to question and to understand everything that is. A person moved to gratitude for the full Light that is foreshadowed in my own little searchlight of a mind and heart. A person moved to love Him-who-has-always-been-within. Even when my eyes are clouded, as they usually are.

To pursue like a hound this movement of the mind is, I think, to plumb what being objective and rational and questioning means, all the way down.

I didn't mean to give a sermon. I am not trying to persuade, but simply to clarify.

We still have a lot of brandy to drink together, Heather. I thank you for the invitation.

FOUR

Heather's Spirited Reply

Soon after our first conversation on atheism, Heather Mac Donald replied with elegance and force. In upholding her end of the conversation she had launched, Heather brought even more energy than earlier. Her objections roar in like angry waves upon the shore. Some of them need to be heard all together, to feel their full effect:

- You don't have to believe in a god to see yourself in the other. The golden rule is based on empathy and self-interest, not on divine revelation. Will it break down? Of course. It is no guarantee against injustice, mass killings, and torture, but neither is Christianity.
- How does Mr. Novak know that behind the appearance of "God's cruel kindness and empirically unjust justice" lies a different reality: God's "ultimate kindness"? Is there a single piece of evidence available in the world to justify the conclusion that the ultimate reality of God is far different from what we see every day?
- Religious institutions and beliefs are, however, human creations. They grow out of man's instinct for system and order, as well as out of the desire for life beyond death and a divine intervener in human affairs. Our striving for justice is one of the great human attributes. Far from imitating a divine model, man's every effort to dispense justice is a battle against the randomness that rules the natural world.
- I do not understand how by "permitting" human choices that

in his "simultaneous present" he has already willed, God passes responsibility for tragedy onto fallible humans (like the hapless L.A. driver whom Mr. Novak seems to blame for his fatal car accident). I understand even less how humans "choose" to become victims of natural disasters or accidents wholly outside of their control.

- I am going to take it as a Christian truism, then, that God's will is manifest in the most minute detail of human events. Nothing happens without—at a bare minimum—his "permission," and everything that happens, in God's view, is "good, and he loves it," to use Mr. Novak's phrases . . . And thus I conclude that as a model for judge, lawgiver, or simply compassionate being, God leaves a lot to be desired.

- But let us test the idea of God's "ultimate kindness . . . justice, and benevolence" against natural events. How is it for a child's "good" to be born mentally retarded, or with a fatal blood defect? . . . But if courage in the face of a fatal disease is such a "good," why don't we wish it on everyone? And how did God choose only some children for the good of early mortality and not others?

- An elementary definition of justice is treating like cases alike and treating unlike cases differently . . . In the case of God's justice, however, we see like cases being treated differently and unlike cases being treated the same all the time—or so it would seem to a human eye . . .

- I am happy to live with a conception of God as completely inscrutable, as long as that conception is consistently applied. But I constantly hear believers confidently interpreting God's intentions when something good happens to them or to others. But if God alternates between mysteriousness and transparency, why assume that it's in the happy outcomes that his will is readable?

For the reader, it might no doubt bring speedy relief to reply to these questions immediately. But after experimenting with that approach, it seemed wiser to postpone my direct replies until after a few preliminary comments. Thus, first, I must sketch the framework with which I approach such questions, as contrasted with Heather's framework.

Two Different "Backstories"

Admiring once again the clarity of mind and persistent attention to evidence that characterize Heather's writing, I note that her queries, taken together, raise three sorts of background questions. One set insists that the autonomy of reason is moved by its own "innate" (as she puts it) search for justice, truth, and solid empirical evidence.

Another set asks about the reasonableness of the Christian faith, and its ability to persuade others of its claims.

A third set challenges me to deal with the differences in philosophical outlook ("metaphysics") that divide us. In this section we will deal with the first two backstories. In the next section, we will take up the third.

The first two of Heather's challenges go to the meaning each of us gives to "reason." In coming to my own views, I have been much helped by Bernard Lonergan's *Insight: A Study of Human Understanding*. Lonergan treats the experience of insight as an empirical datum. An insight (getting the point of a joke, for instance, or seeing at last the solution to an algebra problem) is not quite a sense datum, but it is an experience at least equally vivid. A more complex form of insight, also experienced vividly, is to conclude reflection by making a judgment; for instance: "Having heard the evidence, I conclude that your story is demonstrably false." "I conclude that witness number one is a good man—but his associate is not to be trusted."

The experience of insight and the steps involved in reaching a sound judgment are important to recognize in one's own mental life. Beyond that, based on evidence we recognize in our own inner life, these steps offer important evidence for the judgment,

Who do I understand myself to be? A mistake in *this* judgment deeply affects our judgments about God, his nature, his existence.

Our acts of insight are different in kind from acts of sensation. This difference suggests that our inner life goes beyond sense knowledge. It also suggests that what the ancients meant by "spirit" or "soul" appears most clearly today in a virtually unlimited drive within us—the drive to raise questions, to have insights, and to reach sound judgments about what is true, what false. These common human drives instruct us about our true nature, who we really are. They also aim us in the direction of what an acceptable idea of God's nature is. At the very least, He must be capable of insight and judgment. He is nonmaterial, and may be outside of the space-time continuum.

These are not matters of Christian faith or theology; they appertain to the branch of secular philosophy called "metaphysics," by which I mean considerations of reason, apart from faith. I mean the "background assumptions" about nature and history that are implicit in everything each person thinks and writes. I mean competing conceptions of God, some of which are to be judged better than others. In such explorations, the Greeks and Romans of old were far braver and more persistent than all but a small band in modern times.

Among the chief participants in Plato's dialogues, such differences in metaphysics are starkly drawn. If the participants in these dialogues are to make progress in their this-worldly arguments, it is necessary to bring their underlying metaphysical differences to light. Plato found that the artful presentation of a back-and-forth conversation is the best way to bring out these differences. Bringing these differences to light is a work of reason, even if it is not exactly empirical reason.

In short, most of what Heather requests in her spirited reply does not hinge on conceptions of Christian faith. Most of it must be discussed in secular terms. To employ Christian faith in setting forth my own views in fullness would be a great pleasure. But in the world in which I work, I have for years found it better to keep such matters tacit. They are unnecessary for most of the arguments I am called upon to make. (My professional provenance includes "Religion, *Philosophy,* and Public Policy.") Nearly all that Heather asks of me relies more on philosophy than on religion. And I agree with Heather that one should usually argue within the confines of reason alone about practical, this-worldly matters such as why capitalism is superior to socialism as an economic system, the costs and benefits of the minimum wage, personalized Social Security accounts, childbearing outside of marriage, mandatory national health insurance, and the like. The world of reason has its own relative autonomy, which must be respected.

Experience shows, however, that substantial numbers of the public have learned to think in religious categories, that is, in the categories of Jewish and/or Christian faith. Such persons are often to be highly admired, yet one does regret that some are a bit hostile to "merely" rational empirical thinking, which they find cold, bloodless, and mostly a way of rationalizing what one really wants to do but doesn't dare to express. For instance, in arguing in Latin America about capitalism, I have found Hayek's splendid arguments on behalf of economic liberty not convincing to many, because while they sound nice, they are too secular. Some people want to weigh the religious bearing of Hayek's arguments. How do his arguments fit into a religious scheme of things? For some audiences, an ability to explain things in religious terms (due account being made for audiences of different religions) is indispensable for getting one's words a fair hearing.

In this respect, Heather seems to be making matters a little too comfortable for herself when she insists that everyone should learn to speak her language of reason and empiricism. Hers is a very sound option. Yet experience teaches me that her way is not sufficient for large numbers of people, in this country and abroad. And on this earth, there are many more religious than secular people.

In this book (as in most pluralistic conversations), however, I am happy to play by Heather's rules, and stick to evidence, the ways of reason, and the empirical method. It would be wrong to use my Catholic faith where the proper autonomy of reason suffices. (This is the traditional way for Catholics to proceed, beautifully laid out by, among others, Thomas Aquinas.) One thing that is characteristic of the Jewish and/or Christian faith, and certainly of Catholic life, is its insistent identification of the Creator with *logos,* insight, reason.

Some scholars even argue that for thirty-five hundred years before the modern scientific era was born, biblical faith taught entire cultures to trust reason and to pursue it—habits without which the scientific enterprise would have no mooring in human habits and expectations. Jewish and Christian faiths bear witness to the vision that from the one Creator spring light, reason, insight, and *logos,* and that humans are made in the image of the Source of this light, and are naturally inclined by this heritage to follow reason. Hidden in all things, even the most contingent and puzzling, are reasons why things are as they are. These reasons, although some are far beyond our ken today, await patient discovery by legions of highly disciplined, dedicated, scientific, and wise inquirers. Europe's first universities were founded by Christians to pursue precisely this vocation.

Thus, Heather's affirmations about the sound morality worked out by the "innate" power of reason are a fruit of the classical education shaped by Catholic educators for some twelve hundred years. During various episodes in Christian history, some prominent leaders have turned against reason (some fideist Catholics as well as some Protestant Reformers), just as today in some postmodern, secularist circles. But the confidence of Christians in reason—learned in part from the Jews—long found in Aristotle, Plato, Cicero, and Seneca kindred spirits.

In too simply lumping all religions together, it is possible that Heather does not adequately distinguish between Christian traditions committed to reason versus those (in America especially) that are suspicious of reason. In reason's place, some persons prefer to cling exclusively to the Word of the Bible. It is also possible that I may not grasp well enough what Heather means by "reason." Thomas Jefferson included among philosophers of "natural right" such classical authors as Aristotle and Cicero, whose works were treasured by generations of early Christians. However, by 1935, preeminent American philosopher John Dewey turned sharply away from the classics in order to concentrate on empirical science. I believe that Heather prefers the empirical, pragmatic tradition of Dewey, or something like it. She is certainly not one to mock reason as the postmodernists and some Christian fundamentalists do. (Remarkably, some Christian thinkers welcome postmodernism because it makes both reason and faith equally "subjective." What a foolish mistake!)

We turn now to Heather's third background story: the importance of judging which religions are true—and which false.

THE THIRD BACKSTORY

In the debate that followed her article in *The American Conservative,* Heather raised some powerful questions about the role of reason even within the bounds of Christianity. "I do not understand why religion should get a pass from the empirical and logical demands that we make toward other factual propositions," she wrote. "Doesn't it matter whether it is true or not, or is it OK to live in error as long as one is happy? . . . Do Catholics, for example, believe that the angel Moroni gave Joseph Smith a pair of magic spectacles in 1827 with which to read the mysterious golden tablets from God? And if not, why not?"

Heather, I silently expostulate, are you kidding? The comedian Lenny Bruce used to joke that his boyhood Catholic friends belonged to "*the only* One True Faith." The Catholic Church has always claimed to be true, and it has always offered evidences thereof. Maybe not strong enough evidence for Heather. But evidence that is first addressed to reason rather than to faith. Further, the Catholic Church steadily down through the centuries, much to the annoyance of many, has put on record where (in its view) other faiths or philosophies fall short of truth, or are just plain false. This concern for using reason as a partner of faith is one of the attractions that draws so many intellectuals and artists to the Catholic faith.

Catholics hold that other Christian communities share with Catholics many affirmations of Christian faith, but not all. We cherish this community of beliefs, but pray that the shared circle of belief will grow larger. We hold that our Catholic faith does not make sense unless the Jewish faith is also true. We share with some atheists their clear commitment to reason. Truth is indeed crucial to Christian faith. But it does matter to our consciences which church is closest to the truth. As the aphorism puts it, faith does not take away from reason, but brings it to completion (*gratia non tollit sed perficit naturam*). A quite imperfect analogy is how eyeglasses, microscopes, and telescopes do not demean eyesight, only carry it where it could not go alone. For Catholics and some other Christians, reason is to be honored. Which church is true is a crucial judgment of reason.

In approaching questions of reason and faith, however, many background assumptions divide Heather and me. These have mostly to do with the conception of God accessible to human philosophy. These conceptions are frequently argued over in the history of philosophy, both outside and inside Christian ranks. Those that meet the findings of human experience more exactly than the others are counted true, and those that do not meet this standard fall by the wayside as inadequate or false. Some materialistic thinkers once identified God with "prime matter." Some idealistic ones identified God with the sum of all the intelligibility in all things (as it were, its unified mathematical structure). Others identified God with many different forces in nature such as winds, rain, tornadoes, lightning and thunder, the ferocity of panthers, or long, writhing serpents. Heather's concept places God in time, employing foreknowledge, and exercising His will long before the events willed by Him occur. Thus, in her eyes God foreknows that an auto will crash in Los Angeles. Yet He wills it in advance (at least "permits" it) just as a human would. Therefore, God is culpable just as a human would be, only more so.

Some atheists, of course, dismiss discussions of "backstories" as "mumbo jumbo"—meaningless metaphysical meandering—intended to hide the question of God's injustice behind an octopus's ink cloud. But when some atheists postulate an infinite number of universes in infinite time as a way to avoid a first cause, they, too, propose "meaningless metaphysics." And when others reduce the natural order to material things, they also leap beyond science to metaphysics. That everything is matter is not a scientific finding but a metaphysical preference.

Heather's practical question is this: Does God act unjustly toward men? If we judge Him by human standards, the answer is yes, and He concedes this Himself in the Bible. But, according to human reasoning, in what ways do "divine standards" actually diverge from "human"? The issue here is how we should think about God. Heather is inclined to cut God down to human size and judge Him by human standards. Sometimes, in grief, we all do this. Our conceit is that we have a keener sense of justice than God does; that we care for other human individuals more than their Creator does.

Independently of Judaism and Christianity, Plato and Aristotle had a far higher idea of God than that. They had a much sharper sense of the difference, real and conceptual, between the human, which they could see, and the divine, which no one can see, but only infer. They, like us, had experienced tragedy and irony, both in the course of human affairs and in their own lives. They also felt the weightiness of an unappeasable force they called Fate. Sometimes they later came to judge more favorably certain events that, when they occurred, seemed to them cruel and evil. Similarly, for instance, a middle-aged father recently wrote that after days of self-pity, he came to see the cancer that had suddenly befallen him as God's greatest gift to him. Never before had he seen the priorities of life more clearly, nor tasted its daily joys more sweetly. He was glad to get his purposes straight before death came. Having

railed against God, he now thanked Him. Antigone, too, experienced reconciliation.

It is common but unwise to imagine oneself more just than the
Source of all Justice. Even Plato and Aristotle came to understand
the divine as a force that attracts us (as "final cause") to higher,
better practices. Later, the Jewish/Christian revelation about God
gave rise to the notion of human progress. It did so by writing an
"In the beginning" into the narrative of a people working toward
great events to come. The spinning cycles of endless return in
which pagan cultures were confined were snapped by Judaism.
Human history became not a repetition of cycles but a story with
beginning and end. The Source of all Justice, ever up ahead, became for all historical strivers the measure of full being, truth, justice, and love, attracting us to Himself by His beauty. This standard
measured true progress from decline. Further, this standard kept
raising the historical bar, as the human pilgrimage moved ever forward, notwithstanding substantial periods of decline. In the Jewish and Christian imagination, history is more like a slightly
inclined spiral of ups and downs than a straight line upward.

Thus, Heather is close to the mark when she manifests deep respect for human conscience, for the human quest for truth and justice, and for "innate" drives for goodness and concern for others.
The metaphysical questions is, Where did these drives come from?
What sort of world is it in which such drives appear? Heather frequently finds the world of human experience absurd and meaningless. The all-too-visible law of the jungle that marks our
universe does not seem to her promising for progress in truth and
justice, but within it Heather sees bursts of human energy, drive,
and aspiration. What justice there is in the world is put there by
humans, she holds.

This opinion leads me to the question, What is it about hu-
mans that makes them *so* different from other animals, fish, birds?
Given an irrational cosmos, whence comes the human quest—
Heather's quest—for the good and the true? Behind what our eyes

see, there seems to be an invisible dimension of the cosmos, imparting to human beings a moral thrust. Heather seems to me to be led here, like Christopher Hitchens and so many others who call themselves atheists, by an impressive reverence for the driving power of justice and the fearless light of truth. The Jewish and Christian God may seem to them unattractive, even repulsive, by comparison with their own vision. They sense something far greater, cleaner, more attractive, even if in the end dark and hidden. I have great sympathy for this approach. That is why I call this inquiry *No One Sees God*. There is some power, some force, some energy, some light, in comparison with which they judge the Jewish and Christian God to be unworthy. Some philosophers have called this "the God beyond God." It is sufficient to call it the God of night.

What we know is that questions continue to gnaw at us. Infinitely, it seems, insatiably. It is from that experience that the force of religion continually wells up in human history. Humans gain from that experience an obscure sense of the divine, the thirst that no finite good satiates. In the light of this powerful drive to ask questions, atheists with no trouble poke holes in the careless concepts of God they encounter around them. They seek something greater, more beautiful, and closer to the infinite than those.

As we saw earlier, Albert Camus pointed out an unavoidable duality in human experience, which gives rise to what he calls the Absurd. On the one hand, we feel the undeniable longing for truth, beauty, goodness, justice, wholeness, love, that rushes powerfully within us, even under the most unpromising conditions (as in the Gulag, under torture). On the other hand, these aspirations cannot avoid crashing head-on with the cruel randomness, desolation, and emptiness that we are often forced to confront. We can evade this unhappy duality for a long time by distracting ourselves with pulsating music, card playing, ceaseless activity, shopping.

Yet sooner or later we are driven to ask: Why are we here? Why are so many abandoned children crying in the night? Why the everlasting boredom, and the incessant rain of nothingness upon the windowpanes of our consciousness? Why so many jading daily routines, such petty strife, such pointless quarrels, such office pretenses?

Without both these sides of our consciousness, Camus taught us, we would not come to rest on the razor's edge of the Absurd. Keeping the two sides in contact is crucial to our truthfulness. The Absurd arises from our longing for meaning and beauty held in contact with the absurdities we meet every day. Remove one or the other, and the tension falls limp.

Heather would like to shift onto *my* shoulders the burden of explaining the evil and absurdity in the world, which her reason discerns steadily enough. Yet even when she has eliminated God from the scheme of life as she sees it, she has not diminished by one iota the evils, sufferings, and injustices we both see around us. She does not explain how they fit into her fairly rosy view of human progress, reason, and hopefulness. A faith she dares not express seems to tell her that this progress is indefinitely upward, ennobling, worth contributing to, quite enough purpose for a good life.

Yet, irony of ironies, meaninglessness squared, what if our visible "progress" is hurtling us toward the most awful end of history any apocalyptic writer has ever imagined? What if progress is not progress at all, but ultimate madness? (Heather may well hold this darker assumption, not the rosy one.) I am not trying to diminish the glory of modern progress; without certain new pharmaceuticals, I would be dead. On the contrary, I am trying to make myself conscious of the underlying metaphysics on which progress depends—the vision behind it of the upward direction in which history tends, its underlying dynamism, and its ultimate kindliness toward humankind. Heather seems to share this vision when she writes of human reason and progress as benevolent. Heather herself suggests that the true problem before us is not the problem of evil but the problem of good. Why is there so much good?

In my experience, however, the problem of evil does in fact

bother Jews and Christians, because it goes contrary to what faith teaches about the goodness of God. Evil may not be a problem for my atheist friends. For them, the evil of the world is just there. Insofar as evil matters metaphysically, it destroys arguments for the existence of a good God. To their minds, absurdity forms the backdrop for their heroic human Sisyphus who, against all odds, keeps rolling progress up the hill, only to watch it slide back down into meaninglessness.

At the beginning of this chapter we listed Heather's eight especially tough questions, and we are now better prepared to reply to them, although far too briefly. Let me repeat the questions and then reply.

(1) You don't have to believe in a god to see yourself in the other. The golden rule is based on empathy and self-interest, not on divine revelation. Will it break down? Of course. It is no guarantee against injustice, mass killings, and torture, but neither is Christianity.

Heather expresses pretty well here the Catholic idea of natural law and natural reason. A very powerful ethic can be generated by natural reason alone. Nonetheless, Thomas Jefferson made two claims about the ethic of Jesus, and it is well known that Jefferson believed neither in the divinity of Jesus nor in miracles. Simply using straight common sense, he wrote that the ethic of Jesus is "the most sublime and benevolent code of morals which has ever been offered to man" (*The Life and Morals of Jesus of Nazareth,* 1820).

In particular, the American founders (Jefferson included) admired the teaching of Jesus for its powerful emphasis on the inner realm of conscience—that is, not only on outward actions, but also on aspirations, intentions, and inner compunction for shortfalls. They also thought the Jewish/Christian emphasis on the individual is indispensable for teaching personal responsibility, self-starting initiative, and self-government.

In another context, Jefferson said that Christianity is the best religion for preparing people for a Republic. Better than any other narrative, it helps people to understand the ethic necessary for a Republic, and to form the requisite habits.

More than Jefferson, founders such as Benjamin Rush, John Adams, James Madison, and Alexander Hamilton emphasized the human propensity to certain classic vices. Yet Jefferson, too, appreciated the utility of "checks and balances" and other precautions. While Jefferson more than the others nursed a vision of human perfectibility and societal progress, he admired the unique balance of realism and hope instilled by Judaism and Christianity. The Founders hoped that their new form of government, undergirded by biblical habits, might at least *reduce* the "injustice, mass killings, and torture" of preceding ages. As Heather writes, where human beings are concerned, "no guarantee" is possible. Her view and the founders' seem to accord better with the biblical Enlightenment of Britain than with the purely secular Enlightenments of Germany and France.

(2) How does Mr. Novak know that behind the appearance of "God's cruel kindness and empirically unjust justice" lies a different reality: God's "ultimate kindness"? Is there a single piece of evidence available in the world to justify the conclusion that the ultimate reality of God is far different from what we see every day?

A large pattern of evidence cited by George Washington in testimony to the benevolent role played by Providence during the American War of Independence is one evidence. In several official public statements, Washington reminded Americans of what they had all *experienced* in the war just past. To his mind, Americans more than others owed a debt of gratitude to the Creator for so many "interpositions" on behalf of the American cause and many "signal" acts of benevolence:

> No People can be bound to acknowledge and adore the invisible hand, which conducts the Affairs of men more than the People of the United States. Every step, by which they

have advanced to the character of an independent nation, seems to have been distinguished by some token of providential agency. (FIRST INAUGURAL ADDRESS, APRIL 30, 1789)

Whereas it is the duty of all Nations to acknowledge the providence of Almighty God, to obey his will, to be grateful for his benefits, and humbly to implore his protection and favor . . . Now therefore I do recommend and assign Thursday the 26th day of November next to be devoted by the People of these States to the service of that great and glorious Being . . . That we may then all unite in rendering unto him our sincere and humble thanks, for his kind care and protection of the People of this country previous to their becoming a Nation, for the signal and manifold mercies, and the favorable interpositions of his providence, which we experienced in the course and conclusion of the late war, for the great degree of tranquility, union, and plenty, which we have since enjoyed . . . (FIRST DECLARATION OF THANKSGIVING, OCTOBER 3, 1789)

Washington included in his prayers thanks for the care of Providence even in the great disasters that so often befell his army and the unbelievable sufferings he saw among his troops in the winter snows of 1776 and 1777.

During my seventy-four years, I have met extremely few people who are not grateful for the very fact of life, fresh air, the taste of water on a dry day, the stars and moon at night. It may be surprising how often even people who are very poor, or who suffer mightily from cancer or other illness, give thanks for the good things they have received from the Almighty. There are not many people who think everything is bleak, that death is better than life, that nothingness is better than being. Just existing has a sweet taste to it, even in extremities.

The philosophy professor Anthony Long has written about evolutionary theory in the world of ancient Greece. He makes the point that no one in that world was an atheist. All experience and all reasoning led them to God's unseen reality. He adds that when they thought about Him they sketched parameters within which any concept of Him matched their experience in the world. They came up with the following requirements: God must be "everlasting, blissful, supremely intelligent, and paradigmatically excellent, meaning living a life that serves as the ideal for human beings to emulate."

I find it hard to believe that every day Heather fails to see the sign of God's care even in the midst of the most outrageous suffering she encounters. Possibly she expects a far more perfect world than this, a world of no suffering, no tragedy, no personal betrayal, no sin. But it is not really open to her to blame on God the "rule of randomness" she encounters everywhere, or the pervasive irrationality we all so often encounter. For she seems to reconcile herself quite well to that rule of randomness, and even makes it the foundation of her philosophy of life. Perhaps, then, she expects God to do better than randomness does, in order to qualify in her eyes as a good God.

But perhaps I am missing Heather's anguish.

The Bible describes this world as a vale of tears. Heather finds that sort of world unworthy of a good God. Yet even in this vale of tears, without God, Heather finds much that is noble, intelligent, admirable, hopeful. True humanism may reveal God's presence in the world, too.

(3) Religious institutions and beliefs are, however, human creations. They grow out of man's instinct for system and order, as well as out of the desire for life beyond death and a divine intervener in human affairs. Our striving for justice is one of the great human attributes. Far from imitating a divine model, man's every effort to dispense justice is a battle against the randomness that rules the natural world.

Who can deny that a religious institution, the Catholic Church for instance, is in a huge degree a human institution? On the other hand, were it solely human, its sins are so great—aren't they?—that its constantly revitalized energy would be a wonder. If religion is of human origin merely, entirely an invention of man, that would make it a fraud. As a sign of the transcendent God, it would be worse than worthless.

On Heather's grounds, however, if the Catholic Church is made solely by human hands, its very humanness gives cause to congratulate the humans who built and guided it. For they are responsible for quite substantial human achievements. Which institution has generated a body of art equal to the one that the Christian church has inspired, supported, and offered to the human race? Which institution has created so many hundreds of religious communities dedicated to feeding the hungry and caring for the sick? The abuses and sins of the Church should be candidly rebuked—and, it is to be hoped, reformed. Or the whole thing should be crushed. History records virtually a never-ending round of rebukes of the Church, from inside it as well as outside. Pooping on the Church requires no more than a pigeon's courage.

Heather is utterly correct that one of "the great human attributes" is striving for justice. For many, this striving has been one of the abiding signs of God's reality at work on earth. It is otherwise not easy to see how such an improbable quest, such an impossible dream, grew with such strength in the human creature, whose intellect tells him that randomness rules all. Is randomness unjust? It would seem that randomness knows neither justice nor injustice.

Here Professor Harvey Mansfield of Harvard, who has known more than enough suffering from the irrationality of life, and whose words we shall again recall in chapter seven, seems wiser than most:

> In the contest between religion and atheism, the strength
> of religion is to recognize two apparently contrary forces
> in the human soul: the power of injustice and the power,
> nonetheless, of our desire for justice. The stubborn exis-
> tence of injustice reminds us that man is not God, while

the demand for justice reminds us that we wish for the divine. Religion tries to join these two forces together.

The weakness of atheism, however, is to take account of only one of them, the fact of injustice in the case of Epicurean atheism or the desire for justice in our Enlightenment atheism. I conclude that philosophy today—and science too—need not only to tolerate and respect religion, but also to learn from it.

(4) I do not understand how by "permitting" human choices that in his "simultaneous present" he has already willed, God passes responsibility for tragedy onto fallible humans (like the hapless L.A. driver whom Mr. Novak seems to blame for his fatal car accident). I understand even less how humans "choose" to become victims of natural disasters or accidents wholly outside of their control.

The fundamental choice the Creator had to make is either to make this universe habitable for human freedom and to make human beings free, or to restrict the freedom of humans solely to producing happy outcomes. In other words, all lunches would be free. As long as He allowed humans to be free, He had to allow for unintended consequences as well as for cold-blooded, deliberate evil acts. As long as He made humans free, He had to recognize in humans their own personal responsibility. Let us stipulate that the Creator gave liberty to the poor unfortunate driver in Los Angeles, whose story Heather admirably relates with so much sympathy, an immigrant who somehow missed a traffic signal and drove his auto with wife and two children into the path of an onrushing train. I doubt if Heather expects the Creator to keep playing the deus ex machina to rescue all humans from all bad decisions, however inadvertent. Freedom is freedom, and consequences are consequences.

Heather is on firmer ground in refusing to believe that humans "choose" to become victims of natural disasters or accidents wholly outside their control. Of course they do not choose disaster. Many pray to be spared from it. Even when some accidents do happen through someone's free act—talking on a cell phone or eating a sandwich while driving—the victim has not chosen his victimhood. These events, as George Washington often described them, are the hardest to bear: "The determinations of Providence are all ways wise; often inscrutable, and though its decrees appear to bear hard upon us at times is nevertheless meant for gracious purposes" (Letter to Bryan Fairfax, March 1, 1778).

Examining these matters, we are like people behind a tapestry, where all the threads run helter-skelter and seemingly at random. It is only on the other side that the pattern becomes plain to us, as the artist sees it. A great many parts of the Bible are directed toward helping us to understand reality as it is, not merely as it appears to our eyes.

In real life, what we see seems sometimes ugly. We do not understand how mad the world then appears. We protest against evils that cause us revulsion. Yet, no matter what we do, welcome them or hate them, the facts remain the same. To a world of fact, where "randomness rules," unbelievers and believers must in the end submit. At this point, the unbeliever submits to randomness, while the believer submits to the inscrutable will of the Creator. Both must submit. The latter shows more confidence both in intelligence and in the intelligibility of all things.

But perhaps another way of looking at randomness is this one, proposed by Stephen Barr, the physicist:

> To be responsible agents means being able to impose our own ordering upon events. This requires that some apparent "disorder" be present in the situations that confront us as the raw material upon which we can act. A world without disorder, without "chance" and "random" events would be a world in which everything unfolded according to a single, simple, and predictable pattern. But a world in which many wills are acting cannot have a single, simple pattern. It must of necessity be a multifarious world, a world with

many patterns, and plots, and chains of causation existing side-by-side, occasionally impinging on each other and intersecting each other and throwing each other off course. That is precisely what "chance" amounts to. A world without chance would be a world with a single overarching and controlling pattern, one plot without sub-plots, one storyline rather than a tangled web of storylines. Everything marching in lockstep. Such a world would have no scope for freedom. It would also have no scope for courage, or hope, or vigilance, or daring, or human providence.

Another problem that bothers Heather also bothered me for a long time. When I first tried to think in terms of eternity, it was hard for me to conceive of a region outside of time, and all the more so a region in which the parade of events in time are seen in one simultaneous glance.

Once, from a mountaintop, though, I looked down upon an entire panoply of valleys, in which a train puffed along in one direction, while on an intersecting highway, out of sight around a curve, three or four autos seemed to move at a speed that would bring them directly across the path of the train. Neither the train engineer nor the drivers of the autos could yet catch sight of each other; they did not see what I could see. I had the sensation of watching a slow-motion anticipation of present and future moments in a simultaneous glance. This example is not, of course, exact. But it helped.

There is one sentence of Heather's, though, that especially voices my own original confusion. She writes: "I do not understand how by 'permitting' human choices that in his 'simultaneous present' he has already willed, God passes responsibility onto fallible humans." The problem arises in her use of these last three phrases: "permit," in His "simultaneous present," and He "has already willed." The confusing sequence of tenses perplexes her. The way I now think of this perplexity is as follows: God wills a world in which free agents act freely. He doesn't only "permit" things to happen. He empowers free agents to act, even with less attention than they ought, or against His laws, or simply without common sense. Free agents acting freely, despite the frequently resulting irrationality, is what He now wills and has always willed. He does not *command* irrational (or evil) action. But He certainly brought into being, consciously and (I think) beautifully, a world in which free acts can occur, and evils and misfortunes are frequently transformed by courage, generosity of spirit, and charity into occasions of great human beauty. As I write, amid the horrific flames engulfing southern California (late October 2007), videotape shows many triumphs of the human spirit in the words and acts of so many (but not all) of the victims.

The tradition holds when a human chooses X, then God allows X (permits a human to act, even if He does not like the results). That is, God does not force human acts into existence. Free humans act freely. God does not will into being action by humans, until those humans choose to act on their own. That is the only way, as best I can see, that human freedom is real. Heather's phrase "already willed" reveals that Heather has slipped back into placing God *within* time. She imagines that God "already willed" the deed, even *before* the immigrant driver makes his error of inattention. So God, in Heather's view, is actually responsible. God is then trying to "pass responsibility" on to the driver—that responsibility which is really God's own.

In my way of looking at the same tragedy, when the driver missed the traffic light, which he in law was bound to observe, he certainly did not do so deliberately, only involuntarily. Thus the L.A. authorities would not, could not, charge him with deliberate murder. He did not mean to maim or kill his family. His was not a premeditated act, only a careless act—a normal careless act. I see no serious grounds on which God Himself could blame him. It would be presumptuous of us to imagine that *we* care for this poor man and his family more than their Creator does. In addition, the Creator has resources for showing them His care in ways we cannot. Heather may blame God; that is natural enough. But some of the rest of us will trust Him to transform evil into good, even when we do not see how.

More profoundly, as Stephen Barr has pointed out:

> The really more relevant metaphysical point here is that God wills and approves *the whole.* He does not will the death of the unfortunate man at the railroad crossing for its own sake, as an end in itself, and as something good in itself. Considered in themselves some events are obviously not good, but horribly tragic. But before we condemn God, consider this: We ourselves set up, and approve as good, systems that have as necessary consequences the occurrence of painful and tragic events—for example, educational systems and economic systems. When the professor flunks a student and dashes his life's hopes, is he doing evil? Does he want the student to fail? Is any system unjust in which that happens? That it contains much tragedy is not an argument for the badness of the world.

Jewish and Christian faith do allow for trusting in God's mysterious ways. Jews and Christians hold that the inscrutable workings of God always lead to an ultimate good, though the individual believer may be unable to see that himself. I certainly cannot see how the event at the railroad crossing worked to the good of the two victims, or of the anguished survivors. From my own experience with evils suffered, however, I sometimes (not always) find that there was good in it, not in any way I could see at the time. In any case, Heather is correct. We must see Providence in the bad as well as in the good. Both when it is a torment to accept, and when it is a joy.

I would quickly assure Heather, if it were true, that human reason can equal or surpass God's reason. But our own experience teaches us it can't. The Greek and Roman philosophers found out the same. So here we face the choice: Shall we cut God down to human size and judge Him by human standards? Or shall we admit our own narrow limits, while in awe of an order and a beauty far beyond our ken, to whose measure we are not yet close to matching up? We complain and kick against the goad. We push back. But often there is nothing we can do but submit to facts. What is done is done. What happened happened.

(5) I am going to take it as a Christian truism, then, that God's will is manifest in the most minute detail of human events. Nothing happens without—at a bare minimum—His "permission," and everything that happens, in God's view, is "good, and He loves it," to use Mr. Novak's phrases . . . And thus I conclude that as a model for judge, lawgiver, or simply compassionate being, God leaves a lot to be desired.

"God leaves a lot to be desired" if you believe that God's ways are, or should be, our ways. Does it really seem to Heather that human judges, and human social engineers, do all that wonderful a job at building utopias, in which there are no evils, no unintended consequences, and no hint of injustice? I would have thought the contrary: that it is failures of justice in ordinary human life, human to human, that give rise to that hunger for justice in the human heart which says there must be justice somewhere. The thirst for justice gives rise to visions of God, no? Atheists may say, No, it doesn't. Whence, then, comes their thirst for something that no nation has ever produced, nor any man seen—perfect justice on this earth?

My own view is that this thirst arises from a sort of residual memory of one's origin in the font of justice, truth, and love—in God. In the Source of all existents. So, at least, thought the Greeks.

(6) But let us test the idea of God's "ultimate kindness . . . justice, and benevolence" against natural events. How is it for a child's "good" to be born mentally retarded, or with a fatal blood defect? . . . But if courage in the face of a fatal disease is such a "good," why don't we wish it on

*everyone? And how did God choose only some children for the good of
early mortality and not others?*

Three really tough questions here. Each is above my pay grade,
but let me try. I have seen retarded children transform the house-
hold in which they were born and generate in all around them a
taste of "suffering love" in all the radiant splendor Dostoyevsky attributed to it. And I have seen those children basking in the satisfaction of being loved, even though their range of awareness and
activity was not so large as those of their siblings. Thus, such unhappy events can be transformed into a kind of family joy.

Of course, there are probably just as many cases in which such
transformation is not even close to happening. I know of at least
one family in which the disabilities of such a child drove a wedge
between the parents, debilitated both, and at the poor child's death
ended in family dissolution.

Since we do not wish suffering on anyone, nor demand of anyone heroic virtue, we do not pray for fatal disease to fall upon anyone, no matter if it might become transformative. The more
normal path is much to be desired, that of a healthy child and a
healthy mother. But it would be a poor philosophy that did not
prepare parents for the worst, and did not know how to transform
a tragic defect into a potential positive. No one knows why God
chooses some for this, and some for that. The "normal" course of
events is a healthy child and average mortality. Is that not sufficient
reason for giving thanks and recognizing the goodness of God "in
the round"? The difficult cases, the abnormalities, are far harder
for us to swallow. Yet if God is God, He is with us as much in one
case as in the other, hard as that may be for us to see and take comfort in.

Professor Gelernter comments with great learning:

All we know is that the evil and pain of this suffering world
force us inward, onto the one path that leads to knowledge of
self and God. What we *don't* know: Would true self-sacrificing

compassion exist without misery and suffering? Could moral heroism and concomitant strength and depth of character exist without it? Now we face a good question from doubters: even granted that we owe the existence of compassion in this world to suffering, is the gain worth the price? Or: granted, the price for human freedom is human suffering; is freedom worth the price? Or, in the words of a famous question posed in the Talmud: would man have been better off had he never been created? The two famous schools of Hillel and Shammai argued the point (as usual), and reached a conclusion: Man would have been better off had he never been created. But the rabbis know that their vision is limited, and their task is to take the world as God made it.

(7) An elementary definition of justice is treating like cases alike and treating unlike cases differently . . . In the case of God's justice, however, we see like cases being treated differently and unlike cases being treated the same all the time—or so it would seem to a human eye.

Actually, judging is often a matter of grasping the unique circumstance in any individual case, and tailoring the judgment to fit angular reality. If justice were merely like adding sums of arithmetic, like with like, computers could do it without intervening judges. And to ask how God chooses to do this, not that, is to wish to stand in the shoes of God. Or, perhaps, just to stand behind him like an umpire, calling balls and strikes. Such questions, alas, diminish what even the Greeks and Romans meant by "God." Not to mention Jews and Christians, who introduced into human consciousness an awareness of conscience, interior liberty, and freely chosen (or freely rejected) friendship with the divine.

(8) I am happy to live with a conception of God as completely inscrutable, as long as that conception is consistently applied. But I constantly hear believers confidently interpreting God's intentions when something good happens to them or to others. But if God alternates

*between mysteriousness and transparency, why assume that it's in
the happy outcomes that his will is readable?*

Heather, you have hit it on the head. This is a good sermon to
give to Jews and Christians. Either they believe that God is sovereign and not merely the servant of their will, their needs, and their
interests, or in the place of God they have built an idol. God's will
is present in all things, in good things in one way, in evil things in
another. He does not admire all acts equally, nor, we are told, "reward" them equally in the final accounting.

Yet it is only human to burst out in thanks when good things
happen, and to retire a bit in inner confusion when pain and just
plain evil strike very hard. It is not so much, sometimes, that one
wishes to deny the will of God. Rather, it is only that it is so hard
to accept, and one is not sure that one is up to talking about the
pain in public. Maybe later. Not now.

Professor Barr offers a richer and more lyrical response:

Why do we thank God for good fortune but not blame
Him for bad fortune? We ought really to thank God at
every moment of our existence for our very existence at
that moment, for all the blessings that we enjoy—the ability
to think, to see and to hear, to taste and to touch, to move
and to act, to know and to understand, to love and to be
loved. Everything we have at every moment comes from
God, and we should be thanking Him at every moment.
But being as we are, we forget and largely take things for
granted. It is when we have a "near miss" and almost lose
something important, that we remember to thank God that
we have it in the first place. When the car swerves and narrowly misses the oncoming traffic, we say "Thank God."
We are really just remembering to thank God for all of the
life He has given us up to that point, and for allowing us
some time more to live. If, however, something happens

that takes away our health or wealth or even life, we have no legitimate claim that God has "robbed" us of anything. What we have lost was His free gift to begin with, not something to which we had a right.

IS GRATITUDE THE DIVIDING LINE?

During the autumn of 2007, I was privileged to observe an inter-faith meeting at the Catholic Cathedral of Louisville, Kentucky, organized by an executive director who is a Quaker (born secular and Jewish) and presided over by local religious leaders from some sixteen different religious communities of the area: Muslim, Hindu, Native American, Baptist, Methodist, Jewish, Catholic, Unitarian, Episcopalian, and others of Asian and African roots. The theme of this year's annual prayer service was "Gratitude to God," and each of the presiders read from a sacred text of her or his tradition expressing that gratitude. It was a beautiful evening, both in its unconscious evocation of this nation as a "planetary people," and in its immediate local leadership. Not a single one of these local religious communities lacked an eloquent way of thanking God for ordinary things—for life, for the gift of existence, even for the lessons to be learned in suffering.

I loved the complementary melodies of gratitude that I listened to in Louisville, and so the thought came naturally enough to fruition: Is the ability to give thanks to God, even the natural aptitude for giving Him thanks, the bright yellow line between atheism and knowledge of God? For those who hold that meta-physically everything is random, rooted in chance, without design or narrative line, and based upon a fierce competition for survival, to What or to Whom might thanks be given? If any thanks are due at all.

This vivid experience brought to mind a penetrating passage from an astute review by Theodore Dalrymple of several new books. Dalrymple describes himself as an atheist, but he is an unusually congenial, fair-minded, and discerning critic. A psychiatrist, he faults the new atheists for depriving billions of human beings of a crucial civilizing agency, the desire to express gratitude:

> The thinness of the new atheism is evident in its approach to our civilization, which until recently was religious to its core. To regret religion is, in fact, to regret our civilization and its monuments, its achievements, and its legacy. And in my own view, the absence of religious faith, provided that such faith is not murderously intolerant, can have a deleterious effect upon human character and personality. If you empty the world of purpose, make it one of brute fact alone, you empty it (for many people, at any rate) of reasons for gratitude, and a sense of gratitude is necessary for both happiness and decency. For what can soon, and all too easily, replace gratitude is a sense of entitlement. Without gratitude, it is hard to appreciate, or be satisfied with, what you have: and life will become an existential shopping spree that no product satisfies.

For those who know God, by contrast, life is a conversation. They are never far from raising their affections toward the Almighty, directing their will to Him: "Thy will be done." For them the world is personal, through and through. It is about friendship, and staying in close touch with one's closest Friend. Prayer is like breathing, like easy conversation with one's Beloved. Even to love another human being, spouse or child, is to love them in and through and with the divine origin of all love: *Deus Caritas Est.* God is that particular form of love called *Caritas.*

In this perspective, "globalization" comes not only through international Declarations of Rights (such as that of the UN in 1948), nor only through economic trade. It is also, and much more deeply, a growing community of those who participate, each in an individual way, in the Transcendent One, who in the vastness and greatness of His vision includes them all. Indeed, Heather Mac Donald has observed this bright yellow line in her own life:

> The one compelling ground for religion that I can see is the need to give thanks. I know that I have led an extraordinarily privileged life. I have had everything given to me. I've had to do nothing for myself. I've been given every possible opportunity. I have nobody to thank for that aside from my parents. When you realize how fortunate you are, there is a desire to give thanks in a broader way.

A few decades back, this unfulfilled desire was also echoed in a reluctant discovery by Jean-Paul Sartre, when he was reflecting in old age on how difficult the practice of atheism had been for him. He had often found himself spontaneously, naturally, giving thanks to he knew not whom—some transcendent presence interpenetrating all around him. A splendid sunset could propel that outward movement in his heart. Sartre instantly dismissed the thought, of course, as unworthy of a rational person. But in honesty he noted it.

In my own old age, I have discovered, to my surprise, how difficult it is for many outside the Christian tradition, brought up in completely secular surroundings, even to imagine what a "sense of the transcendent" might be. They try, but they get only to this: How can otherwise intelligent people believe that there is a God worth thanking? Knowers of God are a mystery to them.

The typical answer they give themselves, as Heather puts it in an online interview, is that believers are somehow "willing to put aside their rationality because they have a deep emotional or psychological yearning for a belief in a transcendent being who has responsibility for our world. It's a part of the brain that does not involve empirical reasoning."

But this method of explaining away the mystery begs two questions. First, to affirm a narrowly understood form of "empirical reasoning" is to confine oneself to the world of matter. But such an affirmation is a metaphysical proposition. And it requires evidence to support it, not mere assertion. But true enough, if we are metaphysically amputated to a way of knowing limited to the material world alone, then it is impossible to find evidence for the transcendent in and around us. Thus, this affirmation begs the question about the meaning of "empirical."

Second, why assume that it is intelligent believers who "put aside their rationality," rather than the atheists? And that it is only the believers who experience "deep emotional or psychological yearning"? There is plenty of evidence that atheists also have deep emotional and psychological yearnings, leading them to decisions that (even in their own eyes) fly in the face of their own experience.

Why are atheists compelled to have such a narrow understanding of "reason," "empiricism," and "rationality," even against their own common sense and that of humankind? Why do atheists yearn to assume the pose of a defiant Prometheus? Is the kick they get the robustness of John Milton's Lucifer: *"Non Serviam!"* ("I will not serve!")?

"Have you noticed that the more intelligent people are, the less religious?" an interviewer asks Ms. Mac Donald. "No. It is therefore to me a mystery that very intelligent people can be religious," Heather forthrightly replies.

For myself, I have met tons of dull-witted people who are atheists, some uneducated, some educated only to the point of vulgar conventional wisdom. Yes, there are many quite brilliant people who are atheists, many of whom I have not only met but in some jobs been surrounded by. I admire nearly all of them. But still they are a mystery to me. How can they *not* see what so many others see easily, and some others only after great difficulty, yet in the end successfully?

Some humans seem to gain comfort from thinking of the beauties of our natural environment as "the extraordinary development of billions of years of evolutionary complexity." They feel no other sense of gratitude and wonderment.

Other humans seem to gain a clearer sense of their own "centering" in the heart of reality, becoming better attuned to the truth of things, in a world much more complex than materialistic philosophy and the narrow reading of what counts as "empirical" allow. These others count as "empirical" human experiences such as insight and judgment, a sense of wholeness, and the experience of the world interpreted as radiating personal love and personal presence.

They also want to appeal to something quite "empirical." They urge the atheist—what has she or he to lose?—to experiment, to try it for a while. "Taste and see that the Lord is sweet." Turn inward, converse, keep open and attentive. Listen to the stillness within. Let the universe speak to you from its depths.

Naturally, of course, those who choose against giving themselves *that* inner identity reject that vision. Close their eyes firmly against it.

That is no doubt the bright yellow line. But there is something of a mystery surrounding it: Why do some step to this side, others to that? The ranks divide, by their own free will. Does it do any good, then, to practice reductive psychology on one another? It seems wiser to listen to one another with a bit more reverence. There is a mystery here. A puzzle.

Perhaps, then, we should inquire more intensely into the natural human impulse to express gratitude—gratitude toward nature at large, gratitude toward the whole of which we are a part, perhaps even toward the loving Source of all that is. In that intellectual landscape may lie hidden the key to the inner door.

In such dark terrain, we come closest to the deep recesses of human freedom, at the inmost core.

THE GOOD DRAWS ALL THINGS TO ITSELF

Among the early pagan philosophers, Plato in particular was stunned by the beauty in things, the forms visible everywhere to the inner eye, the perfections toward which things of every kind tend. Indeed, so splendid to him did this orderly beauty seem that it felt to him as if life on this earth, lived by empirical reason alone (which he never disdained, but honored), was like life in a cave, shaded from the brilliance outside its door. An inner fire of the *eros* of inquiry drove him to seek something more and something higher.

Something like Plato's vision, I think, lies buried in Heather's own metaphysics. She really does see humans as aspiring to "forms" such as truth, justice, fairness, judiciousness, amity, and the concern of one human for another. She measures progress by approximation to these forms. Out in the future, she seems to see these forms beckoning us onward, toward ever more inspiring progress.

Heather in print seems impassioned by conscience, justice, and the careful use of reason, pleased most by progress in reducing the suffering of her fellow human beings. She insists that these inner strivings are "innate," not really earned but given. This fierce belief of hers does not blind her to the ways in which the reality of the ideal of justice is obscured by human backwardness, recalcitrance, and resistance to the light of reason.

In my view, Heather's own conscience and noble longings for the good—which seem so different from, and superior to, the "randomness" she claims to believe in—are signals of the divine. Such signals led Plato and many another non-Christian philosopher to conclude that, in the end, the fundamental force at the heart of things cannot be considered purely evil. On the contrary, the force of the good is an attraction that slowly pulls the human race onward and upward toward the divine. As gothic steeples point upward.

I do agree with Heather that building up a human ethic could conceivably be accomplished by a combination of reason and lofty human sentiments. Maybe neither the Christian nor any other faith is needed. President Washington in his Farewell Address was, however, skeptical. In fact, he much more trusted the opposite proposition:

Of all the dispositions and habits which lead to political prosperity, religion and morality are indispensable supports. In vain would that man claim the tribute of patriotism who should labor to subvert these great pillars of human happiness—these firmest props of the duties of men and citizens. The mere politician, equally with the pious man, ought to respect and to cherish them. A volume could not trace all their connections with private and public felicity. Let it simply be asked, Where is the security for property, for reputation, for life, if the sense of religious obligation desert the oaths which are the instruments of investigation in courts of justice? *And let us with caution indulge the supposition that morality can be maintained without religion.* Whatever may be conceded to the influence of refined education on minds of peculiar structure, reason and experience both forbid us to expect that national morality can prevail in exclusion of religious principle. (emphasis added)

Washington's caution makes one hesitate. A law of moral inertia *is* operative in human affairs. Cups of tea cool, mountains erode, distant stars die, and across the generations, during some periods, human character declines. For a purely secular morality, weakened by the cluelessness of relativism, moral decadence is a heavy downward pull. Perhaps not in certain individuals of a particular character, but in the general public, moral decline is normally discernible over time. At first, awakenings and upward thrusts may occur. Later generations try to live up to the heroic models of their predecessors, but soon enough ardor cools.

In our day, in any case, Washington's proposition is being put to empirical test. Under the often observed law of moral inertia, can secular societies survive? We shall puzzle out this subject in our final chapter.

I do not wish to end on a note suggesting that religion is an indispensable means to the survival of the Republic. I am not ready to assert that spiritual claim. I don't mean, either, to argue for re-ligion on account of its social utility. My aim is solely to linger awhile on the source of Heather's own goodness of spirit, and on the fidelity of such moral heroes as Sharansky, under torture in the Gulag.

To what, exactly, was Anatoly Sharansky exercising fidelity when he felt pain in every part of his body and soul? His tortur-ers tried ingeniously to undermine every hope he might have in truth, justice, and fidelity to conscience. "Why don't you just give up, as all the others do?" they asked again and again. "Everything is random, isn't it? Whatever you do will make no difference."

Sharansky came up with his own answer.

As must we all.

The problem of good is as perplexing as the problem of evil. Before we wrestle with that problem, though, further conversa-tions raise other questions. But we cannot leave this conversation without gratefully observing how well Heather conducts an argu-ment, with respect and openness, with spiritedness and with clearly put dissent.

In the next chapter, we must try a fresh approach of our own. Those of us who believe that there is a God—on the grounds of philosophical reason alone—have strong reasons for so believing, even if those are rejected by atheists.

Many of us (two billion in total) hold also that God revealed Himself in history, in the Jewish prophets and in the person of His Son, Jesus Christ, true God and true man. Although Christian faith is not the subject of this book, our atheist colleagues so often bring it up that some preliminary discussion may be useful. But a full-fledged argument for the truth of Christian faith will have to be searched out not here, but in hundreds of other books.

PART THREE

Who Are We, Under These Stars?

"Atheism is a cruel and long-range affair," Jean-Paul Sartre writes in The Words. *"I think I've carried it through." But now that he has carried his project through, how does his state of mind differ from a believer's? Is atheism a more truthful, more human project?*

How does one answer such questions, faced with the prospect of a single, short life which it is necessary to live well? One does not want to misconceive the nature of life; one does not want to choose badly. What direction shall one take? In the end one's decision springs from, and determines, who one is. An inquiry preceding such a decision requires clarity about one's starting place.

—Belief and Unbelief, 1965

FIVE

Horizons, Blicks, and Ockham's Razor

Belief is opposed to unbelief as one radical interpretation of human destiny to another. By belief in God,
a man accepts the universe as radically personal; he
believes that a Person who is the intelligent source
of the world draws men, through whatever evils, to
himself. In nonbelief, a man interprets the universe
by an image of impersonality: of chance, of function-
alism, of the laws of physics, of the absurd.

—*Belief and Unbelief,* 1965

It is time now to make some proposals of my own. But allow me
to repeat: A few of the most virtuous, brave, and generous people
I know are atheists, scrupulous in following inquiry where it leads,
and in bowing only to evidence.

In addition, the presence of atheists in the common dialogue is
of extraordinary benefit to Jews and Christians. It awakens them
from complacency, forces them to confront new arguments and to
think more deeply about older ones. It tempers the hubris, self-
satisfaction, and unreasoning enthusiasm too often visible among
people of faith. It pops balloons of airy assumptions and facile answers. It hoists complacent believers on the petard of their careless
self-contradictions. It invites the minds of believers to become
firmer, sharper, and tougher.

And now to my proposal. The logic used in deciding whether
to link one's identity to atheism or to God is sui generis. The ar-

gument is *not* whether there is one more object in the world (God), or one less (atheism). The center of the argument concerns whether I should think of the universe as impersonal and indifferent to me, and ruled by randomness and chance. Or whether I should interpret it as personal through and through, in such a way that all things that are (and have been, and will be) dwell in the presence of God, a Person (not in a literal but in an analogous sense) who understands and chooses all that He brings out of nothingness into existence. "Existence" here means being "alive in the presence of" our Creator. I apply the term now to conscious human persons, not to all existents.

For the believer, this world is personal. All of human life is an interior conversation with our Maker. Personality—whose defining traits are understanding and deciding (or creative insight and choice)—is the inner key and dynamic force in all things.

To the atheist, all this seems hot air. Solipsism. Fear of death. Illusion, delusion, poison. The unbeliever's universe (say they) is far more bracing, invigorating, and challenging. Each brave spirit is like Prometheus, snatching a burning stick of justice from the nothingness of the night. The atheist believes that human beings put into a random, purposeless universe all the good that has ever been, is now, or ever will be. Using Ockham's razor, the unbeliever slices off God: "We have no need of that hypothesis." The unbeliever holds that the most elegant, most economical, and most chaste explanation is likely to be best. Ockham's razor seems to be in tune with the way things are. Into the bucket below the guillotine drops the head of God.

The believer, however, does not regard God as a "hypothesis," an "explanation," or even an "entity." Rather, in the horizon of the believer, God is the inner dynamism of inquiry, understanding, and love in his (or her) own life, but also in the lives of all others. Dante Alighieri described God as "the Love that moves the sun and other stars." The believer sees God as the inner mathematical and creative light—and the inner, dynamic striving—of all things.

Yes, that special sort of love that is proper only to the divine: *Caritas*.

In short, unbelief and belief are not two rival theories about phenomena in the universe. They are alternative "horizons." A horizon describes all that an intelligent, inquiring subject can experience, imagine, understand, and judge to be real, from the point at which that subject is currently situated. A horizon is defined by two parts: the attentive, conscious subject, and the range of all that that subject can experience, imagine, understand, and judge. Human horizons are "systems on the move." The horizon you now have has changed by a great deal—in range and in intensity—since you were ten, twenty, or forty, or even sixty. Ideally, one hopes one's horizon will keep reaching out and growing until death.

The horizon of the unbeliever has within it no answering personal presence (because the unbeliever thinks God is an illusion). By contrast the horizon of the believer is permeated by an obscure sense of living within the presence of Another. Thus, if the believer strives mightily not to cooperate with the Lie, even under torture, even in prison with no possibility of escape, pain leads her to see that the inner light to which she tries to be faithful comes from beyond her pain or her own strength, burning Insight that fires her whole being. In being faithful to the truth, she is being faithful not only to herself, but also to Him who is the central light and energy and love within her.

These are two radically different ways of living in the world. Two very different horizons. And—if I may say so—two very different blicks.

A. Flew, R. M. Hare, and "Blicks": The Atheist, the Deist, and the Reality-Based Blick

Antony Flew's essay of 1950, "Theology and Falsification," has been called one of the most influential philosophical essays of the past fifty years. In it the leading atheist of his era made the case that when believers assert the existence of God and/or the goodness of God, they seem to admit no possible circumstance that would make such statements false. Thus, these statements are merely empty, so much hot air. Believers may think that they are explaining something by uttering these statements. But they offer no falsifiable evidence that allows others to see what real difference these words make. Nothing in the real world changes whether such assertions are believed or disbelieved (although there may be changes in the psyche and the actions of believers). Therefore these assertions explain nothing.

As a counter to Flew, Professor R. M. Hare, a theist, invented the term "blik." A blik is not, Hare posited, an explanation; it is the way by which we decide what *counts* as an explanation. Here persons of good will and sound judgment often disagree. Hare credits David Hume with drawing our attention to the inevitably personal character of certain important kinds of judgment, which we use in daily commerce with the world as it is. For some, their "common sense" puts them nearly always on target. For others, their inner eye is astigmatic or wandering; they always see things partially wrong. Hare may be on to something here, but I don't think he gets it quite right.

Nonetheless, the philosophical literature on the nonfalsifiability (and, therefore, emptiness) of theological utterances, and also on the interesting but much disputed concept of bliks, is quite vast. (Those interested may search the entries for "Flew" and "Hare" on the Internet.) In any case, I propose to take a somewhat different road. To mark that difference, I want to employ the richer concept "blick." A blick is part of an intellectual habit, the part that shapes one's pattern of judgment concerning what is real or not real, true or false, credible or lacking in credibility. It guides what leaps into the foreground and what recedes into the background of an individual's judgment concerning what is to be credited as true and what is to be dismissed as false. A blick is deeper and more sweeping than a single factual assertion. A blick is a way of viewing reality that is not usually overturned by one or more

pieces of countervailing evidence. It constitutes a rival way of seeing the world, such that some facts seem more salient, and more
probably true, in our way of judging daily reality, and some facts
less so. It springs from a personal horizon, that point in a person's
long voyage through life from which he currently discerns all realities within range of his intelligence: the sum total of everything
knowable to him at that point of his ascent.

In this way, I propose, atheism is one blick, so is deism, and so
(in the third place) is Christian or Jewish faith. The whole world
looks rather different to those habituated to one blick or the other.
Atheists report that in their eyes the world seems random, uncaused, impersonal, and yet oddly progressing upward. To the
deist, the whole world springs from one unchanging, eternal intelligence, which accounts for its remarkable, often mathematical,
intelligible unity. For the deist, there is an impersonal God, intelligently propelling a rising curve of evolution (toward more complex, interpersonal, and cooperative, sympathetic conduct among
higher species). Such a deist does not at all accept Jewish or Christian faith. He (or she) does not assess the nature and destiny of man
as Christianity does, nor the nature of God as Judaism does.

As it happens, a good example of these three different blicks
was provided by Antony Flew during the course of his lifetime. In
1950, his blick was crisply, clearly, and challengingly atheist. In
later years, advances in science obliged him, he said, to alter his ha-
bitual outlook (blick) in regard to evidence all around us. Scientific advances were revealing ever more patterns of design, on the
one hand, and on the other, many increasingly complex and intelligible patterns within evolution itself. He found himself, he insisted, by no manner or means a Jew or a Christian. He saw
himself closer to the intellectual position of Aristotle. And in this
new blick, atheism no longer had the ring of truth. A kind of impersonal Designer with a forward-looking vision seemed to him
more in keeping with reality. To emphasize that his god was not
the God of Abraham, Isaac, Jacob, and Jesus, Flew chose to call
himself a "deist" rather than a "theist," emphasizing the imperson-

ality of his god, and this god's lack of concern for human lives and moral goodness.

In other words, Flew's first view of what counts as evidence might be described as the atheist blick. His second view as the deist blick. And the blick he explicitly rejected, the blick of Jewish and Christian faith, was in his eyes a faith-based blick (for which the term "theist" is sometimes employed). Specifically, this third blick holds that the Creator created humans free so that they might be invited to walk in friendship with Him. The Creator knew each of them by name, before Time was. This world is under the direction of a loving, personal God concerned with the good living, daily governance, and final judgment of human persons. The Creator is concerned about the divinely inspired moral quality of their daily lives, on whose integrity and sense of responsibility He renders final and undeceivable judgment. This third blick was too much for Flew to swallow. Nonetheless, Flew's own life career brings out rather well the utility of the concept of blick, to distinguish his first horizon from his second, and both from the third.

Christopher Hitchens provides a dramatic case from his own ninth year of life, when he first became aware that he did not hold a theist blick. This awareness struck him profoundly when his teacher Mrs. Watts, taking her young charges on a nature walk, exclaimed happily how grateful she was that God had created a world of so much blue in skies and water and so many restful shades of green in forests and grasses, in order for humans to derive from them a great deal of pleasure.

In a stab of light, Hitchens saw how Mrs. Watts had got things exactly backward. There is no God who makes dumb scenery to please humans. There are only the chances and hazards of evolution, making it necessary for earlier creatures to adapt themselves to those elements that contribute to their own survival in a harsh world. Among these elements are certain colors, shapes, and qualities of air to take refreshment from. A certain pride in human adaptiveness should get the glory. God is owed no thanks. That is the atheist blick, as contrasted with the deist blick, and even more with the Jewish/Christian blick. Believers hold that the human person, though infinitesimal and seemingly insignificant among the galaxies, is the interpretive key to the universe and to the presence and activity of God. In the conduct of their lives, nonbelievers value the human person as much as believers do. But they refuse to reason from that lived value to a belief that the human person is an image, however weak, of an infinite God, the Source of the universe and the Friend of man.

The concept of blick is not best explained by the limping metaphor that I am about to set forth, yet, despite its flaws, this metaphor might point the mind in a helpful direction. Imagine a black circle drawn by a compass on white paper. Then place within that circle a round black spot. Now look at that spot as if it were recessive, so that the circle around it seems to descend inward. Then change your perspective. Imagine the spot as high in the foreground, with the circle fading to the background. Change your point of view back and forth and watch the figure change from a cone rising upward and out toward the viewer to a spot descending into a deep tunnel.

This metaphor fails, since a blick is more than a perspective. A blick is built up by all sorts of earlier judgments, tested in experience, and on the whole offering a reliable guide for those practical decisions about reality that one has to make every day. Do I expect the greedy, unscrupulous person to get his comeuppance, or do I half expect that the evil persons of this world often prosper? How much justice do I estimate that there is—or can be—in this world? Consider three further examples.

In one blick, a person is inclined to see everything around her as at root random and absurd; while, even so, she turns her face against fiercely hostile winds, in the direction of an ever fuller justice she helps to prevail.

In another blick, this same instinct for justice is seen as a sign of the divine life active in the poor stuff of this world.

In a third blick, the Creator is a bungler, cruel, and not good

at all. For instance, He does not use His omniscience and His omnipotence to spare His "children" from suffering and pain, as a
normal human parent would do.

In Flew's second blick, there is a Designer and Creator, but one
who is impersonal and cannot be judged anthropomorphically by
human standards. Flew finds it possible to exempt Aristotle's God
from the problem of evil, but not the God of Jews and Christians,
Who is said to be kind and gracious. We sometimes excuse a human father for not fully understanding the circumstances, Flew
writes, or not having the resources to halt an impending evil. On
neither of these counts can we excuse God. He is omniscient, and
omnipotent. He has no excuses.

I wish I had the talent and the actual knowledge to set forth in
schematic form all the characteristic differences between the blicks
of the atheist, the deist, and the Jews or Christians. If we had such
a map, we would be able to see much more exactly where we each
disagree. And we might address by indirect arguments why it is,
and where, that each blick is superior to, or weak in the face of,
the others.

COMPARING AND CONTRASTING BLICKS

In *Whose Justice? Which Rationality?*, Alasdair MacIntyre has set
forth a method for testing the relative strengths and weaknesses of
contrasting views of justice. Just because we often encounter passionately held contrasts in ways of making moral judgments, we do
not have to turn in despair (as Hume wryly proposed) to a game
of backgammon. Some blicks have strengths that others lack. They
hold up better under long and diverse human experience. They
have a broader extension of explanatory power. For such reasons,
blicks are not simply biases or choices of preference or will. They
have an often unnoticed intellectual power. Some blicks, for instance, nudge their possessor to notice the weaknesses, the limits,
or the hidden self-contradictions in rival blicks. Over time, richer

and fuller experiences lead persons in one blick to discard that one, in favor of a more intellectually satisfying one, which sheds more reliable light upon life in the world as it is.

The proof of this point is that rather frequently persons do convert from one of these blicks to another, for reasons that to them seem more liberating, and that also offer them a fuller and richer sense of reality. Moreover, these changes from one blick to another are frequently achieved through mutual argument, inquiry, and (above all) attention to new or heretofore neglected evidence. Blicks are not prima facie unintelligent or unreasoned; neither are they guided purely by desire or interest. They may be all those things. But that they are cannot be a reasonable presumption; such deficiencies in human judgments need to be demonstrated, not merely assumed. And they need to be demonstrated to mutual satisfaction. Otherwise there is no dialogue, only serial monologue.

The best book I have ever encountered on the problems of blicks—which are something like a still photo of his "illative sense"—is John Henry Newman's classic, *The Grammar of Assent.* In the order of daily living, we may sharpen our abilities to reason appropriately, make sound judgments, and over time be on the lookout for the verification or falsification of our own practical decisions. Some of these demands cut deeper than merely notional or conceptual understanding. They seek out a more lustrous and experienced imagination, a practiced familiarity, a nose for the practical truth, a sound and uncorrupted desire to get things right. To become a better human is to have been converted often, by evidence from life itself.

In such matters, I observe, conservatives' tendencies may differ from progressives'. The latter may tend to think our forebears morally inferior to ourselves, because human moral life is on a more or less steady upward ascent. That is why they style themselves "progressives." Conservatives on the whole have a tendency to believe that our ancestors were at least as wise as we, sometimes more so; and that most bright new "reforms" go badly; and finally that we ought to test bright new ideas against probable unintended consequences, about which history is so eloquent a teacher.

Those sharing the atheist blick find all sentences that assume that there is a God to be false or misleading. Yet many atheists do at times, if they are self-critical, recognize that many of their own moral aspirations are "as if there were a God." It is not so easy to distinguish a large part of their moral life from that of Christians. Typically, atheists want human beings to seek to alleviate, even to eliminate, sources of human pain and suffering. They want human beings not to act solely for their own crass self-interest, or competitive survival. They do not want them to use any and every means available. They would wish human beings to teach themselves, even against the current of their own genetic and tribal makeup (their "selfish gene"), to become cooperative, other-regarding, sensitive to the needs of others, neither self-preening nor arrogant in their judgments of others, kind, open, unafraid, daring, enterprising, even self-confident about the human future. In such matters mere science alone does not offer atheists much support. Some findings of science do suggest that "human survival" depends on such virtuous "habits of the heart." But others disclose that "survival" can also be the battle cry of hungry and bloodthirsty wolves. *Homo homini lupus.* ("One man to another is a wolf.") "The life of a man [is] solitary, poor, nasty, brutish, and short."

Many who share the blick of atheism, therefore, cleverly smuggle into their blick moral values of a specifically Jewish and Christian origin, conception, and long-tutored experience, to which their atheist and Darwinian views do not, by themselves, entitle them. To be sure, they can take moral instruction and comfort from the Stoics, Epicureans, and even Aristotelians of the pre-Christian world. (Yet virtually all such ancient teachers shared the blick of deists or theists. Virtually none were atheists.) The Jewish scholar (and a practicing Jew) Philo of Alexandria, born a generation before Christ, taught that the teachings of Moses did not describe merely a special revelation to one people, but the law of moral nature itself, with universal relevance to all human beings everywhere. In sharp contrast, modern atheists tend to borrow the noble ethics of the ancients, while rejecting their intellectual ground in the first cause, Intelligent Maker, and Source of all good, who draws all things upward, toward the divine.

Naturally, those who share the atheist blick find grave flaws in the Christian and Jewish blicks. Some also find flaws in the deist blick of Antony Flew. (Actually, the number of conversions from the atheist blick to the Jewish or Christian blick, as well as to the deist blick, is remarkably high in our time; but there are also many conversions in the opposite direction.) In his rebuttal, Flew himself felt obliged to follow the evidence where it led; and it led, he judged, to ever more signs of design and intelligible upward direction in the world in which we live. This evidence made him no Christian. But it did lead him to renounce the blick of atheism, and to look at the world with the blick of a deist. It is quite astonishing how dramatically altered familiar realities appear after the exchange of one blick for another.

Sometimes what triggers a change of blick from one to another originates in one tiny clue, and then another one, and then another, until we are moved to take up a different point of view than the one we have comfortably cherished up until now. We begin looking at things within a different horizon. Perhaps something has changed within ourselves—one pole of our horizon. Sometimes we notice a number of changes in matters that surround us, changes that oblige us to shift the way we have been seeing things—the other pole. Often these fairly large shifts in our habits of viewing things are first prompted by a tiny clue, to which later more clues are added. Let me conclude this chapter by mentioning two such tiny clues that may prompt in others the sort of shift they prompted in me.

Clues: Johannes Kepler and Ockham's Razor

Often in life we notice seemingly trivial matters that are a little out of place, that jar us, that plant a question in our subconscious—whose full significance we do not grasp until later. Sometimes we need to learn more about the background, the context, the story line, before we can see the point of the discovered clue. In this case, the fuller implications of these two clues may—or may not—burst upon us in the next three chapters. Each clue, to my mind, helps to set off one blick in contrast to another. Each is like a little *click* of recognition that opens up wonderment.

1. *Johannes Kepler.* The first clue is the summary of a short passage by Johannes Kepler, the German astronomer (1571–1630): *All nature can be read as a book.* At the moment of one of his greatest discoveries, Kepler prayed: "I thank thee, Lord God our Creator, that thou allowest me to see the beauty in thy work of creation."

One may have full confidence in the human mind's ability, over time, to learn everything the book of nature has to teach. Nature is itself a revelation into the mind of a supremely ordered and wise intelligence, of great acuity and penetration and reach. Science, therefore, like nature, tells us much about God.

As the sociologist Rodney Stark has observed, the Jewish and Christian Creator is different from the gods of the folk religions of Asia, Africa, and other regions. He is *Logos,* a Light giving birth to Insight (the inner Word), and bound by reasonable laws that flow from His own being. He is to be thought of as Light—the light of intelligence, insight, mind. He comprehends and orders everything. That is why the practice of scientific exploration can be relied upon. Scientific investigation is not doomed to meaninglessness and frustration, but, on the contrary, is favored by God.

2. *Ockham's Razor.* Many atheists make appeal to Ockham's razor. They use it as a handy instrument for ruling out of existence spirit, mind, God, and other such unnecessary beings. There are several

different foundations of "Ockham's razor." (Ockham was the nom-
inalist philosopher—1288–1349—whose work formed a watershed
between medieval and modern philosophy.) One of the most
common is: "One should not multiply entities unnecessarily."

But what makes Ockham's razor true? Why should it be re-
garded as an apt and trustworthy instrument of a searching mind?
There is a worldview implicit in the assertion of Ockham's razor.
There is a blick behind it.

The implicit understanding is that the world is a unified intelligible whole, and that briefer is better: The world's inner laws favor simplicity and economy. If the solutions are jerry-built and
multi-caused, there is some probability that they have not yet
reached the heart of the matter, but are only approximate, a little
verbose, overdone.

Another implicit premise is that the universe is tight-knit.
Everything is related to everything, and there are few wasted mo-
tions. The universe is organized in an obscure yet highly sophisticated way. A very great deal of it can be described by mathematical
expressions, of increasing simplicity and extensive reach.

Why Blicks Are Useful

As I wrote years ago in *Belief and Unbelief,* in some cases the real,
exact differences in the actual lives of believers and nonbelievers
are surprisingly few. (In other cases, of course, they are dramatic.)
Consider the problem of evil. Whether there is or is not a God, a
serious Christian or Jew and a serious atheist will both have to
confront the same visible, indisputable facts: cancer killing a young
mother with three children; an auto hit by a train and all within it
killed; a long and lingering death from leukemia; a crippling accident from a fall against a rock in a recreation park; a sudden onset
of schizophrenia. There are human sufferings enough for everyone. Sometimes they are all but unbearable.

Now some may think that at such moments the believer finds
in faith much "consolation." In actual practice, believers may suf-

fer an even more acute pain. For they know that God is good, but cannot see any good in so much pain so close to them, sometimes in their own families. For some atheists, actually, the "problem of evil" may not really exist; some already begin by holding that life is irrational, meaningless, and heartless.

Let us suppose that the unbeliever sacrifices herself to help the poor, or care for the sick (like Dr. Rieux in *The Plague*), and is in other ways almost indistinguishable from a devout Christian, except for not going to church and never seriously praying. In such cases, by their conduct one can scarcely tell apart serious believers and serious unbelievers.

Still, a profound difference may lie buried within the inner life of each. The unbeliever may hold something like this: I will make the world as humane as I can, and I will try to reduce the suffering of this much-afflicted world, at least by a little. Evidence, especially scientific evidence, obliges me to say (the unbeliever may conclude) there is no God. The world is impersonal. It is irrational. It is uncaring. That's just the way things are.

The blick of the serious Jew and serious Christian is different. The believer may agree with the unbeliever on the facts of life. But he will interpret these facts differently. That is the force of looking at the same facts through a different blick. For the believer, despite admitted evils in front of him, sees the world we live in as personal through and through, as conversational breathing in and breathing out. The world in which humans dwell is meaningful. It is purposeful. And it is transformative. It can transmute evil into good, in ways we do not now discern.

It is as though the present human condition is like that of the close-to-the-earth catepillar, before the bursting into freedom and light of the monarch butterfly. "We have not here a lasting home." Our next step heads elsewhere, but only through the fire and the darkness.

A Proposal

I do not understand why atheists, deists, and Jewish and Christian theists cannot argue calmly and reasonably about such matters. Mapping out the chief differences, and the obstacles in the no-man's-land between one blick and another should—with perhaps an additional case of brandy slowly sipped—be accomplished in a decade or less. Such a discussion need not convert anyone. But it should lead to a much higher quotient of mutual respect among all three parties than we have seen for many generations now.

Several more difficult switchbacks await us on our ascent up the mountain.

SIX

Nothing Is by Design;
Everything Is by Chance

Daniel Dennett has averred that the work of Charles Darwin advanced the cause of atheism further, and more quickly, than any other event in the history of religion. With two grand swaths of his scythe in his explanation of the workings of nature, Darwin seemed to have cut down any need for God whatever. First, by his hypothesis of natural selection by random variation and, second, by his postulate of a dynamic principle—the prospering of the most fit and the weeding out of the weakest—he dramatically changed the worldview behind cosmology and biology. He changed the background assumptions with which we approach reality. He changed the basic presuppositions of metaphysics.

World processes, he seemed to be arguing, move forward not by a design grasped in advance, but by myriads of events acting randomly, one upon the other. To be sure, these world processes show an upward-tending nature. By the weeding out of the less fit and the upward adaptation of the most fit, every species is constantly being improved. Best of all, Darwin's principles allow for steady upward improvement without an inner-directed goal—sheerly by random behavior.

These fresh intellectual triumphs achieved two long-desired liberations for progressive and secular persons. They established a dynamic of cosmic historical *progress.* They removed from the necks of the enlightened the supervening governance and *moral judgment* of an all-seeing, omnipotent Designer. Everything is random, not foreseen. Everything is moving forward, except those weaker beings that deserve to perish, on account of their weakness. There is no longer any need for the primitive conception of a supernatural Lord and God. Everything can be explained without Him.

Science had at last replaced metaphysics and religion. The atheist could at last feel superior to the believer. The new scriptures teach: "The fool hath said in his heart, 'There is a God'" (Psalm 14:1, KJV).

We have already seen that Richard Dawkins uses as a knockdown argument for atheism the principle that in nature motion does not proceed from an advance plan to an inexorable conclusion. Rather, through the random interactions and buzzing collisions of life, the more advanced forms emerge from the less advanced. Thus the "final cause" is not present at the beginning of the process. It emerges by chance only at the end of the process. God's action, in the light of current scientific knowledge, does not cause things to be and to act. It cannot be the first cause. Rather, evolving beings and random collisions among them *result* in a design that did not exist at the beginning of the process. What people used to call "God," so to speak, is a result, not a cause. Intelligibility emerges as a result of world process, and was not present at the beginning. Here is Dawkins: "Far from pointing to a designer, the illusion of design in the living world is explained with far greater economy and with devastating elegance by Darwinian natural selection." And again: "Any creative intelligence, of sufficient complexity to design anything, comes into existence only as the end product of an extended process of gradual evolution . . . God, in the sense defined, is a delusion; and . . . a pernicious delusion." Thus, Dawkins triumphantly attributes to believers a simplistic and wholly unnecessary concept of design.

Contrary to Dawkins's perception, however, it can quite comfortably be argued that some Jewish/Christian concept of Design is at the heart of rational scientific discovery. The God of Abraham, Isaac, Jacob, and Jesus pulls back the veils upon His own inner life to reveal at least this much: that He made all things with attention to detail, and saw that they were good, and loved them, and drew them to Himself. Every small thing has been conceived of and willed by its Creator since "before Time was." Everything is intelligible—and more than that, actually *understood,* by One who created it in kindliness and love.

Note that behind this conception lie two lessons for human beings: The world beyond our ken is not inspired by an evil spirit bent on our humiliation or destruction, but by some degree of kindliness. Second, to be creative and inventive is not only permissible; it is the action by which we imitate the divine.

These two convictions have been a powerful impetus to scientific investigation. They help to explain why it was the nations touched by Judaism and Christianity that became the bold and adventurous explorer nations, full of confidence in their Creator. These convictions help to explain the mysterious confidence in progress among early modern (still Christian and Jewish) scientists—a confidence that has continued among contemporary atheists, who have few scientific grounds for optimism. If everything is chance, if nearly all species perish in due time, how do we know that the cockroaches will not inherit the earth?

What the ancient pre-Christian, pre-Jewish philosophers figured out with unaided reason, then, and what many nonbelieving moderns still figure out, is that there is a radiance of intelligibility in all things, prompting our minds to seek out passionately all their inner secrets. There is an *eros* (an inner drive, a burning hunger) of the understanding, before which all other forms of *eros* seem secondary. Second, this radiance of intelligibility found in all things seems to be interconnected, as though all intelligibility available in this universe is part of one unified field. The world has an intelligible (often mathematical) structure.

What is meant by this word "intelligibility"? Suppose you catch a snowflake upon your black mittens and examine it with awe. Suppose you see a pot boil on an open fire and note that when someone puts a lid upon the pot that lid is sometimes lifted up by some force within. Suppose that someone is telling a joke, and you are on the edge of the group and, although hearing every word, cannot quite get what everyone is laughing at; and then you ask the person next to you, and they whisper a word or two, and then later than the others you laugh, too. In all these cases, the mind can see that something is going on and wants to know what it is, and begins to formulate certain questions. The mind is then shown to be relentlessly eager to satisfy its drive to understand. Everything that is has a point. (In a "shaggy dog" story, the point of humor is that there is no point.) Everything unlocks wonders, teasing the mind to penetrate within.

Hold two or three grains of sand in the palm of your hand, in the bright sun along the curving shores of the Atlantic. What wondrous colors, shapes, and uniqueness you notice in each of them, when for once you take the time. Look with wonder at a single leaf, studying its veins and the lighter color and rougher texture of its underside, compared to the shimmering smoothness of its outward side. Study its tips, its petiole. Compare it to other leaves. One shortly suspects that there is an entire science here. Or study caterpillars, ants, or wasps. Wrens or seagulls. Wonder about them at least a little. In these cases, too, one begins to understand that there is more to be understood in each of these humble things than in our normal rush and unseeing utilitarianism we had earlier paused to notice. There are many different kinds of roses, and from these roses many different fragrances—vast differences. To learn how and why, and even simply to classify, is to begin to plumb the layers upon layers of intelligibility that are infused in all things everywhere.

Some of the ancients thought that this radiance of intellectual light in all things is what men really mean by God. God is not separate from the earth but is the twinkling, teasing glimmer of light hidden in all things everywhere. The inner light in things "will flame out, like shining from shook foil" (cf. Gerard Manley Hopkins, "God's Grandeur"). Man may follow this prey like a beagle, pounce upon it, chew upon it, back up in awe of it. The mind can be at rare times enraptured—as by the first sight of the Hubble photographs—a humbling, mystifying glimpse into our nearly boundless universe, the heavens vast, the furthest stars appearing close enough to touch.

The God reached by Aristotle and Plato might well have been, for all they knew, eternal. The most satisfying penetrations by the greatest of the Greeks conceived of God as the inner core of the Universe, its inner intelligence. They did not think of God as a Creator, but as an abiding intellectual presence. Their vision was not quite pantheist; they held that God is more than the sum of all the intelligibility in the universe; God is more than an inner part of the universe. They seemed to think that their eternal, immutable, radiant, all-seeing *nous* must, in fact, be separate from the earth as cause is from effect. That cause may be *present* everywhere in its effects—as the heat of a fire can extend to the farthest corners of the room. But the fire is not identical with the heat. They thought God is not identical with the universe, but present everywhere, within all things. Not a personal God, but a God whose nature is intelligence and a capacity to choose.

The Greeks could not imagine God to be moved by some cause outside Himself. He is a "necessary being," as they named Him, in comparison with perishable things. Yet even in diffusing his being and his intelligence into all things, the imperishable, unchangeable God of the Greeks allows contingency and freedom. He is not, like the God of Islam, Pure Will, before whom the only possible response is submission. He is intelligence—*Logos*—the source of all the intelligence in conscious agents, and of all the intelligibility in inanimate things.

God's free will was a little less clear to the Greeks than his intelligence. But then it was also not clear to them how *human* will is paired with human intelligence. Foreign to Plato was the cry of Saint Paul: "For what I do is not the good I want to do; no, the evil I do not want to do—this I keep on doing" (Romans 7:19, NIV). This common experience, stated so clearly, led Christian thinkers to recognize that simply knowing the good is not enough. To meet the data of human experience, a more sophisticated conception of the weakness of the will must be worked out than was achieved by the Greeks.

The Greek *nous* (in its highest, purest formulations) is *not* the biblical God. All by itself, the god the unaided human mind conceives of is closer to being a light infusing all things (by way of the radiant intelligibility poured into all things) than to a Creator who governs human affairs, watches over them as a kind Providence, and at death summons every human individual to a piercing Judgment, in which God is not deceived. The *nous* of the Greeks is by contrast relatively unaware of human conduct, even unconcerned with it. This serene intelligence is neither within history nor overly concerned with history. The *nous* is eternal, unchanging, impervious to concerns emanating from his creatures. The *nous* is the god of irony and tragedy.

The Greeks believed in the efficacy of human action, especially in the defense of liberty, as in the wars of Sparta against the Persians, and of the Athenians against all comers. In this sense, the Greeks were not entirely fatalistic, passive, supinely submissive. Yet they did recognize the sometimes tragic blade that descends upon humans, willy-nilly. They believed in fighting to the bitter end, refusing to submit to the passivity called fatalism, defying Fate until their last breath. From that fight, they thought, springs heroism. As in Sisyphus, Prometheus, and Antigone.

In that fight, they displayed true love for liberty, in its raw, basic form.

The Greek conception of God, at its highest, is quite beautiful. Sometimes atheists who do not believe one bit in the Jewish/Christian God find the Greek god admirable, attractive, noble. That is why some hesitate to call themselves *atheists*. They do not believe in eternal life. They do not believe in the Christian God, or any sort of personal god. But they do not want to close their minds to every other concept of God. The conceptions of Plato, Plotinus, Lucretius, Marcus Aurelius, Seneca, and others appeal to them. They take no time to make a study of metaphysics, to define precisely all the contours of their background beliefs.

WHY DO ATHEISTS HATE DESIGN?

One of the first things atheists attack in believers is the "argument from design." This seems odd, since the same atheists claim to value science above all things. It would be *very* odd to think that science is not interested in a study of laws, designs, regularities, and even (by a kind of reverse-mirror insight) deviations from the norm. Indeed, skills in *empirical* research these days seem to pale in comparison with the uses of sophisticated mathematical modeling. There is no design in mathematics? You have to be kidding.

It is not science that opposes the discovery of design in all things, even in purely random events. But there are three prejudices that, if allowed to color science, do supply ways to mock design. I call these three prejudices the materialistic fallacy, the fallacy of placing God in time, and the fallacy of utopian designs.

Scientists who love science and exercise the scientific habit with distinction do not have to be materialists. The science lovers who are materialistic are a distinctive breed, the offspring of an odd marriage. One of the most impressive characteristics of a contemporary scientific article or textbook is how terribly little these writings offer to the senses and the imagination. They are very cerebral, indeed. One regrets not having learned more mathematics than one did, more equations, more trigonometry and chemistry, and a host of other mentally demanding disciplines. Of course, articles in journals such as *Scientific American* are surrounded by photographs (whether of distant galaxies or of insect life) of startling beauty. Such beauty exemplifies marvelous patterns, symmetries, and mathematical proportions, of the sort that ancient and Renaissance artists carefully studied in formulating their own artistic codes. So highly formal and mathematical does contemporary science appear, indeed, that it seems to us, mere amateur lovers of science, as the human habit furthest removed from being matter-bound, sensuous, touchy-feely, and graspable in purely materialistic terms. It is certainly not proportioned to the human senses. Science is an achievement par excellence of mind.

My *Webster's* distinguishes three definitions of "materialism." The first is the *philosophical* theory that the facts of the universe are sufficiently explained by the existence and nature of matter. The second is the *ethical* doctrine whereby material well-being, especially of the individual in question, should rule in the evaluation of conduct. The third is the *tendency* to give undue importance to material interests.

As I say, I am a mere amateur in science, but it does seem to me that the solid, tangible world that one used to signify by holding aloft physical things—thumping on a table or weighing a book in one's hands—is not exactly what science discovers when it analyzes tables or books or any other physical things. When some of my teachers said "objective" in those old days, they knocked their knuckles on something solid. If I am not mistaken, the atomic particles that "constitute" matter and the subatomic particles "within" them, and the fields of energy and light within which these cohere, appear to be far more porous, and have been formed and constructed by mind. They certainly don't feel as solid as the objects that nineteenth-century materialists used to rap upon. The term "objective" does not ring the same way it did before the formulation of quantum mechanics and the analysis of molecules, atoms, and beyond.

You might ask a physicist if the pencil he is holding is better described as being made up of matter or of mind? He may smile and repeat a new but already hackneyed refrain:

> *What is mind? Doesn't matter.*
> *What is matter? Never mind.*

The truth is that many scientists tested materialism as a philosophy for explaining scientific habits, and they found materialism lacking. No doubt, it is indispensable to science to take into account the material side of all earthly things. No doubt, sensible experiments under laboratory conditions are the single best tool for making scientific progress. These facts do not require that one adopt materialism as a philosophy of life, of existence, and of intellectual horizon. Much less in ethics and in relegating "material interests" to their proper place.

In life, in existence, and in normal intellectual horizons something else seems to be active besides mere matter. Even in the photographs of nebulae, galaxies, and starbursts in scientific magazines—not to mention sunsets, the Grand Canyon, the marvels of the insect world, the patterns within a grain of sand along the shore—human insight grasps far more than the mere materiality of what our senses report. The world of our experience seems to be suffused with intelligibilities, which it takes our questioning minds a long time to plumb. All material things seem suffused, if an intellectual metaphor may be used here, with light. As when, at the moment an insight of ours grasps the inner unities that had eluded our understanding just a moment before, the metaphor we reach for is a light suddenly going on. Suddenly we see what had been in front of our eyes for a long time, without our being able to see it.

This is not to say that God's creation does not take a wild, unpredictable, highly contingent adventure through history. But it is to say that the Creator's relation to his creation is not that of a human being in time, as Dawkins, Harris, Hitchens, and other atheists normally imagine.

Heather Mac Donald transforms the cuteness of "God acting before" into a charge against the goodness of an infinite, omniscient God who allows preventable suffering: "The claim that we are overseen by an omniscient, omnipotent God who *also* loves every human being and treats every human being with justice does not square with the slaughter of innocents that I see every day."

The god of Plato, Aristotle, and on through Einstein, is not a "person." God does not have passions of sympathy, compassion, love, or kindness. God is the all-permeating *nous* radiating intelligibility into all things, and inspiring in our breasts the restless, unconditioned drive to understand. The way humans reach "union" with God is by way of questioning, coming to insight, understanding. Our finite minds catch a sliver of the great radiance that shines through all things: the beauty of the structure of the world. We admire.

For the Greeks, there is no Hebraic God who governs the affairs of humans in history and cares about human conduct and destiny. (Plato, though, is a little closer to thinking of God as the Good, knowing all things, inspiring in conscious, discriminating human beings the pursuit of goodness and justice. Humans never quite reach these goals, but keep being drawn toward them.)

For the atheist, the "problem of evil" is transmuted into a practical matter. If children cry in their beds at night, then in order to exercise our secular compassion on their behalf, we should take the practical steps to diminish their number. The role of the secular saint in alleviating suffering in this world, not only through science and medicine, but also through advances in agriculture and in water purification, and by a thousand other humane means, is no petty thing. On the contrary, like Dr. Rieux in Albert Camus's *The Plague,* the secular saint casts a very noble light.

For the atheist, though, the problem of goodness creates an intellectual problem. If everything is by chance and merely relative, why is it so natural for so many to be good—if not all the time, at least remarkably often? Why do some atheists try so hard to be good—good and public-spirited—and why are they so insistent on being credited with moral good?

For those atheists who are not nihilists, the intuitively obvious moral good—or at least the most *reasonable* good—is to promote human flourishing. Learning to be a person of conscience is good, for without conscience not even scientific papers would be reliable. Learning to cooperate with others is good, for in cooperation humans flourish much better than in a (vulgarly defined) Darwinian "jungle," where dog eats dog and only the fittest survive. The evolutionary value of compassion, charity, solidarity, and other high human virtues has been boastfully pointed out by contemporary atheists, not least by the biologists among them.

Thus, the newest evolutionary biology turns out to be not so opposed to Christianity as atheists used to think. On the contrary, contemporary atheists are eager to show that any high virtues that Judaism and Christianity promote are better promoted by evolutionary biologists. In other words, you can have the distinctive historical virtues of Judaism and Christianity—for which both religions were once mocked—without necessarily believing in the God of Abraham, Isaac, Jacob, and Jesus. You can even believe in an impersonal *nous* who is identified with the beautiful and brilliant intellectual structure of the universe, without accepting the Jewish and/or Christian God. Anything Judaism can do, atheism can do better. Atheists can do Christian stuff better than Christians.

It is quite stunning how again and again contemporary evolutionary biologists confirm the findings of classic Jewish or Christian morality—not in all respects, but in nearly all the most central ones. Indeed, they do so not only in ethics, but in the design they find so beautiful in the structure of the universe. They explain this design as completely and solely the result of chance. This is an implausible claim, to be sure, but they insist upon it. *And then they add*—and this is the kicker—that, yes, the design they detect does look *as if* it had been designed by a designer, but their science shows that it really wasn't.

You don't believe me? Reflect on these four passages from Daniel Dennett (easily replicable in Harris, Hitchens, Dawkins, and others). The first is this:

> It just stands to reason (doesn't it?) that all the wonders of the living world have to have been arranged by some Intelligent Designer? It couldn't all just be an accident, could it? And even if evolution by natural selection explains the design of living things, doesn't the "fine tuning" of the laws of physics to make all this evolution possible require a Tuner?
> (THE ANTHROPIC PRINCIPLE ARGUMENT)

Dennett is pretty firm in his reply: "No, it doesn't stand to reason, and, yes, it could all just be the result of 'accidents' exploited by the relentless regularities of nature, and, no, the fine tuning of the laws of physics can be explained without postulating an Intelligent Tuner" [243].

His second quip is snappier: "Not one sperm in a billion accomplishes its life mission—thank goodness—but each is designed and equipped as if everything depended on its success" [59]. (Not a single one of them will stop to ask for directions.)

Dennett's third point begins thus: ". . . evolution provided animals with specific receptor molecules that respond to the concentration of high-energy sugars in anything they taste, and hardwired these receptor molecules to the seeking machinery." Then he goes on: "Not all plants 'chose' the edible fruit-making bargain, but those that did had to make their fruits attractive in order to compete. It all made perfectly good sense, economically; it was a rational transaction, conducted at a slower-than-glacial pace over the eons, and of course no plant or animal had to understand any of this in order for the system to flourish."

Now comes the great conclusion, with a fanfare: "Blind, directionless evolutionary processes 'discover' designs that work. They work because they have various features, and these features can be described and evaluated in retrospect as if they were the intended brainchildren of intelligent designers who had worked out the rationale for the design in advance."

Finally, Dennett praises chance over Shakespeare: "The wonderful particularity of individuality of the creation was due, not to Shakespearean inventive genius, but to the incessant contributions of chance." But not to worry: "That vision of the creative process still apparently left a role for God as Lawgiver, but this gave way in turn to the Newtonian role of Lawfinder, which also evaporated, as we have recently seen, leaving behind no Intelligent Agency in the process at all." Dennett finds comfort in heartless fate: "What is left is what the process, shuffling through eternity, mindlessly finds (when it finds anything): a timeless Platonic possibility of order. That is, indeed, a thing of beauty, as mathematicians are forever exclaiming, but it is not itself something intelligent, but wonder of wonders, something intelligible." Now Dennett does not wish us to conclude that he is blind to beauty, sacredness, wonder, affirmation. He praises Benedict Spinoza, who "in the seventeenth century, identified God and Nature, arguing that scientific research was the true path of theology." Later, he asks: "Is something sacred? Yes, say I with Nietzsche. I could not pray to it, but I can stand in affirmation of its magnificence. The world is sacred."

On these passages from Dennett, Professor Barr pens some trenchant words:

> Dennett here makes two claims. First he claims that Newton replaced the idea of a Lawgiver. That is nonsense. In physics—and that is what he is talking about—all explanations account for orderliness by appealing to a more comprehensive and more beautiful and more profound mathematical orderliness at a deeper level of nature. For example, Newton explained the wonderful laws discovered by Kepler, but only by showing that they followed from even more wonderful laws. It is Laws all the way down! And indeed it is more and more beautiful laws all the way down. If anything, the discoveries of Newton and his successors strengthen the case for a Lawgiver. That was Newton's own view. It was the view of Faraday and Maxwell, the two greatest physicists of the 19th century, who were also devout Christians.
>
> Dennett's second point is that "recent" developments have even done away with any idea of lawfulness in nature. Here he is grossly misunderstanding what he has heard about the so-called "multiverse" idea, in which the universe randomly picks laws in different parts of the universe (hence Dennett's "process, mindlessly finds"). But if he knew what he was talking about, he would know that the multiverse idea if it is true (and at the moment it is speculation) is based on the assumption that deep down the whole universe

shares some ultimate set of laws. It does not get away from lawfulness.

A completely naïve person might think that if something looks designed, and acts designed, and seduces the inquiring mind by the intricate ways in which it is designed, then it rather emphatically seems to be designed. Such a person might also be unable to imagine the millions upon millions of years, the "eons," and the alternate universes, that the atheist biologist continually postulates in order to maintain his belief in a designerless design. A simple person might even wonder if the existing evidence gives the present universe anything like enough "eons" to produce randomly all that evolutionists attribute to time alone. Hearing the atheist's interpretation of the data, the naïve person might imagine that "evolution" rests on a rather mystical process, whose whole range nobody ever sees because it happens over so many eons that no records exist, or in such conjectured alternative universes as perhaps never really happened. These long lengths of time—almost like eternity—and these alternative universes, never subject to empirical testing, require a lot of faith. To believe in an intelligent, conscious, purposeful Designer—"Artist" is better—seems far cleaner, far closer to what science actually shows us. Ockham's razor.

True enough, the designs this Artist displays are marked by probabilities, not necessities, by failures as well as by successes, by evils and sufferings as well as by joys and delights. In fact, Christianity actually dares to propose that the key to the design really intended by the Artist is *the cross* on which Jesus is crucified—the just man, the innocent man, made to suffer terribly just as, long before, the prophets of Judaism had suffered and been rejected. The cross is the key that fits into a universe of many contingencies, accidents, sufferings, evils, and heartaches, and opens up the door to understanding. So this is what it all means!

Now that is a shock.

It is also an appeal to our liberty: "Come follow me." Jesus invites all. He gives us free choice. If you so choose, suffer with me on your own cross (each of us is sent plenty of crosses down the years). One picks up one's cross not for the sake of suffering, which would be masochistic, but for the sake of transforming suffering into divine love, which the accepting of such suffering (Dostoyevsky's "humble charity") unlocks.

It is not hard to sympathize with atheists who find abundant reasons, on many levels, to turn away from Jesus. Many humans have done so. Possibly a large majority. What is harder to sympathize with is the oversimplified image of a bumbling naïf, which atheists fantasize, whose rosy purposes are undercut by evil, failure, contingency, chance, the absurdities of human life, and by all the cruelties of that "nature red in tooth and claw," in which so many animals are torn apart by other animals. A more sophisticated image of the Artist should emerge from the awful and bloody realities believers see around them, not the schoolboy rationalism of their teenage years.

If you do not believe in the Lord of the Absurd, contemplate what He allowed to be done to His only Son, on the cross. The Artist God in whom Christians believe is this Lord of the Absurd, this Lord of the suffering Son of God, on the bloody gibbet.

Jews, too, by their own path, reflecting on the long historical sufferings of the Jewish people, know that their God is no Pollyanna, no Pretty Boy, no Promiser of rose gardens. He made the earth to be a place of trial.

Then again, two further points. First, belief in the Lord of the Absurd so thoroughly squares with human experience and with the findings of science ("chaos" theory and all the rest) that it frees the mind to confront with equanimity both the "chance" and "directionlessness" and the radiant intelligibility in the structure of the universe. Combining both, the Jewish/Christian faith in an intelligent and kind Creator goes more directly to the heart of what scientists and mathematicians actually experience. (We must return to this point.)

But beyond that, belief in the Lord of the Absurd also answers deeper questions in the human mind, which science is not equipped to understand. Atheist writers describe the designer god of their imagination as if he were intended as a deus ex machina, some sort of hypothesis to explain what makes things work. Thus, when they show step-by-step that such a god is not needed to explain *this,* or *that,* and not even *that other matter,* they stop questioning. They have the (scientific) answers they need.

Okay, no deus ex machina exists. God is not a scientific hypothesis. Agreed. We have stipulated that. The biblical God is not a deus ex machina to bail out temporarily puzzled scientists. He is not even reachable by scientific inquiry. Science is on the wrong wavelength.

On Darwin

Before we proceed, we must linger a moment on the terms of the debate. "Darwinism" and "neo-Darwinism," physicist Stephen Barr reminds us, "properly refer to scientific ideas, not philosophical ones. 'Darwinism' means the theory of evolution by natural selection, and 'neo-Darwinism' merely the modern form of Darwinism that is based on the synthesis of Darwinism and Mendelian genetics."

Professor Barr offers four good reasons not to use the words "Darwinism" and "neo-Darwinism" to denote philosophical ideas.

First, to do so would leave no word to refer to the mere scientific theory of evolution by natural selection, in which an overwhelming majority of scientists—including those who are faithful Christians—believe. It would force those who have been persuaded by the evidence to believe in God and also in the methods and findings of modern science into the difficult quandary of having either to denounce "Darwinism" and be seen by many scientists as rejecting "facts," or to identify themselves as "Darwinists" and be regarded by their coreligionists as having abandoned the cause. This usage would chip away at the middle ground.

Second, use of these terms would lead to costly and unnecessary misunderstandings. For example, when Catholic Cardinal

Christoph Schönborn denounced "neo-Darwinism" in the *New York Times,* he was understood to be attacking a scientific theory, and this mistaken impression caused shock waves that were unnecessary. Third, this inflamed usage runs counter to the definitions most dictionaries have accepted across many decades. Finally, believers cannot allow atheists to own the word "Darwinism." Darwin's theory is widely viewed as an enormous accomplishment and a pillar of modern science. For believers to lock themselves into a rhetorical stance against "Darwinism" is wholly unwise.

Though many students of the humanities, accustomed to terms such as "neo-Platonism," "neo-Thomism," and "neo-Kantianism," make the mistake of interpreting "neo-Darwinism" as a philosophical reference, we should acknowledge that the term is most properly understood as "the synthesis of Darwin's theory of natural selection with modern genetics."

If one assumes there is no God, no design, and no future plan in the structure of the universe, as Dennett and the others do, then one needs two new principles for the impressive dynamism, the movement, the change we see around us. First, what makes things *go?* Second, what makes progress happen? That is, what makes evolution tilt *upward?* "Natural selection" satisfies both needs.

Moreover, there is a very neat offset: If there is natural selection, there is no God. And if there *is* a God, then natural selection is one of the possible ways through which He might have organized world process.

But these two propositions are not symmetrical. The first one does away with God, on account of natural selection. But the second keeps both God *and* natural selection.

Well, partisans of the first proposition might say: If we have natural selection, we don't need God. "Do not multiply entities without necessity."

To which the riposte might be: At its deepest level, partisans of the atheist position who rely on Ockham are assuming a very high degree of intelligence at work in the world, economical, tending toward elegant simplicity. How do they explain this assumption? Ockham's razor is based on it.

On a less profound level, another riposte is possible: Such partisans seem to imagine that the terms "God" and "natural selection" are two different "explanations" for the same thing. Thus, the rule of Ockham's razor says that one of them must go. But while natural selection may articulate the *method* by which species make themselves more fit and improve their capacities, and so forth, the human mind still requires an answer to the question, But what kind of intelligence and dynamism might have implanted "natural selection" as a law of nature, at the very beginnings of biological life? Did the law of natural selection—*pop!*—just suddenly appear?

Then, too, where do partisans of "natural selection" come up with the loaded term "the fittest"? Such a term requires an energizing Source of intelligence and dynamism that puts in place an absolute standard, by which given states of development are adjudged progressive or regressive, backward or avant-garde, worse or better. Without such a standard, there is no nontautological way to separate what is "more fit" or "fittest" from "whatever happens to be." On its own terms, natural selection has a fatal ambiguity within it. It seems to display a circularity in Darwin's thought. If X is "fittest," X is more likely to "survive." If X survives, that shows that X was "the fittest" among competitors. Fittest = survivors. Circularity?

Besides, is it true in our own experience that the finest human beings we have known outlive the thugs that prosper among us? That seemed not to happen in Stalin's Soviet Union or Hitler's Germany. The morally good were often put to painful death, while the malicious prospered.

So what does "survival" prove about the moral good? "Fittest" depends upon "fittest for what"? And mere survival is not a very high moral standard.

But this point about what makes individuals "fit" can also be made about species as a whole. There may be many other living creatures on this earth more "fit" to survive than human beings. Maybe the cockroaches. If humans disappear from earth, it is unlikely that all life will cease.

THESE ARE JUST A HANDFUL of observations that call for work beyond the Darwinist account of human life and its origins. To further examine its claims, let us take some instruction from a very bright Australian philosopher, Dr. David Stove. Professor Stove, an atheist, found no difficulty in accepting Darwin's theory of evolution for galaxies, plants, and animals. But as regards human beings, Professor Stove found that the theory of natural selection based upon brutal competition, in which only the few fittest survive, utterly fails to pass the test of what he sees with his own eyes. Professor Stove, in his penetrating analysis *Darwinian Fairytales,* calls this mistake "Darwin's dilemma," his failure, his insupportable proposition.

No other book on Darwin I had earlier read woke me up so sharply as Professor Stove's. I had not fully grasped, in the detail he lays out through eleven tightly argued chapters, the disjunction between the phenomenon of human life and the other parts of the universe. Apes don't devote years to educating their young. Chimpanzees do not build medical clinics. Wrens don't become doctors. Alligators have not formed schools of monks to copy painstakingly from fragile, ancient scrolls. Even eagles do not inspire a hundred thousand nuns to lovingly care for eaglets suffering from incurable disease. Bears do not form modern states and organize into great bureaucracies to hand out benefits to the needy, to help the vulnerable survive and even prosper, or to ease the sufferings of the poor or down on their luck. Frogs do not form hospitals to ease the pain and suffering of their tadpoles and elderly. It seems highly unlikely that the lions of the world would care, without any discrimination whatever, for lambs and other species not their own. The problem with animal rights, after all, is getting the animals to respect them.

By contrast, perhaps a third of the human race is caring for the weak and the down-and-out either through government services or nonpublic institutions—and sometimes by volunteering on their own. Far from human life being a harsh, dog-eat-dog struggle for survival, in which only a few survive, enormous human energies are expended through sympathy for the needy, keeping many from perishing who otherwise would. Such care also tends lovingly to the feeble-minded, the delinquent, the alcoholic, and many others whom strict Darwinism would identify for weeding out, for the sake of a healthier gene pool.

Not even Dawkins and Harris can bring themselves to turn their backs on the suffering. They are living disproofs of a significant part of Darwin's conception of man. Perhaps not the most heroic disproofs, but disproofs nonetheless.

To a considerable extent, then, one might argue that contemporary atheists—even those who most viscerally hate Judaism and Christianity—have nevertheless absorbed from the culture in which they live and move and have their being the moral sentiments of Deuteronomy, the Gospel of Matthew, and even Adam Smith about loving their neighbors (even strangers) as themselves. Recall Smith's emphasis upon the sentiment of "sympathy":

> And hence it is, that to feel much for others, and little for ourselves, that to restrain our selfish, and to indulge our benevolent, affections, constitutes the perfection of human nature; and can alone produce among mankind that harmony of sentiments and passions in which consists their whole grace and propriety.

> When the happiness or misery of others depends in any respect upon our conduct, we dare not, as self-love might suggest to us, prefer the interest of one to that of many. The

man within immediately calls to us, that we value ourselves
too much and other people too little, and that, by doing so,
we render ourselves the proper object of the contempt and
indignation of our brethren.

Confronted with this radical error in Darwin's incautious
sweeping of human beings into a net better woven to catch stars,
grasses, flowers, serpents, grasshoppers, sparrows, bass, salmon, and
all other nonhuman animals from rabbits to rhinoceri, the spontaneous reaction of Darwinists is to voice horror at a kind of outrage committed against their master. "This is terrible. This verges
on libel!" When they actually get to defending the proposition
that the Darwinian thesis about humans holds true, Stove has discovered through many years of experience in debate, they usually
try one of three gambits.

The first defense is: "Yes, of course, people today have learned
how to associate, cooperate, and take care of each other. But this
is only after many centuries spent living in caves as Neanderthals,
brandishing clubs. Brutal competition used to exist. Only recently
has human life been made more caring and considerate—and
atheistic science must take much credit for that."

But a theory explaining everything cannot be salvaged by taking refuge in such an exceptional twist at a certain point in time.
Surely, the fundamental theory needs a quite vital amendment to
account for the human tendency to overcome primitive Darwinism, a Darwinism valid only for cavemen (if even that part of
Darwinism is true). At this point, it appears that Judaism and
Christianity offer a far more nuanced theory about the good and
evil in man's nature than Darwin did, at least at first.

The second defense is the "iron fist in a velvet glove" defense:
Well, it may *look* like human life is civilized and well-mannered,
as in the Victorian era, but if you step outside the drawing room
you will see that in industrial circles there really was "social Darwinism"—it was dog-eat-dog, a jungle out there. And if you visit

the chancelleries of Europe, you will see Realpolitik mapped out as if humans were pure self-interest, who use ideals as smoke screens, and whose placid public surface masks plots, counterplots, intrigue, espionage, arms races, and cleverly disguised imperial exercises. Yet this defense, too, essentially admits that the Darwinist account is partial and incomplete. So far are its darker impulses from being the whole story that they must operate only by subterfuge, as subtext within a larger paradigm. Is the human longing to show compassion and to give loving care to those who suffer actually explained by Darwin, or is it far too lightly brushed aside, in order to keep simple and clean the background theory for which Darwin has real affection? A theory that brushes aside facts that loom so gigantic is in need of fairly dramatic modification.

The third defense is a softer one—too soft either to deny the charge or to modify the theory. It usually goes something like this, with an introductory wave of the hand: "Oh yes, that's true of course, but that undercurrent of dog-eat-dog is really fundamental in human life. And except for humans, it's universal. So let's not quarrel over the details."

But these are "details" only on the supposition that there is no God, no Judaism, no Christianity, no ethical humanism. The "soft defense" still suggests that humans should abruptly dismiss any search for "meaning." They should set aside any hope of making sense of their capacities for goodness, compassion, and truth. When it's over, it's over, just as it is for dead chipmunks.

But this defense actually rests on an unscientific assumption that atheism accurately describes the human predicament. Whether there is a God or not falls beyond the range of science. If something more than atheism predicts is going on in humans who show compassion, practice justice, and seek truth, then as a theory of human existence Darwinism quite simply, and dramatically, fails. For the rest of nature, Darwin's thesis may provide the best explanation yet available for the inner dynamic of evolution. For human beings, it leaves too much out to satisfy the inquiring mind, rooted in a multitude of daily experiences of care and compassion, some secular, some religious. How can something so central be waved aside, purely to save a flawed theory?

In addition, there are three moral objections to Darwinism, when it is presented as an alternative to traditional ethical systems based upon reason, common sense, and careful reflection on Jewish and Christian revelation. The first objection is based upon the horrors unleashed by the eugenics movement of the period 1896–1945, first supported by many of the most accomplished and socially esteemed elites of New York and Boston, and then so horribly abused by Adolf Hitler.

The second objection opposes the rationale for the First World War presented by the German General Staff, which argued that the strongest races had a moral duty to supplant the weaker ones, in order to further a healthier natural selection of the fittest. A duty imposed, no less, by Darwinian natural law.

The third objection confronts the effect upon young and imbalanced minds of being taught to admire atheism, nihilism, and natural selection. Two such were Nathan Leopold and Richard Loeb, the brutal young murderers in Chicago in 1924. This objection was raised by Clarence Darrow, in his defense of these tragic youngsters against capital punishment, on the grounds that their minds had been unfairly poisoned by readings assigned them at the University of Chicago.

The point of these objections is that, if Darwin's theory of natural selection were applicable to humans as to the other animals, in order to weed out the helpless weak, nothing would be morally wrong with the use of eugenics. Nor would anything be wrong with a strong nation's practice of justifying by the law of natural selection the depredations it inflicts upon weaker nations. Nor would anything be wrong in the dreadful, murderous conclusions drawn by Leopold and Loeb from the texts they had been assigned to study. But the spontaneous sentiments of the human heart, once the relevant information is before it, cry out that these are evils to be opposed. These evil impulses are not "natural" duties to be obeyed. Whatever its strength in other areas, something is seriously wrong with an unmodified Darwinian social theory about human beings.

Pressing on, we find that many of our most irrepressible inquiries push beyond the bounds of science: Why do human beings, since it is said to be so futile a longing, nonetheless long for eternal life? Why is atheism so hard to live by, since spontaneously even the atheist heart on some surprising occasions involuntarily breaks out with "Oh! Thank God!"? Jean-Paul Sartre candidly confessed in *The Words* how hard it was to remove all religious instincts from his life.

Again, has nature instilled religious aspirations, beliefs, and longings in us only in order to frustrate them? Their power in us makes a large majority of humans take them as evidence of a dimension of existence about which science, at least so far, is in denial.

Why do we, knowing well our private, deeply hidden betrayals of our own deepest principles—our honesty, our courage—still long for forgiveness and for a fresh, clean start? Why are our consciences, even under torture, so insistent on not becoming complicit in the lies our torturers demand that we confess? Why does fidelity under duress become so supremely important, even under threat to our very lives and (since some tortures are intended to maim us) to our future health? To *what*—to what vagrant impulse, to what fleeting whim, to what law of nature—are we trying to remain faithful? And why?

Why are atheists in the same prisons sometimes so brave, so forthright, so courageous, in standing up to torment? What is it in them that makes truth seem so important, when their fidelity to it does not in fact help them to survive but, on the contrary, threatens to overwhelm and to destroy them?

No doubt, there are secular, atheistic answers to such questions. And also to Immanuel Kant's three questions: *Who am I? What ought I to do? What may I hope?*

And yet there is an odd imbalance: The believer in the Lord of the Absurd, the God cherished by Job and Jesus, gives up nothing by embracing all that science qua science reports. Whereas the atheist who rejects Judaism and Christianity loses access to those deeper, more existential questions that science does not, and cannot, address. An atheist may think that that loss is trivial. He may not even miss it. And he may partially ignore these irrepressible questions of the human mind. He may quiet them by having many pleasant lunches.

Nonetheless, the atheist does lose quite a lot. Perhaps he likes it that way. The Lord of the Absurd sees clearly the atheist's choice. Such a choice is allowed. It is a choice the Lord does not take away. Such a choice serves very well the design by the Designer that entirely by the free will of individuals some accept friendship with God and others say, "No, thank you." The "Designer" is more like an Artist of human liberty and the testing of character.

The God who made a world fit for human freedom—freedom tried by fire, winnowed like wheat, tested, stressed—was not building Disney World. He allowed, instead, for Auschwitz, Dachau, the Gulag, and Chinese and North Vietnamese "reeducation" camps. The hardest thing to grasp is how some human beings can be so mercilessly cruel to fellow human beings. Should limits not have been set to human cruelty? Could not the Creator have set—and enforced—them? Even at the cost of limiting human freedom?

A FINAL QUERY

A final query lies in this. Atheists are fond of offering psychological "explanations" for the practices of believers. That is the work of Sigmund Freud in *The Future of an Illusion,* as well as of Dawkins, Dennett, Harris, and Hitchens in our own generation.

Do any atheists also study the psychological "explanations" for the beliefs of atheists?

Is it fear that motivates atheists, the dread of being judged? It can scarcely be a mere resentment of "heteronomous" law. For in science there are many binding scientific laws for whose discovery individual scientists win perduring fame. By their own obedience, they even reverence them with pride. As we have seen, evolutionary biology tends to verify the utility for human survival of most of the Ten Commandments, as well as the utility of such biblically approved practices as cooperation, solidarity, and compassion. Even altruism.

What is it, then, that makes atheists so *angry* at believers—at least at Jewish and Christian believers? Read Dawkins, Dennett, Harris, Hitchens—it is their lashing fury that stands out. Hitchens in describing religion as a toxin "that poisons everything" might just as well be writing hate speech, except that hatred for religion seems in this generation's moral ecology not to count as hate. Why on earth do atheists not just feel sorry for the poor folk whom they consider benighted—why be so angry at them?

Perhaps it is a question of numbers. In the United States, at least, there are so many believers. Beyond this, the number of believers in the world just keeps growing. The total body of Christians on earth in 1054 AD at the time of the Great Schism between Byzantium and Rome was about eighty million. The number of Christians today, just Christians, is more than two billion.

Meanwhile, the population of Muslims (about one billion) also keeps growing exponentially, more by demographics than by conversion. The number of Catholics is now the highest it has ever been, much of this growth through conversion (not in Western Europe, where it is losing ground, but nearly everywhere else). The same is true of Protestantism, especially of the evangelical type. China is today becoming a field of steady and rapid Christian growth.

All together, just over one-third of all the people on earth today are either Christians or (in a tiny minority) Jews. Add the one billion Muslims, the hundreds of millions of Buddhists, Hindus, and a wide variety of other religions, and the atheists of the world are a shrinking proportion of the whole.

If evolution predicts the flourishing of the fittest, why are there not more atheists in the world? And why is their demographic profile so discouraging, their rates of childbirth among the lowest in the world?

My own guess is that there are fundamental human questions troubling human minds that science does not address, and by its canonical methods, cannot address. That is why even the atheists of our generation typically do *not* place all their trust in science and only science.

There is plenty of reason, then, for believers and atheists to begin to approach each other anew, with mutual respect and openness. The world around us is too vast, and often too absurd, for any one of us to think that we "possess" the whole truth. We may each try to be faithful to the truth, at least to that sliver we are able to discern. We ought each to be happy to learn a little more of that truth from others who are equally serious in its pursuit.

The long and short of it is, the atheist and the believer often help each other by the different questions they raise and the humanistic discoveries to which each contributes. The course of history until now would seem to have demonstrated that. Furthermore, today's massive threats against liberty of conscience (not only from religio-political jihadists, but also from some atheists, such as in North Korea and Cuba) counsel close cooperation among atheists and believers who share the thirst for liberty and inquiry.

SEVEN

Thinking About God

Even if it is no longer appropriate, some atheists call themselves "brights," and describe themselves as the "reality-based" community. But of course both these claims are exactly what is in dispute. (To his credit, Hitchens upbraids Dawkins for thinking of atheists as "brights.")

By "reality-based," colleagues of Dawkins mean verified by scientific method. But this creates a problem for the brights' metaphysical claim, namely, that all reality is exhausted when we know what is verified by scientific method. That claim cannot be verified by scientific method. It is not a scientific claim.

And there is a further consideration. By 2000, surveys showed that 87 percent of the world's population considered God to be real, a full 5 percent higher than in 1980 (82 percent). The brights hold that all these growing billions of people are captured by an illusion. The brights alone are in touch with reality.

Interesting.

Does even one of them, during the night, sometimes ask himself: Could I be wrong?

Further, when you consider that just a short time ago atheism was the official metaphysic of more than half the world's population—in the former Soviet Union and all its satellites, along with a billion Chinese, plus North Koreans, Cubans, and others—the fact that 87 percent of the world now (so soon afterward) holds that God is real is rather stunning.

Just a few years ago, in half the world, proselytizing on behalf of God was a crime punished quite severely—by beatings, public humiliation, and long imprisonment. In fact, scores of millions were put to death solely for being religious, on the ground that religion is a threat to the totalitarian state. "First thing we do—we kill all the priests." Nonetheless, all the State's tanks could not convince the people under their guns that atheism is true.

Again, why does the scientific community, even in the United States, have such a hard time persuading a relatively captive audience that its findings are fully believable? We are invited to assume that those who accept these findings and the metaphysic that may accompany them are brights, while the large majority of the skeptical are dims. That is not quite persuasive. Science and scientism are not the same thing.

Dawkins and his colleagues invite us to conclude that the brights are in touch with reality, in a way that the dims are not. But on a matter as practical as "Who *are* we human beings, under these stars?"—a matter with such important consequences for what we dare to do with our lives—one would expect common sense and the common experience of humankind to count for something. Do they not? Do the commonsense beliefs of ordinary people amount to nothing, just nothing at all?

It does not take Ivy League genius to see that empirical science is far from being the sum total of our knowledge of reality. The gap between science and reality is especially visible to those who learn by practical experience. In guiding our daily lives, we often find it wiser to rely on common sense than on scientific experts.

What is it, then, that makes atheism so unpersuasive to hundreds of millions of well-educated people, including, as Alister McGrath shows, almost half the scientists in the United States? Atheism brings with it many attractions, after all. Atheism removes the fear and dread of meeting God. It removes the unpleasant idea of being judged, perhaps even for one's deeds behind closed doors, even for one's secret thoughts. Atheism permits a far broader range of sexual acts (though maybe personally restrained); since Marx, it has sometimes been paired with "free love." Atheism is also seductively presented as an act of extraordinary honesty and spiritual bravery. It has the attractive ring of defiance and independence, which to the younger mind can seem exhilarating. It bears the mark of adolescent rebellion. And *still* it is unpersuasive to a rather immense majority.

May I offer a friendly suggestion, simply as a possibility to be explored? It may be that the ideas of God presented by atheists are so incredible that the atheists' own reputation for good sense is tarnished. Whatever the reason, atheists—even when they are given control of all levels of education, even free rein for uncontested indoctrination—are remarkably unsuccessful in persuading others of the larger picture of human life that they present. If atheists gave better evidence that they knew with reasonable accuracy the God from whom they turn away, their testimony might carry greater weight. Carelessness in thinking about God injures their cause.

Consider five common but insulting ways of speaking about God.

FIVE OFF-PUTTING WAYS OF SPEAKING ABOUT GOD

1. *God as Scientific Entity.* God is spoken of as an object for scientific discovery—like discovering a new planet, or a new layer of atmosphere around the earth, or perhaps a heretofore unrecognized form of energy—say, psychic "waves" of some sort. The point is, God is taken to be just another object for scientific investigation.

2. *God as Redundant.* God is the gap-filler in scientific theories and philosophies of science. A little like a utility infielder, God is played in whatever position He is needed, wherever there is a gap in existing explanations. As the circle of explanations grows, God is less and less needed. His utility shrinks.

3. *The God of Infinite Regress.* God is the plug in the bath to halt any infinite regress of explanations for "where the world came from." He is the answer to the question, "Yes, but who made the world?" An Indian sage once whimsically replaced God in this role with a

giant turtle that holds the world up, lest the world plunge down, down, down into nothingness. In this vein, some think of God as the plug that prevents infinite regress. Others take the sage's point to be more subtle—to dramatize the ridiculousness of supposing that there is one more turtle to hold up the turtle that holds up the world. And one more after that, ad infinitum, all the way down. The bottom turtle standing on nothing at all. Absurd!

4. *God as Superdad.* God is man writ large, a superhero who knows more, and can do more, than any ordinary human being. Yet He is to be judged by the same standards as humans are judged. If He is a "father," then He should be held to the same standards as other fathers. If He is a "Creator," then we should note the things that (from our point of view) He has botched up, and review His work critically, just as we would review the work of any other artist.

5. *God as Subjective Feeling.* God is the object of an ecstatic experience—highly personal, purely subjective—which gives its subject evidence that can scarcely be transmitted convincingly to others, if at all. Either you have known it yourself or you haven't. Beyond rational communication. Mute.

All these conceptions of God simply pump up anthropomorphic images to Giant Size. Most of all, they skip over the term "existence," and do not reflect upon its peculiar nature and power. Instead, they remain preoccupied with supplying concepts aimed at capturing, as best they see it, the essence of God. A false or misleading *concept* is guaranteed to frustrate any questions concerning God's *existence.* A false concept sends seekers down fruitless paths. And makes failure inevitable.

A further problem is that there is a vast yawning distance between *essence* and *existence,* between the concept of a thing (its essence) and that thing's actually springing into being, a substantive reality (existence) springing out of nothingness for a limited time. How to analyze this difference is a problem beyond the methods of science. It is not, for this reason, unimportant to human reasoning. This distance is as important as the difference between a "what-IS-it?" question, on the one hand, and a question that asks for proof of the reality of the matter: "Is that so?" The first question involves forming an accurate hypothesis. The second involves an act of virtually unconditional judgment: Yes, it exists; or no, that concept has been falsified.

For some readers it may help to explore in their own experience the difference between reaching an insight that allows them to conceptualize an experience they have had, and reaching a judgment about an actually existing reality. Imagine, for example, sleeping in a tent on a hot summer night, and just before dropping off to sleep hearing what seems to be a quiet buzz near one's ear. The question posed by the purported sound is, Is that a mosquito? Seeking verification, you carefully raise a hand and slap down hard over your ear. The sound stops. Then, as sleep begins to come, again that quiet buzzing in the ear. Slap again! But this time you pick up a flashlight and look for any evidence of an actual mosquito. You see nothing, hear nothing, find not a shred of evidence that there ever was a mosquito. Was it, then, some anxiety caused by something you ate? Are you imagining a mosquito? Are you even imagining the buzzing sound?

Perhaps this question isn't important enough to spend much more time on. You pull the sleeping bag up a little higher on your upturned ear, and fall asleep. But analyze what just happened.

You have no problem with the concepts here—mosquito, indisposition. The question about what actually exists is quite different. Tired as you were, it was too difficult to resolve at that time, in that circumstance. You were quite sure about your two plausible hypotheses. But to reach a judgment about reality (existence) was at that point beyond your strength.

The problem in thinking about God is also twofold: First, how should we conceive of Him—that is, which hypothesis are we testing? Second: What is the method of verification—the method for reaching a judgment about God's reality?

Both questions are operative in the scientific method as well as in the methods of common sense. In both science and common sense, these two questions operate in sequence. We need to be clear about what we are looking for and where we might find it, and then we need to search for evidence about whether such a being actually exists.

The most cherished definition of God was actually formulated in the Torah: *"I am Who am."* That is, God is purely and completely *existence.* This definition was almost (but not quite) reached by the philosophers. They were preoccupied with getting straight about the essence of God. Questions about the nature of "existence" did not yet have their full attention.

God's "nature" (so to speak) is not the same as the nature of created things. God *is,* always is. Whereas for fragile, temporary, fleeting creatures such as ourselves, existence is derivative, borrowed, freely given us from elsewhere.

As the ancients saw it, all other existing things flow from God's abundance, borrowing for a time their existence from Him, as many candles may borrow from one single candle to turn a darkened room into a room of soft, splendid light. Perhaps better (but still faulty): All briefly flickering flames depend on oxygen. Should the oxygen be withdrawn, darkness. Were God's active existing withdrawn, all creaturely existence would end.

In the world as we observe it, all the things we see and hear exist only for a time, then vanish. Put otherwise, God brings the natural things He has made to participate in existence only for a while. Those with intellectual consciousness may grasp the poignancy of such a brief, dependent existence.

The answer to the question "Does God exist?" depends on the answer to two prior questions, asked in sequence: "Who is God?"—that is, "How should we think of Him?" The by now classical proposal is that we should think of Him as "He Who Is." Second, "What is an adequate method for judging whether a being of that nature—He Who Is—actually does exist, is real, towers out of and over, and surrounds nothingness?"

This discussion probably makes those trained only in the scientific method uncomfortable. Still, the general form of its movement—from experience through understanding to judgment—actually follows a paradigm not unlike that of science. It moves from observable experience, to a hypothesis that captures the essential features of that experience, to a judgment that the hypothesis fits the facts. From experience and reflection we come to an understanding (held as a hypothesis) about how to think of God. Then we judge whether that understanding meets the facts. We may form an idea about God, a hypothesis. But does God, under that hypothetical understanding, exist? Put more exactly, can we with validity and force climb out from the realm of essences and hypotheses when we speak of God, up into the realm of existents?

So now is the time to climb a little higher, to gain a new perspective on what we have so far discovered. The method to be followed is like the ascent of a mountain. We do not assault the peak in a straight line upward. Instead, we switch back and forth from side to side, but always upward, as steeply as we can. At each terminus we come to fresh vistas of the terrain—both below and above. Through repeated switchbacks we gain several fresh angles of vision. From above, the images we held as we toiled back and forth down below now appear to be quite incomplete, even misleading.

After thinking about the lay of the land, I have spotted eight or nine short switchbacks that might help us to cover quite a bit of the upward ground.

CLIMBING TOWARD A BETTER VIEW

The hypothesis upon which our path ascends was marked out long ago by Aristotle, Socrates, and Plato: To be satisfactory to our searching minds, the God we seek must be immaterial, composed in some way of pure insight (understanding) and outward-going energy, the Cause (Source) of all the energy in all we can discover, that is, throughout the whole knowable universe. Such an understanding of God calls for a single, universal, immaterial, insightful, and benevolent generative power, capable of exerting upon human minds a powerful attraction toward ever greater understanding, and ever more attractive human goodness. Here is Aristotle's vision of God in his book on the principles that lie behind physics, that is, behind the world of nature such as we know it. Such principles, and only such principles (or others very like them), account for nature having come into existence at all. That book is *Metaphysics* book XII, chapter vii (10–25).

Permit me to paraphrase that text. The first mover must exist ceaselessly ("by necessity"), Aristotle writes, since the things moved into existence by it are fleeting and fast disappearing. These nondivine things do not cause their own existence. They depend upon something steady and noncontingent. "On such a principle, then, depend the heavens and the world of nature. And it is a life such as the best which we enjoy. But we enjoy it only for a short time (for the first mover is ever in this state, which we cannot be)."

Being animated by the active motion of the divine power is also a delight. And for this reason we find attentiveness, perception, and inquiring most pleasant, and "on account of these, hopes and memories are also pleasant." Inquiring itself is "that which is best in itself, and inquiring in the fullest sense is that which is best in the fullest sense."

In other words, our inquiring is well matched to reality and can gently press itself into all the folds, angles, and nuances of the things of nature. In a sense, our understanding and the intelligibility of nature are made for each other. They become one in the act of inquiring. For the intelligibility that resides in every object around us lights up our own mind in a happy union. From paraphrasing Aristotle, we move again to a direct quote from the same chapter.

Thought reflecting on itself shares the nature of the object of thought; for it becomes an object of thought in coming into contact with and inquiring into its objects, so that thought and object of thought become one. For inquiry is capable of *receiving* the object of thought, i.e., the essence of the thing. But inquiry is *active* when it *possesses* this object. Therefore the possession rather than the receptivity is the divine element which inquiry seems to contain . . . The act of contemplation is what is most pleasant and best: our receptivity to reality, the divine light-giver thrusting his light into us. If, then, God is always in that good state in which we sometimes are, this compels our wonder; and if in a better, this compels it yet more. And God *is* in a better state.

And *life* also belongs to God; for the actuality of thought *is life,* and God is that actuality; and God's self-dependent actuality is life most good and eternal. We say therefore that God is a living being, eternal, most good, so that life and duration ceaseless and eternal belong to God; for this *is* God. (emphasis added)

The argument here is that whatever God may be, He includes in His nature what is best in creation, and in particular what is best in those creatures possessed of powers of inquiry, insight, reflection, and choice. These are the best powers in the universe. They cannot be greater than God's powers, for God is their source. Whatever is best in us, and in the rest of the universe, therefore, points us (from however great a distance) in the direction of God's own nature. It would be foolish to hold that the best things known to us are unknown to God, foreign to Him, and not included in the powers of His own nature, for it is from Him that they acquire their own motion.

This, then, is how the ancients reasoned their way to the divine Author of all that is.

It might also be well to note that for the ancients, especially Aristotle, the most characteristic feature of everything called "nature" is motion. "Eppur' si muove!" Galileo protested; "Still, it moves!" And many different *kinds* of motion are discernible in nature, in all its variety. Hot tea cools. Spreading oaks from tiny acorns grow. Nourishing vegetables spring from tiny seeds—even huge melons from a seed smaller than an aspirin. Cats prowl. Meteors blaze across the sky. Eyes blink. Rocks slide down a hill. Some forms of rock may also slowly erode, under a constant beating of water or, perhaps, of acid rain. The constant scraping of countless young feet on the marble stairs of a school may, after decades of wear, make depressions at the places where hurrying students pivot on the balls of their feet.

But here, now, is a particularly instructive example of one limited type of motion. One billiard ball, struck by a pool cue, may clack loudly into another, which in turn glancingly touches a third, pushing it gently into the side pocket. An observer may note that the movement imparted through the cue to the first ball and the movement imparted from ball to ball are different in kind. One may also observe that the cue stick is moved by a superior mover, not only by the practiced movements of the two hands, but also by the guiding inner movements of calculation, deliberation, adjusted intention, and the complex decision: which ball to single out, with which degree of force, and what precise trajectory is best designed to glance off the second ball, so as to brush it gently against the third, just sufficiently to drop it in the side pocket. (Too much force would drive the third ball to bounce away from the pocket.)

In other words, when several bodies are as alike as pool balls, there may be "the movement of equivalents" imparted by one body to another along a certain plane. This was the force of the Indian's joke about a turtle standing on the back of a similar turtle "all the way down." Every turtle was like every other. His story took no account of any superior cause, of a different order and higher potency.

But there are also "superior movements," such as the deliberate premeditated force and direction imparted to the three billiard balls by a human mind, through the practiced movements of the hands upon the cue. This sequence of superiors—mind to hands, to cue to billiard balls—is of a wholly different hierarchy of complexity and skill from the "movement of equivalents" that impels the first ball into the second, and the second into the third.

The classical argument from movement in the universe trades on these ever more unequal powers of movement. Nonetheless, the classical argument begins with a simple fact. The fact is that movement happens, can be observed, and anyone would seem dense who did not observe movement throughout all natural things. But there are scaled "levels" of movement, governed by different orders of complexity and driven by ever more potent powers, often invisible except in their effects. These different powers, in turn, work in remarkably different ways, by different laws, and under different concrete circumstances.

Imagine that there are in sequence four or five different levels of movement, such that the "first mover" in this bracketed sequence is of a different order from the one lower in line, and that one from the next below, and so forth. We should not imagine all movements as if they were like billiard balls striking billiard balls, all alike, and on the single plane of a green felt table. Rather, fourth movers (such as the billiard balls) have lesser potencies than tertiary movers (the cue sticks, moved by practiced hands). The secondary mover (the human power to reflect, choose, and impart intentional direction) has powers greater than all that are lower on the scale, and of a more intentional and spiritual order.

And yet such human powers did not always exist. Human life has not been coextensive with history but appeared on the world stage rather late in the history of the earth (as we now know it)— and much more so, in the history of the cosmos. Darwinian evolution may very well explain *how* human life evolved from its earliest beginnings to its ever more complex and sophisticated powers of inquiry and reasoned choice. But the very fact of such higher powers as inquiry and calculated choice coming into existence raises questions beyond the scope of science. Were these set in motion by a yet more potent and more intelligent mover?

Of course, maybe there is no such first mover. In that case, no lesser order of mover is moved by the first. But simple observation shows that there is motion, all around us. If the principle is valid that "Everything that is in motion is moved by a mover," what put the world's discernible movers into action?

I do not offer this as a "proof" of anything. But it does mark out fairly well, I think, the "way" the human mind was led upward along the chain of more complex movers, suspended from a first mover. This first mover is complete in itself, possessed of contemplative and active intellectual powers, and already and eternally in pure act, unmoved by any other. Such a mover must have been capable of imparting movement to an entire resplendent, variegated, and jerkily evolving universe, a universe marked by myriad contingencies and happenstances, allowing remarkable liberty to human individuals—those humble and dependent, but nonetheless self-directing originators of their own actions.

All these conclusions, be it noted, were once reached without faith, by unaided reason alone. Philosophers down the ages have found some fault in them, and some merit in them. They are a landmark at which one is well-advised to linger, along the switchbacks up the mountain. Something like them seems to be needed to satisfy the hungry mind, even of some of the most intelligent inquirers in human history.

What Philosophy Learns from Judaism

Jews and Christians have a different source for thinking about God, but their sources do not seem to contradict or to cancel out the view reached by Aristotelian and Socratic reason. In fact, this Jewish/Christian source of light adds to the earlier view achieved by reason, improves upon it, poses many new avenues of inquiry for it, and adds a great deal of concrete and intellectual detail. Further, this source of light better explains some features of human life and philosophy than the ancient theories did. (That is why so many learned Greeks and Romans were converted to "the new philosophy.") Even today one is free to reflect on this new way of thinking about God, to test it by experience, to trace out its implications for human behavior and for social inspiration. In fact, after the collapse of the virulent atheistic regimes of the twentieth century (supposedly an enlightened and advanced century), no one in formerly totalitarian nations is any longer *forced* to avoid questions about the meaning of life. In fact, many survivors of that dreadful period are inclined to find atheism not only unpersuasive but repugnant. Perhaps this is a mirror image of the repugnance that Judaism and Christianity inspire in some atheists.

However that may be, one can discern on brief inspection that Judaism and Christianity do claim that there is *one* God, one Creator, for the whole universe. That is, the God they have formed an understanding of (correctly or incorrectly) is a God of universal reach, spreading His blessings upon all nations, and inviting all peoples to turn their minds and hearts to Him. In other words, He is not just the God of one tribe. He is the universal Creator of all. Indeed, even if that knowledge of Him—knowledge of "the true God"—was first nurtured within one tribe, from the very beginning it was made clear to that tribe that this one God is the God of all. Jews are in this sense the first witnesses to a universal God.

It is also significant that no one can come to this God except by personal freedom. Many of His first believers at times turned against Him. A few were faithful to Him freely, often at great personal cost. Every story in the Bible has as its dramatic axis an act of liberty. At one time the same human being is unfaithful to God, and at another faithful, and the suspense in the next chapter is, What will he or she choose to do this time?

Even if one is not, and does not intend to be, a Jew or a Christian, it has proved useful for philosophers to test certain Jewish or Christian ways of thinking about God—and, correlatively, to explore Jewish/Christian ways of thinking about human nature and destiny. To trace out all these cultural interactions is not our purpose here. Yet such studies ought to be more commonly and regularly carried out, since even the Enlightenment is in important ways a child of Jewish and Christian ways of thinking. Where else did the Enlightenment ideas of "fraternity" and "equality" come from? Turn away from Judaism and Christianity as one will, it is not admirable to be dishonest about one's intellectual debts.

Jews and Christians call God "He Who is." And also: Justice, Governor, Creator of all things, Father, Providence, Way, Truth, Life, Lamp unto my feet, Friend, and even Love itself.

Yet it is also true that both religious traditions are painfully aware that no believer sees God, neither with the eyes in our heads nor the eyes of the mind. Humans cannot touch God, nor see Him, nor hear Him, nor taste Him, nor discern the scent of His presence—except by way of metaphor. No one sees God. We cannot reach God through our senses. For that reason alone, to seek God through the ordinary methods of empirical science is pointless. Wrong method. Wrong tool. Wrong way of thinking about who God is.

Even those evangelical Christians who say that in Christ humans did in fact see God, hear God, even touch God, must note that many of the people who saw or heard Jesus Christ in the flesh did *not* detect God in him, but walked away. More, apparently, walked away than believed. Even though there is a way, metaphorically, of "seeing" God—by faith—it seems much better in ordinary language to say that in trying to see God believers are in a night as much as the atheist is. In this darkness, God does not appear. We have already read many testimonies to that point in earlier chapters. Here Saint John stresses it again in his first epistle, and points us to a better way to come to know God, indirectly, not through sight, but rather by the fruits borne by believing lives.

No one has ever seen God. Yet, if we love one another, God remains in us, and his love is brought to perfection in us. This is how we know that we remain in him, and he in us . . . God is love, and whoever remains in love, remains in God and God in him . . . If anyone says, "I love God," but hates his brother, he is a liar; *for* whoever does not *love* a brother whom he has seen *cannot love God whom he has not*

seen. This is the commandment we have from him: whoever loves God must also love his brother. [Emphasis added]
(1 JOHN 4:12–13, 16, 20–21, NAB)

To put this in another way, eye has not seen, nor ear heard, what
a person-to-Person encounter with God is like.

AGAIN, GOD CANNOT BE SEEN

The Bible says that Moses saw God in a burning fire. But when
you read that book, you must understand how to attend both to
the literal word and to the proper usages of genre and metaphor.
You must read inquiringly, intelligently, wisely.

Moses never saw God. All he saw was flame, flickering and
roaring upward, spiraling and disappearing, a never-ending font of
coruscation. Moses had to turn away. It was only a burning bush,
but it was too much for the eyes of Moses; he had to turn away.
Moses didn't see even a sliver of who God is. As a drop is to the
ocean, so compared to God is a dancing flame.

If God appeared face-to-face before it, the human mind (left to
itself) would shatter like crystal. Darkness is the *normal* mode of
Jewish and Christian belief. Nor is darkness quite the same as
doubt. Even if one has not the slightest doubt about the presence
of God, still one feels the pain and abandonment of not *seeing* God.
Our minds are not proportioned to the divine mind.

Brave and persistent men can come to *know* that God exists. (I
repeat, *know* it. Not *believe* it.) They can know unmistakably that
God exists. That much is within the powers of human reason.
They know it by the fruits of God's presence in their own lives and
those of others. Meanwhile, some who claim to be atheists act as
if there *is* a God, and some who claim to believe act as if there is
no God. As a literary friend has written in a note:

A text I always turn to in times of doubt is "By their fruits
ye shall know them." It seems to me that it would be unrea-

sonable of God to expect ordinary folk to have the brain-power to follow the arguments of the philosophers and theologians for His existence, so he has given them a much less doubtful guide in the form of a commonsensical injunction to pay attention not to what people say but to what they do. Those who say they believe and yet do ill are commonplace—mere hypocrites like most of us. But those who say they believe and who act with love are the ones we should pay attention to, since they have defied hypocrisy. They're the ones who mean it.

If you follow that guide, you find—at least I find—that it will infallibly lead you to admire men and women of faith over those without it. There is a beauty in their lives whose example still has the power to inspire admiration and emulation years after their deaths—as did your own brother in Bangladesh, whose example is still remembered there today. To paraphrase Hume, it would be more of a faith in the miraculous to believe that the power of their example was not connected to their belief in God than to believe that it was. To believe that that belief could produce such mighty and lasting spiritual effects if it were only fancy or wishful thinking would be wishful thinking itself.

However, humans cannot know, cannot possibly know, *what* God is. Not with God's own self-knowledge, and not even with their own. Humans cannot reach the biblical God, the God of Abraham, Isaac, Jacob, and Jesus, by way of reason alone. Nonetheless, philosophy goes quite a long distance toward God. Many who have climbed mountains into the thin air of reason at its best have seen quite a lot. Most are changed by it. As Professor Anthony Long notes, "No ancient philosopher of the leading schools was atheist or even agnostic." Without God's prior existing and creating, they reasoned, not even our wishes would exist. The ancients figured out, for instance, that God is not made of matter nor bound by time. They regarded the notion of an uncreated material universe as self-contradictory. They did not think of the whole, empirically knowable, material universe as "created." But they were certain that it was not self-caused, could not account for its own existence, and required an uncaused cause constituted by eternal mind, not perishable matter. In other words, an eternal, Existing Act.

Humans are clearly able to reason from what God has made, and what God continues to do, to the fact that He is present within and around humans. They can also learn a lot about what God is *not*. To anyone with any honesty of spirit, it has to be pretty clear that God is not a stone idol, nor an idol of bronze, not a golden calf, nor a thick serpent, nor a jaguar—not a *thing* either, not one more object like everything else in the universe. Nor is God the object of mere wish fulfillment. What sort of God would *that* be? Not one to take seriously.

The ancients painstakingly figured all this out before God pulled back the veils in the biblical tradition and humbled Himself as if to speak to little children, to His human family. He then revealed Himself in two ways. First, by an inspired written text, the Bible, a complex set of narratives written over many centuries and in many different voices and different genres. Second, He revealed Himself by the life and death of His Hebrew prophets and of His beloved Son. By those two paths, God let out many of His inmost secrets, in ways that humans could understand. That is, if they wanted to and were not willfully resisting the insight. Their choice.

Furthermore, a great many signs about Who God is have been sown like clues in His creation. Long before any self-revelation on God's part, His good servants—Socrates, Plato, and Aristotle, among hundreds of others, without so much as having in their hands a single scroll of the Bible—discovered for themselves from humble observation and undistracted reason that God exists. They recognized that God is present in every blade of grass and grain of sand and living thing.

Summarizing the work of many others, Aristotle discovered

that God must be self-actualizing, eternal, immaterial, not only intelligent, but drawing all intelligences and all intelligibility to Him as their destination (final cause); and good, true, just, and even loving. All this from evidence of natural things that the ancients observed around them. They even saw that their own self-knowledge is the best and truest clue to what in their keenest vision God's nature must be like. Well, only remotely, and by analogy, but still. God must be more like human consciousness, insight, a sense of humor, good judgment—more like a person imperishably immortal—than like any other creature on this earth. Why? Because no other known creature acts in so complex, self-conscious, intelligent, and self-critical a way. God must be *at least* like that, and far greater.

In the end, though, it was important to God that His Son (who is one with Him) became human and dwelt on the earth, even to suffer and die. In this way, Christ parted the veils for humankind, so that humans might see in his way of living, more clearly than in any other way, what God is like: like suffering love. The God of Judaism and Christianity is He who can transmute evil into good. As Christ transformed an unjust death into new life, new hope, and new possibilities for the human race.

Nothing like what humans had expected! Not the apostles of Jesus, even. Not the Jews. We never do fathom God's surprises. We find it too difficult to admit, that we are not as smart as our Inventor and Creator. Such limited creatures we are, to be so arrogant! Ungrateful rascals, our pride is our undoing. So unlovably consistent in our betrayals of our better selves.

God knows well the creatures He has made. He *has* to beat us around the ears a bit—if He wants us to understand. We can't seem to get it all at once, only spoonful by spoonful.

We are as God made us, fickle and inconstant, stubborn and proud. Not such a bad sort, to God's way of thinking. He made us independent, to use our own minds and wills.

And now we seekers must take a steep step, so those who can't make it, don't.

What Do You Think of When You Say "Trinity"?

Take a look at this Trinity thing. What goes through your head when you say the word "Trinity"? This was a question a Jewish friend posed to me one sunny day, in an outdoor café in the Rockies. On the upper slopes of this mountain, I learned from this surprising probe to look from a new angle, from a new vantage point, on thinking about God. There really is a point to "the Trinity," for those who reason carefully.

Jews reasonably hold that monotheism means that God is one, literally One; He cannot be Three-in-One. They have a healthy fear that the step to a "Trinity" is a betrayal, a blasphemy, a weak-kneed return to the many gods of the polytheists, among whom they struggled for generations simply to survive. An abomination, therefore, to be resisted mightily.

God's Islamic children are even harsher about it. They consider the Trinity so great a treason to the One God that meting out humiliating servitude for it is far too kind. Infidelity of that sort ought to be exterminated from the earth. Their revulsion expresses the obligation put upon them (so say the hotheaded): Infidelity must be obliterated.

Most of us might agree that the best things in our lives are the loves we have known: of parents and friends, of teammates undergoing great struggles, of soldiers under heavy fire with their "brothers." And especially the most wonderful of all friendships, that between husbands and wives. These loves are the best experiences I have encountered in life. If anything is, they are the most "divine" part of life, the part that is most like God. (Read again 1 John 4, above.) The point God is making in teaching us that He and His Son are one, and that one with them also is the Holy Spirit of Understanding and Love, may thus be a fairly humble one.

To think of God as Trinity is to think of Him as more like an intimate communion of persons than as a solitary being. He is one, but as a communion of persons is one. Our minds struggle here, of course. We barely know what we are talking about. Yet when we hold this belief up to daily experience, it illuminates. It offers us profound lessons for our contemplation. *Deus caritas est.* God is love, and whoever lives in love lives in God.

GOD AS THE LIGHT OF MIND

Still again, one more switchback on the mountain. Let us try thinking of God as intelligence suffusing all things—and suffusing them also with love. Did not Aristotle and Socrates and Plato discern as much? Let us build up to this point step by step.

Every human being on earth, we may be sure, detects certain clues about God's presence within him. It's a little like finding a corpse on the green at the fifth hole of the golf course—the green around the bend, behind the trees. This particular cold corpse on this fifth green poses irrepressible questions. Who *was* he? Did he die of "natural causes"? Was he *killed*—by accident?—or by design? Finding a human corpse on a public green isn't like finding an acorn. No, medical assistance must be summoned, the police, detectives. A dead body on the fifth green requires an inquiry. This inquiry is often a fascinating one.

That is how detective stories all begin: with something that must be explained. But why? Why must everything be explained? The assumption behind every detective story is that everything, no matter how tiny the detail, has an explanation. And that that explanation may cast a beam of light upon the meaning of an entire sequence of actions. Every detective story rests on the assumption that intelligence and intelligibility suffuse all things. Everything is luminous with reasons, if you have eyes to see. As Sherlock Holmes did. As Agatha Christie's heroes and heroines did. And many another. Every detective story is a proof of God's existence.

When everything is suffused with reasons, that's the presence of God. Everything ought to be (and is) luminous with reasons—although these are often not so easy to figure out. After all, everything flows from one single intelligent Creator. If one may say so, God knew what He was doing.

Still, we have to recognize: God hates to be too obvious about things. He writes pretty darn good mysteries into almost everything He does. Our fun lies in the detection. Who would be attracted to God if He didn't drop a hint, or plainly plant a clue? And then cover it up again? We have to work for it. Use our brains a little. Keep pursuing the hidden God. God is pursuing us, and wants us to be *adults*. Not wimps. But we keep running from Him.

There is a little verse that presents God as "The Hound of Heaven":

I fled Him, down the nights and down the days;
I fled Him, down the arches of the years;
I fled Him, down the labyrinthine ways
Of my own mind.

That poem nails the reality.

God has been pursuing us. He has been flirting with us. He has been giving us all the hints we will ever need. It is okay to stop and let Him catch us.

HOW TO READY ONESELF TO PRAY

There is one more turn before the top of the mountain (where no one will appear).

I am not very good at prayer, although I try to be praying all the time, like breathing. (In fact, I have at times asked God—when I am too ill or too tired to think in words—to take my breathing as a prayer.) Prayer is an inner conversation, wordless often, marked just by attentiveness. Every detail of every event is speaking. It comes forth from the creative insight of God.

When I want to ready myself to think about God, I place myself quietly and humbly in His presence. I try to shut out other thoughts, and then quietly think about the most beautiful and ennobling and stunning things I have seen in life—all my favorite things. There are two views in the Alps—in Grindelwald and in Bressanone—that I have especially loved. The peacefulness of an ocean on a quiet day, the blue water barely rippling, never fails to move my heart. And the sunsets—in Iowa, in Wyoming, on the seacoast of Delaware—and that most peculiar green sunset on the plain above Mexico City where the sun drops over the edge of the plain before it disappears behind the earth, so that the light during that interval is eerie and prolonged and unforgettable.

I think then of my favorite music, of Mozart, Bach, Haydn, Vivaldi, Dvořák's *Stabat Mater,* the most beautiful of all, written after the sudden death of his much loved daughter. I think of favorite paintings from the Pitti and the Uffizi, and the convent walls painted by Fra Angelico. And sculptors. And poets. And philosophers and other writers whose work has thrilled me. (One of my most unforgettable moments as a young man was reading Maritain's *Creative Intuition in Art and Poetry*; it was so beautiful I had to get up and take a long walk down to the lake, almost speechless in silent wonder.) For several years, every Easter I read one of Dostoyevsky's long novels, followed in later years by *War and Peace* and *Anna Karenina*. I think of God as the Creator of all these great minds and artists. I wonder how much greater than they is God's own mind and sense of beauty. I would love to share in contemplation of such works and such persons for all eternity. And all the more so of His beauty.

Then I think of the loves I have known. Close friends, childhood buddies, grandparents, uncles and aunts and cousins, my three brothers and one sister, my dear parents—and then Karen, whose name means what she is, *Clara,* the clear light of my life— and our solid, noble, and strong children and grandchildren. All these loves make me think that God's love is more than the sum of these, of a different order entirely, and yet the source of all of them. "Where there is *caritas* and *amor,*" the old hymn goes, "there God is." That is my favorite hymn.

Jesus asks us not only to be just to our enemies, not only to be merciful, not only to forgive. He asks us to resist evil, yes, and to be like steel against unjust aggressors—to defeat them thoroughly—but also, in the end, to be able to see that even our enemies are also children of the one Creator. When all the evil has been drained out of their aggression, we need to be ready to welcome them back into the human community.

The United States and our allies did this rather nicely, I have always thought, in regard to Germany and Japan after World War II. If there is ever to be even a simulacrum of a brotherly world—all right, at least a relatively tranquil world—even one based upon fear of greater power, reaching out in tests of amity and voluntary cooperation is a necessity of human life in our time. Here is one point at which I think Christianity led the way: from the first it preached universality and peace. It once united all Europe in a common civilization. It has suffused the secular humanism of our time with compassion and solidarity and individual freedom. It is helping to shape one global civilization, with respect for individual liberty, and for human solidarity.

If I had to pick out one human experience that for me seems most godlike—the best, the highest that I know—I would choose the experience of choosing to love Karen, and being loved by her in return. Second would come acts of insight—those little bursts of fire that come when we are puzzling things through. In many ways, these two experiences are related, but saying here how that is so would delay us far too long. Suffice it to say that those are my choices for the best in life—the achievement of mutual love, and the firing off of insight after insight in pursuit of understanding. That *eros* of understanding is almost as powerful (in some ways more so) than the *eros* of love; yet the latter is primary, and is profoundly influential upon understanding. Understanding keeps love from erring badly, but in the dark, love often leads the way for understanding.

In the Presence of God

With such lines of reflection as these, I try to ready myself. Some call this "placing yourself in the presence of God," through reminding yourself of all that you know about God, from your own experience and from the wisdom of the great writers of the past. Ironically enough, even some atheists find analogous reflections helpful to their own spirits, even though they do not see "God" in their experiences, only peaks in their own inner awareness.

It bears repeating that one reason for such exercises is to accustom one's mind and heart to the interior life. There—and usually only there—is God likely to be found. There have been a few cases of highly dramatic outward incidents, such as when the famous Medal of Honor winner Sergeant York of World War I was knocked off his horse by lightning. He was riding furiously through the rain, just after having formed a smoldering resolution to murder an associate who had terribly and small-mindedly wronged him. Most of us are not suddenly knocked off a horse.

If God is to be found, He is within. He has long been tapping on the windowpanes of our silent souls. It is to avoid that delicate sound that we prefer to surround ourselves with endless Muzak. Silence troubles us. We experience a certain dread when it envelops us.

Time Out for Atheists' Rebuttals

The atheist says: "The obligation to argue me into religious conviction falls on you. The default position is atheism. And with me," they tell me, "you have by no means clinched your case. In fact, you have given me more reasons not to believe in God than I had before." They keep up steady fire, *rat-a-tat-tat*:

"In order to appreciate the stunning beauty of this world, I do not need God. In order to give myself to science, I do not need God. In order to value highly such vital human virtues as honesty, courage, friendship, loyalty, concern for the common good, a sense of community, a thirst for justice, I see no need whatever for any god.

"Too closely connected with belief in God, as I see it around me in the world, is a certain prudishness about the naturalness of sex, narrow-mindedness on any number of subjects, a lassitude and slackness of spirit rather than a hot flame of the *eros* of inquiry. I find cloying the religious person's purrings about 'love,' 'the human person,' and 'the common good.' In order to value altruism, honesty, the cultivation of human communities, and practical wisdom, I need no more than the principles of natural selection—all these virtues have high survival value among the animal species. I can learn all that is necessary about the primacy of human sympathy from Adam Smith, and all I need to know about solidarity with workers and the poor from the humanistic side of social democracy. I do not need Torah or the New Testament.

"Besides, the many objections to religion by other atheists, many of them recounted here in earlier pages, have piled up a superabundance of reasons not to believe. The logic of this present book is too meandering, too strained, to convince anybody but the already convinced. It leaves me cold, I would say, except that it actually makes me angry. Such drivel, however piously intended, provides cover for the worst sins of religious people down through history, including today."

At the Core of Humanism

No doubt the record of the sins of Christian peoples down through history and continuing today gives plenty of cover for atheists, even though many of these would be atheists for other reasons, no matter the bad behavior of some believers. Their sense of autonomy and personal responsibility (they think) demands it. In looking back on the long history of Christianity, however, that huge and wild and tumultuous ride down the long and hard-fought centuries, simple fairness also demands counting up the pluses with the sins. The record of deliberately atheist totalitarian regimes ruling over a majority of this small planet during the twentieth century suggests that Christianity offers a far better intellectual foundation than totalitarian atheism for liberty and human rights, for democratic republics and creative economies, for freedom of association and rights of conscience, for pluralism and for free moral, cultural, and scientific space. In the cultural contest between modern atheist regimes and Christian regimes (even at the latter's worst), Christian cultures, in my judgment, win hands down. Nearly all human progress in liberty and universal friendship has been wrested from savagery and barbarism through Christian cultures, in whose bosom secular scientific culture has also taken form, and prospered mightily.

Let me pause here for another point much neglected in anti-Christian circles. If it had not been for the great battles fought between the fall of Jerusalem in 1099 AD and the defeat of Muslim armies outside Vienna in 1683, most of Western culture today might now be speaking Arabic and memorizing the Qur'an. It is fashionable today to despise the Crusades, that long chain of wars to block (and for a while to push back) Muslim expansion after 632 AD. The success of these wars kept us until now from going under to a fierce and relentless pre-modern force.

No argument from cultural history, of course, settles the issue of how I today should understand my own identity, let alone the identity and destiny of the whole human race. No consideration of the scarlet sins of others makes me less responsible for choosing my own identity, and trying to bring it to its highest possible development and lustre. Nothing others do coerces me in my response to the friendship that the Creator offers His creatures, as portrayed by James Madison in his *Memorial and Remonstrance against Religious Assessments*, and earlier, by Thomas Jefferson in his *Bill for Establishing Religious Freedom in Virginia* (1779). In that bill, Jefferson observed:

> Almighty God hath created the mind free, and manifested his Supreme will that free it shall remain, by making it alto-

gether insusceptible of restraint: That all attempts to influence it by temporal punishments or burthens, or by civil incapacitations, tend only to beget habits of hypocrisy and meanness, and are a departure from the plan of the holy author of our religion, who being Lord both of body and mind, yet chose not to propagate it by coercions on either, as was in his Almighty power to do, but to extend it by its influence on reason alone . . .

We the General Assembly of *Virginia* do enact, that no man shall be compelled to frequent or support any relig[i]ous Worship place or Ministry whatsoever, nor shall be enforced, restrained, molested, or burthened in his body or goods, nor shall otherwise suffer on account of his religious opinions or belief, but that all men shall be free to profess, and by argument to maintain their opinions in matters of religion, and that the same shall in no wise diminish, enlarge, or affect their civil capacities . . .

[W]e are free to declare, and do declare, that the rights hereby asserted are of the natural rights of mankind, and that if any act shall be hereafter passed to repeal the present, or to narrow its operation, such act will be an infringement of natural right.

Jefferson's idea of religious liberty flows logically from his idea of a Creator, a Creator in the Judeo-Christian sense. Jefferson's God of liberty ("who chose not to propagate it by coercions") gives His children the choice to choose friendship with Him, the choice to worship Him in gratitude—or not. This choice belongs inalienably to each one of us. No mother or father, brother or sister, aunt or cousin, can take away this personal responsibility. No state nor any other social institution may do so. The invitation comes directly from the Creator to the human individual, Creator to creature.

To any who grasp the actual relation of Creator and creature, the obligation of the creature to be grateful to the Creator is self-evident. This relation is prior to every other human relation, both in point of time and in moral and political precedence. In the words of James Madison:

> Because we hold it for a fundamental and undeniable truth, "that Religion or the duty which we owe to our Creator and the manner of discharging it, can be directed only by reason and conviction, not by force or violence." [*Virginia Declaration of Rights,* art. 16] The Religion then of every man must be left to the conviction and conscience of every man; and it is the right of every man to exercise it as these may dictate. This right is in its nature an unalienable right. It is unalienable, because the opinions of men, depending only on the evidence contemplated by their own minds cannot follow the dictates of other men: it is unalienable also, because what is here a right towards men, is a duty towards the Creator. It is the duty of every man to render to the Creator such homage and such only as he believes to be acceptable to him. This duty is precedent, both in order of time and in degree of obligation, to the claims of Civil Society. Before any man can be considered as a member of Civil Society, he must be considered as a subject of the Governour of the Universe . . .

Jewish and Christian faith—and please note that it is our atheist colleagues who, by their severe accusations against it, have obliged us at times to shift out of the philosophical mode of argument, in order to defend a fair assessment of our community of faith—gives a better account compared to atheist philosophies, gives a better and deeper account of freedom of conscience and religious liberty (inclusive of atheists and members of any other religious faith and all human beings). It shows us—better than any of some atheists' illusions about the goodness of man—the need in a free Republic for checks and balances, and divided powers. It gives us a profounder account than atheism does of the origin and vocation and inner divine power driving science forward. It gives a better account of the human thirst for justice.

Two other features about the Jewish and Christian conception of God, at one with the philosophical conception as far as it goes, captivate my admiration. Because Christianity understands the depth and persistence of human sin in each one of us, it has been faithful to the lesson taught it by Judaism: that God does not turn away from us merely because we violate His word; He pursues us, and calls us to awaken, repent, and convert our way of life.

Again, Judaism and Christianity together offer a very satisfying philosophy of history, with its imperative to learn from past mistakes, and to resume the path toward progress. The kingdom of God within each of us, "not of this world," a new, internal kind of kingdom—the inner kingdom of justice and friendship, and liberty and compassion; of truth and humility—is like a mustard seed; it keeps growing, developing, altering its ways, taking on new insights and fresh changes of direction. Judaism and Christianity bear within themselves their own theory of evolution, of inner transformation, of developments of doctrine, and of advances in self-understanding. Judaism and Christianity are religions of progress—and were so, even when the secular philosophers of Athens and Rome and the Asiatic fleshpots were still frozen in cycles of endless return, with little glimpse of an open future, or any prospect of deep and inward cultural evolution.

Yet even were Judaism and Christianity shown, in the round, not to yield the best vision of human history and destiny yet discovered, I would still be inclined to believe that knowledge of the living God—the living God of insight and intelligence known to the philosophers, without any dependence on the Bible—is preferable to atheism, sheerly on the grounds of consistency of intellect. If you do not really trust intellect, be an atheist. If you think that intellect is out of harmony with a world of randomness and ultimate absurdity, then by all means be an atheist.

But if you trust intellect in its penetration and living presence in all things that have appeared or will appear within the horizon of endlessly inquiring minds, then you should admit that you have caught a sidelong glimpse of what is meant by the existing God.

How Belief in the God of Reason Makes a Progressive Civilization Possible

Further, I am inclined to believe that belief in the living, creative insight of God is the best available and long-tested background belief for the ideals that make a progressive and humane civilization realizable, gradually and by degrees. With the second president of the United States, John Adams, the chief architect of this nation's independence, I am inclined to believe that civilization depends finally upon the regulative idea of truth as a necessary condition for reasoned argument, and thus for social progress over time. This regulatory rule does not imply that any one of us possesses the truth, but rather that all of us agree to make our arguments in the light of evidence available to all. For the gift of this idea, Adams gave thanks to the God of the Hebrews, and so do I.

In contemplating the two possibilities laid out by atheism, either the absurdity and mundaneness of all things, or blind fate, Adams thought the Hebrew idea of truth illuminated the path for both:

> I will insist that the Hebrews have done more to civilize men than any other nation. If I were an atheist, and believed in blind eternal fate, I should still believe that fate had ordained the Jews to be the most essential instrument for civilizing the nations. If I were an atheist of the other sect, who believe or pretend to believe that all is ordered by chance, I should believe that chance had ordered the Jews to preserve and propagate to all mankind the doctrine of a supreme, intelligent, wise, almighty sovereign of the universe, which I believe to be the great essential principle of all morality, and consequently of all civilization.

To that too I say, Amen. And why?

Because civilization is constituted by reasoned conversation. And unless there are rules of evidence accepted by all, no true public reasoning is possible. Civilized peoples are able to reason with one another; barbarians club one another. Experience shows mightily that, as our forebears often wrote, only truth can make us free—the regulative idea of truth, consented to by all.

That is another fact of life better explained by the existing God of creative and universal insight, than by atheism. From this God springs the fiery light of the regulative idea of truth. Put otherwise, the power of the regulative idea of truth—I mean the evidentiary rules of honest conversation—supplies the seeker with a method for discerning that such a creative insight does exist—and efficaciously—since our own insight is a fruit thereof. The regulative role of truth is harmonious with the whole of nature. And fires human minds everywhere, like the sure light of the stars, in the fiercest of darknesses.

We need to reflect a little more on the odd fact of existence—and on the existent. The latter, as opposed to nonbeing: an abrupt disappearance back into the primal nothingness. Even for atheists, primal nothingness is where human existence comes from. Is it not? But atheists then suppose that existence is given to humans magically, by random chance.

By contrast, philosophers who reason to the existence of God see the divine as intelligent and intelligible all the way through, from beginning to end. These are two very different points of view. If I have not well described the differences, perhaps someone can advance the discussion by doing better.

In chapter five, I proposed as an aid in this attempt a term for the different options that atheists (of more than one kind) and believers (of more than one kind) bring to bear in the fundamental questions of divine life and human life. That term was "blicks."

At this point, I would like to introduce two other useful terms for a dimension of reality little adverted to nowadays by pragmatic philosophies: "existence" and "the existent." These terms point to realities grasped neither by perception nor by concept, but rather by a sidelong glance of reflection on what happens in human judging. Suppose one judges that there really is a mosquito in the tent, not a fantasy, or that a bright idea is actually true as opposed to false. In such cases we raise our working minds to an activity distinguishing existence from nothingness, the existent from the fanciful. This dimension of reality is employed by science, but not explored by science. It is a central part of inquiring into what God is like.

EIGHT

Existence and the Existent

NOT ON OUR WAVELENGTH: REFLECTING ON GOD

When I try to think about God, I remind myself of two axioms. First, *God is not to be found as a thing out in the world around us. Nothing that is, is quite like Him.* Always one expects a little resemblance between creature and Creator, but the essential differences are vast. God is on a different wavelength entirely. These words of St. Augustine are like a burst of lightning: "I sought Thee everywhere, my God, never finding Thee, until I discovered Thee within." Not out among all the other furniture of the universe, but within.

If God seeks us before we seek Him—I the sought and He the seeker—then He could not catch me until I looked within.

The second axiom is this: *God cannot be found by any scientific method, since science is by definition limited to what can be known through evidence from matter.* Anything that science discovers is, by definition, in part material. That is not the wavelength on which God is to be found. To say that there is no scientific proof for the existence of God is obvious on its face.

I respect the long tradition of philosophers, many of them secular philosophers, who have spent long hours trying to come very carefully and precisely to an idea of God that met what they experienced within, in the cool depths of their minds. Not by ecstasy, but by calm reflection.

They rejected the notion that God is composed of material substance.

They rejected the notion that God is in time, in the way that material things are in time and space.

They rejected the notion of some of their predecessors that God is embodied in any animal or object in the world. Or that He is an embodiment of the *whole* world.

They rejected the idea that God is simply another name for the whole of everything that exists. They thought pantheism an unworthy idea, compared to the knowledge of God they had already gained.

They rejected the claim that God is simply a name for the intelligibility of the world, its mathematical structure, so to speak.

The more contemporary philosophers have also rejected the modern analogy suggesting that God is best imagined as a watchmaker. For them, it was entertaining to encounter examples such as this modern one, about discovering a watch in a part of the jungle heretofore unexplored by human beings. The question about that watch can scarcely be repressed: *How did that thing get here?* It is certainly a clue that a scientific Sherlock Holmes cannot ignore. The watch certainly cannot have grown organically from anything in its environment. Who had lost it there, or put it there? Even deeper, if one imagines the finder being unfamiliar with the art of making watches, who had known enough to make it?

The watch is without doubt a sign of an intelligence at work. But it is not, for various reasons, a reliable analogy for God. For one thing, the world of our experience is not put together like a clock; its inner logic is not that of a clock. To be sure, there are some regularities in the world (our heartbeats, our range of temperatures, the movement of the stars above, women's periods, laws of chemistry, and so forth) that may be said to "work like clockwork." But there are many other events and concatenations that do not work by laws of that type, but more by accident or chance, probability schemes, sheer randomness.

A more useful metaphor came into use long ago, particularly in light of the beauty that artists create out of often unlikely materials. These are the metaphors of Artist, Author, and practical Governor of the universe, amid its myriad possibilities. Thus, the divine Governor in the contingent affairs of men; the divine Author of all the good (however paradoxical, ambivalent, intermixed with evil) that was, that is, or that ever will be; the divine Artist Who creates living objects of breathtaking beauty; the divine Teller of the adventuresome, unpredictable, contingent, accident-propelled, often surprising and suspenseful stories of practically every human life. Tales told not by an idiot, but signifying a large range of somethings, with many surprising morals dramatized by each story. Lessons even about the absurdities of human existence.

Scientists may be concerned to discover *how* things work in this universe, and to make tools that give men the power of prediction and control over events.

Philosophers are more interested in what *sort* of existent has made possible the beauties and marvels of all other existents. In other words, in what category, on what wavelength, should we think of God? Even prior to making a judgment for ourselves about whether or not we live in the presence of such a One, we need to know a little about what we are searching for.

Professor Dennett (along with Hitchens and Dawkins) brings up Thomas Aquinas at this point. In all propriety, we should treat Aristotle and pagan philosophy first, before turning to Aquinas. But since our colleagues turn their fire on Aquinas and ignore Aristotle, we had best do things out of order, to accommodate them.

Thomas Aquinas

Professor Dennett makes fun of what he takes to be the philosophical argument of Thomas Aquinas about the "First Cause." (As we have seen, you can find an earlier version of this argument in Aristotle's *Metaphysics,* Book XII, written more than a thousand years before Aquinas and nearly four hundred years before the birth of Christ.) It is a philosophical argument, not a theological one. As Professor Dennett reads it, in Aquinas,

[t]he cosmological argument, which in its simplest form
states that since everything must have a cause the universe

must have a cause—namely, God—doesn't stay simple for long. Some deny the premise, since quantum physics teaches us (doesn't it?) that not everything that happens needs to have a cause. Others prefer to accept the premise and then ask: What caused God? The reply that God is self-caused (somehow) then raises the rebuttal: If something can be self-caused, why can't the universe as a whole be the thing that is self-caused?

The answer to Dennett's last question is, if the universe were self-caused it would have to have the characteristics that the ancients (see chapter four) reasoned such a self-contained being must have: immaterial, outside of time (eternal), incorruptible, unmoved by change. The universe we observe does not meet these tests.

Aquinas argues that if there is no First Cause, the mind must rely on infinite regress, and that is irrational. Dennett has two dismissive replies. What's so wrong about infinite regress? Or why not allow for unlimited time back through evolutionary history? Second, if there needs to be a first cause, why invent God? Why can't we just say that the world is its own first cause? Equally plausible, Dennett thinks.

But that sort of ridicule—reductio ad absurdum—was Aquinas's point. Scientists (and the rest of us) don't just turn our eyes away from existents that come into our ken; we begin to inquire about how these existents came to be, and from what antecedents. Existents don't just appear magically, detached from everything else. We assume that every existent lies within a unified field of intelligibility. And so we investigate it. We cannot just brush it off.

Philosophical thought is here a bit different from scientific thought. Like ordinary people, philosophers are often struck with wonder about things. A philosopher can hold a daffodil in his hands and allow its intricacy, colors, scents, and proportions to grip his mind. He can marvel that such a beautiful and in its way perfect piece of work perishes so swiftly. This experience leads him to the idea of the perishability and the fragility of existents.

He sees all around him things that come into existence for a time and then rapidly corrupt and fall, as it were, back into dust, and cease to exist, at least as they were a short time before. Perish, like last Tuesday's wilted flowers now brown in the garbage can.

The next question is no scientific one. But philosophers do marvel about the perishability of individuals, species, and even the whole of the earth. Maybe even of all the moons, planets, and stars. This awareness of *existence* leads the philosopher to wonder if there is some Existent who is permanent, incorruptible, and imperishable, while all other things come into existence and exit from it. In this sense, "existence" is a little different from "being." Being is a more general concept than "existent," for it includes imaginary beings, possible beings, phantoms, illusions.

By contrast, existence is not a concept at all, in the same way that other ideas are concepts. It is quite different from possible beings, imaginary beings, and the like. Concepts are only figments of thought. But existents are propelled into the act of existing in actual space and time. (Only in the case of Who-Is immaterially and timelessly.)

Ordinarily, existents belong to a far more limited field; they are only those possible beings that come in fact to be actualized, which virtually always come into the world of time and space for only a short while, then perish. "Existence" (the act of existing) is that poignant stepping out of nothingness and into reality, here and now, before disappearing again back out of our view, or hearing, or sensing, and dissolving into nothingness.

Albert Camus's sharp sense of the momentary existence of a girl wading in the sparkling blue waters of the bay, droplets of water flashing on her shining bronzed shoulders, her black hair wet as it is tossed aside, her eyes avoiding his and in need of shading from the blazing sun of Algiers—this acute awareness excited Camus's senses and mind and appreciation. He tried to retain it. It would be gone forever far too quickly. His emphasis on this fragile coming into existence, and then going out, is one of the features that won for his philosophy the name "existentialism."

After some years, Camus learned to distinguish this sharp taste of existence, staccato and moment by moment, from ideologies, abstract ideas, general concepts. He came to find the first worthy of his love, and deserving of his protection. He found applying ideologies to human affairs too often murderous.

If we return now to the argument of Professor Dennett, we find his image of reality, by comparison with that of Camus, exceedingly flat. For Dennett, and for those trained in scientific thinking generally, ideas must necessarily be flattened into univocity for the sake of clarity and universal precision and, indeed, for translation into mathematical equations. Camus calls this a "two plus two equals four" kind of thinking. What Camus wants to call into conscious awareness is wonderment about the fragility of existents. The concrete, many-edged, particular, contingent, inimitable character of each existing thing. He wants to inspire admiration for, wonderment at, and the protection of existents, over against "the concept crowd" with all their legions of goose-stepping enforcers.

Dennett and Camus are talking about two different realities. They look at the world from within the horizon of two quite different philosophies of life. The realities of Camus's world have edges and valleys and mountains; the realities of Dennett's are flat.

Aquinas is on the side of Camus here, but he goes even deeper. He, too, had been struck by wonderment that acorns did not have to exist at all, yet in fact he was holding one in his hand, and he knew it could perish. It could die in the soil, and then become transformed into a fledgling oak tree. Or it could rot (as most did) and simply cease to exist. He reasoned that if everything can cease to exist, then sooner or later there would come a time when nothing exists. To bring anything back into existence after that would be unthinkable. There would be nothing that a new cosmos could evolve from. Only nothingness.

The coming into existence of a new cosmos would require a different sort of cause, a cause of a magnitude and type science does not know and cannot know. Plainly enough, the substances we know best have no control over the duration of their existence. They die.

The argument of Aquinas is not, then, as Dennett imagines it. Aquinas is not dragging in a prior cause to put underneath the world, like the turtle of the Indian sage from chapter seven. Such a finite cause in an infinite series is outlandish in itself, and in any case explains nothing. It is absurd. And it simply postpones the answer to the question intelligence is asking.

Besides, Dennett interprets the cause of a cause as if both were the same, like one turtle on another, or one billiard ball striking another. But Aquinas is thinking of *successively more efficacious* powers—up a set of ontological "stairs," until the great gap appears between all secondary causes and the Cause of the existence of all of them (and Cause of their relations to each other and to the whole).

Existents do not account for or maintain for themselves their own existing. But they do, in fact, exist. Look at your own hand. Move your fingers. Become conscious of your own acts of insight and willing. Something must account for the existence of such realities, says common sense. Alternatively, we can accept three propositions: that the world comes from nothing (it just is), that the world is wholly intelligible to no intelligence at all, and that to inquire about a rational cause of all things is useless. In other words, irrationality lies at the heart of reality. An odd move for those committed to rational inquiry in all things.

Does the outcome here depend upon there being a Creator? No. The imperishable Existent reasoned to by Plato and Aristotle may be eternal.

ARISTOTLE

It is easy to misunderstand the word "exists," for its actual discovery as the most penetrating term in philosophy took many centuries, and is one of philosophy's greatest achievements. Nonetheless, among persons initiated into philosophy in modern times, this term is very difficult to grasp. To explain why that is so would be the subject of a very interesting book in itself.

But that is not our task here. Our task is to choose language borrowed from common sense to re-create the sense of the intellectual world in which "exists" came to be so radiant a word, with such unusual explanatory power.

I like to begin by recalling the Latin *ex,* meaning "out from," and the infinitive *sistere,* meaning "to stand forth." In our case, to "exist" is to burst up from nothingness, to come into the world of flesh and blood, to be alive and aware of the sights, colors, scents, sounds around us. And of emotions and passions, and ironic humor, and understanding, and further puzzles.

It is not so hard to think of nothingness. A snowflake lands on the back of my dark blue mitten. Beautiful as it is, its existence in that form is fragile; it dissolves swiftly into the tiniest drop of water. The snowflake, in a limited but helpful sense, no longer exists. In its place there is now something else. Yet *its* existence, too, is fragile. Indoors beside the fire, the speck of water may quickly evaporate, and return to air.

The world of nature all around us is a world of becoming. The ground is hard and I see in it the harsh impress of the tires of a heavy earthmover. Spring rains come, and slowly the rims of the tire tracks erode. Then comes the storm, with thunder and lightning and heavy beating rain. The hard ground that held the sharp impress of the track is now a sea of mud, even a miniature lake. After two or three days of sun and wind, the water has gone but the soil is still mushy, soupy almost. Then its darkness gives way to lighter shades and dustier forms. We have solid ground again. But the tire tracks have disappeared. Our world is always becoming, and perishing. Almost all the objects of our life are like that. The snowflakes, the lilies of the field, the trees. Our dogs, our cats, ourselves. Even stars die. Everything is always becoming, and perishing. "All nature is a Heraclitean fire," the poet sang. All is change. All is becoming.

All natural things are also contingent. Nature, defined by the ancients, consists of all those things that move or are moved. (As hard ground was baked by the sun, and a puddle was formed by the rain, the hard ground was slushed into mush, and the wind and sun again hardened the dusty earth.) But nature also consists of those things that happen only for the most part. In other words, even when laws of nature predict that acorns will become oak trees, a large number of contingencies have to work their way out so that *this* acorn will take root and grow slowly into a stately oak. When an acorn becomes an oak, it violates no law of botany; on the contrary, it fulfills more than one of them. But laws alone are not enough to bring an oak into existence from *this* acorn. Favorable contingencies are also required.

Another way of putting this is that many things in nature are here in the world of existence relatively briefly and then pass away. Here today, tomorrow disappeared. So it is with flowers, summer grass, and autumn leaves. So with the ice on the pond in December. So too it is with us. Just yesterday we were thirteen, and now (it seems impossible) we are past seventy, and oh! so swiftly life is roaring toward its end.

Can you think of anything in nature—any *substance,* that is; not a physical law or mathematical equation—that exists forever? Aristotle thought the stars did—eternal, fixed, lawlike and dependable in their orbits. If there are any things in nature that are eternal, he thought, stars qualify. With the investigative equipment available to him, this judgment seemed empirically true. Today's scientific equipment has falsified that hypothesis.

In our own lives, Aristotle observed, among all the things we do, understanding and the dogged pursuit of understanding—the *eros* of inquiry—is the best, the least destructible, the most immaterial, the least likely to be affected by circumstances. For Aristotle, nothing tops understanding. And when understanding is directed to the fixed, eternal, lasting things—the highest, the best—it finds the most joy. As a further step, Aristotle experimented with the proposal that our understanding of our own understanding—in its workings and in its objects—is the best form of understanding. We find then that our capacity to inquire is infinite. No limits can be placed upon our questioning. In that way, the mind is *capable* of receiving all things, of being one with them. "The mind is in some way all things." But to be capable is only a potency; much better is actually to possess the understanding of all things. This, a human being comes closest to doing by engaging his understanding with God's. Aristotle refers to that activity as "the divine element" in humans.

The actuality of understanding, Aristotle is sure, is *life*—the best and highest and most permanent life. And God is that actuality in its purest and highest form. God is full understanding, in act. And God's existing is solely self-dependent, life most good and most eternal. He says, therefore, that God is a living being, eternal, most good, and that life continuous and eternal belongs to God; "for this *is* God."

From this we know what Aristotle understood God to be. We do not know yet why Aristotle holds that such a God actually exists.

The reason that Aristotle came to think that God is eternal and unchanged, self-dependent, and the source of his own existing is as follows. In us, our understanding plainly depends upon the state of our own bodily system. If we have been felled by a concussion to the head, or if we are drunk or highly agitated, we cannot think straight. Our understanding and our consciousness seem to perish when our bodies perish. Our understanding depends upon our being embodied in a healthy and fit body.

Is it necessary that all understanding be so? Not by the nature of understanding, in itself. When connected to a human body, yes. One can imagine a human body so diaphanous that it makes very few demands upon a man's limpid and active understanding. Some humans in the act of understanding seem almost lifted up out of their bodies, having lost all sense of time and weariness and bodily need. The act of insight can be enrapturing. When one "comes down to earth," one is amazed by how much time has elapsed. One had not been conscious of it.

The same thing can happen with the contemplation of a baby. What father has not looked with amazement at the little ears of his newborn son, the tiny nose, the exquisitely formed fingers, the small breathing chest, the lips, the tongue, the smile that answers to one of the father's own. In contemplation of one's own infant's face, one loses track of the minutes.

In front of a great painting, who has not sat down for half an hour trying to absorb it all, caught in a kind of inner joy and gratefulness, transfixed? No particular thoughts come, no calculations. One is simply trying to absorb each loving detail—details of the color, the strokes, the ordering of shapes, the narrative represented, and its perspective. A great painting is often coiled around a single point of tension, where an act is brought to its greatest point of intensity, and is about to crest into resolution. One must live with a masterpiece in timeless moments, through a form of understanding that may defy verbal expression.

Looking into a woman's eyes, one may glimpse understandings never voiced. One may read commitment, or just simple assent to a fling, nothing more. Or simple flirtation, with nothing behind it whatever. Or indifference, or chill, or *Get lost!* There are forms of understanding that are wordless. There are some people who seem not to be able to pick up the frequencies on which unspoken communications are sent.

Insight is life, Aristotle writes. A very keen intensity of life.

A high intelligence may bring with it much suffering, the more acutely felt because of one's ability to read every painful one of its nuances. Other people may miss half the unspoken drama and half the hurt. Or, perhaps, not reading too much into the event, they take it with common sense and get closer to the heart of the matter. For that reason, some artists portray the man of common sense—the man-at-arms, the sidekick, the valet—to be a happier man than his "master"—Jean de Joinville to Louis IX, Sancho Panza to Don Quixote, Robin to Batman, Jeeves to Bertie.

Aristotle imagines God as pure insight, not in potential but in act. A living flame of light and piercing illumination. Suffusing that light into all things, giving them contingent order, internal intelligibility, and luminous relations with all else. Everything in the universe is related to every other detail, through this divine understanding. See intelligibility anywhere, it directs your mind to the source of its own light. This is why it is not certain whether Aristotle conceived of God as a personal God—able to understand

and to love, to choose—or, rather, as the living core of the whole intelligible order of the world. The bright light at the heart of the music, mathematics, order, and freedom-giving contingency in all things. What Einstein saw when he was enraptured by the unity and order of the universe. An impersonal Understanding that plants intelligibility in all things, and shares His capacity for insight with human beings, lighting in them the *eros* of understanding that, with one puff, ignites inquiry into every detail and, in so doing, drives them closer to the Light at the root of all things.

But does such a God exist? Well, all the evidences that we see about us seem to confirm that such a God is at work, knowing even the solitary lily in the field, and the numbers of the hairs of our head, and every fragment of fossils and exemplum of fauna. Intelligence-in-act, the fruits of which are all around us. As an instance of this, watch how contemporary scientists keep inquiring into new questions.

The Universe Has No Purpose?

Even top scientists, when they think beyond the limits of science, use ideas not so distant from those of the ancient metaphysicians. "Uncreated universe" and an infinite regress of causes—old ideas are coming back.

"There is no purpose in the universe," say some of the scientists writing in a recent symposium. (All the questions in this section derive from statements presented in that symposium.) The director of New York City's Hayden Planetarium, astrophysicist Neil deGrasse Tyson, points out that humans have not been around to ask questions of *any* sort for better than 99.9 percent of cosmic history. And during that long history—a history rocked by devastation, destruction, and death from volcanoes, earthquakes, pestilence, floods, and killer asteroids—well over 99.9 percent of all living species have become extinct. For him, the universe as we now know it looks "more and more random." And the case against purpose in the universe is strong, as is evident to anyone who sees the universe as it is, rather than through sentimental, overly biased human eyes.

Nobel Prize winner and biochemist Christian de Duve begins with Jacques Monod's judgment that the universe was *never* "pregnant with life, nor the biosphere with man." Thus, "man knows at last that he is alone in the unfeeling immensity of the universe out of which he arose only by chance." At bottom, the universe is pure random chance and contingency.

Against this, De Duve considers and rejects the hypothesis that there might be multiple universes, among which this universe arose by chance. He cannot concur that this one merely by chance happened to have the physical constants that allowed life to evolve within it and, within life, allowed mind to evolve. He holds by contrast that "life and mind are such extraordinary manifestations of matter that they remain meaningful." Even the possibility of many trillions of universes "in no way diminishes the significance" of this world's "unique properties." De Duve sees life and mind as "clues to the 'Ultimate Reality' that lies behind them." Science leads us to wonder, and in music, art, and literature, we come to other aspects of this same awe-inspiring reality. "With philosophy and religion, we have become aware of its ethical and mystical aspects." He adds that "love has introduced us into its very heart."

But De Duve sees no need for a creator. "By definition, a creator must be uncreated, unless he is part of an endless, Russian-doll succession of creators within creators." But why not, then, have the universe itself uncreated, an actual manifestation of Ultimate Reality, rather than the work of an uncreated creator?

A professor of physics and astronomy at Case Western Reserve University, Lawrence M. Krauss, wonders why God, if there is a God, left so few clues by which humans could decipher whether there is a purpose at all, and what it is. Krauss is certain that we humans "do not play a central role" in the universe. "We are, as a planet, cosmically insignificant. Life on earth will end, as it has probably done on countless planets in the past."

Professor Krauss adds that "organized religions, which put humanity at the center of some divine plan, seem to assault our dignity and intelligence." For him, a universe without purpose is not depressing and does not suggest that our lives are purposeless. We can *give* ourselves purpose. "Through an awe-inspiring cosmic history we find ourselves on this remote planet in a remote corner of the universe, endowed with intelligence and self-awareness. We should not despair, but should humbly rejoice in making the most of these gifts, and celebrate our brief moment in the sun."

Does not the Krauss perspective seem very like a religious perspective? The ethical imperatives with which Professor Krauss endows this world seem very religious: humility, wonder, rejoicing, celebrating the fact that we have not here a lasting home . . .

By contrast, Peter William Atkins, fellow and professor of chemistry at Lincoln College, Oxford, is far more dismissive of any imagining of a Creator, and any and every "purpose" imputed to the universe. "Cheetahs have evolved by the bloody, directionless, unguided processes of evolution . . . Similarly, the universe has evolved over its 14 billion years of current existence by the directionless, unguided processes that are the manifestations of the working out of physical laws." But then he, too, concludes with an oddly religious sentiment: "I regard the existence of this extraordinary universe as having a wonderful, awesome grandeur. It hangs there in all its glory, wholly and completely useless. To project onto it our human-inspired notions of purpose would, to my mind, sully and diminish it."

It would seem, then, that for Professor Atkins our universe is "extraordinary," after all. It would seem that it has a "wonderful, awesome grandeur," and that it sits here "in all its glory." Such sentiments, at least, seem to be shared by both religious people and atheists. The *interpretations* each offers for the attributes of this universe differ radically; the *blicks* of each are rather different.

Physicist Paul Davies of Arizona State University begins with the quasireligious viewpoint almost always expressed by scientists: "Scientists often wax lyrical about the scale, majesty, harmony, elegance, and ingenuity of the universe. Einstein professed a 'cosmic religious feeling.' " Although some scientists say that "purpose" is a word inspired by human discourse, and so reject it, they themselves use alternatives that are also inspired by human discourse: nature is a "mechanism," or a "computer," or a mix of lawlike, mathematically regulated movements and random events.

Davies is uncertain whether there is a purpose or direction in the universe, but he thinks the evidence tips in a discernible direction. The evidence for cosmic purpose, Davies proposes, "lies right under our noses in the very existence of science itself." There is a purpose in practicing science because it gives us real knowledge of the world, helping us to dig out "additional coherent and meaningful facts about the world." The fact that we can comprehend the world, in a steadily improving, methodical way, indicates that the world "makes sense." In this way, evolution singles out science as an especially worthwhile activity. By contrast, "If the universe is truly pointless, then it is truly incomprehensible, and the rational basis of science collapses."

Yale professor of computer science David Gelernter argues that at least one part of the universe does have a purpose: we human beings do, and around us, the earth that made us possible. And what is that purpose?

Namely to defeat and rise above our animal natures; to create goodness, beauty, and holiness where only physics and animal life once existed; to create what might be (if we succeed) the only tiny pinprick of goodness in the universe— which is otherwise (so far as we know) morally null and void. If no other such project exists anywhere in the cosmos, our victory would change the nature of the universe. If there are similar projects elsewhere, more power to them; but our own task remains unchanged.

AS WE CAN SEE from these comments, even the strictest scientists need to put the findings of science in a metaphysical context.

When they are faced with questions about meaning, purpose, and cause, they cannot help themselves. Some speculate that causes may be hidden within other causes like Russian stacking dolls. Others speculate that all the universe should be considered as an uncreated cause, the first cause, of its own existence.

However, when they do metaphysics they invite comparison to the inquiries of ancient and medieval thinkers, who moved more carefully on such matters.

INTELLIGENCE ALL THE WAY DOWN

What we do know is that concrete things exist. We live in the midst of them. And things do not hold themselves in existence; one by one, their period in existence is brief. That fact poses a problem to our inquiring intelligence.

It is entirely possible that one form of existence evolved from another over eons of time, in the way that the new Darwinians picture human history. Aristotle's philosophical argument for the reality of an imperishable existent is actually consistent with a Darwinian exposition of *how* things, once they came into existence in some form, perhaps as a primal ocean, got to where they are today. Can there be an imperishable Existent that infuses temporary existence into all perishable existents? If so, that fact is consistent with theories of either evolution or creation, or both. The philosophy in question is prebiblical. It springs from wonderment at the marvel of coming into existence, and exiting out from it.

The fact it rests upon is this one: You and I unarguably exist.

The mind wants to understand not only the *how* of that fact, not just the brute fact, but the *source* of existence that makes you and me to be. In the argument of Aquinas about the "unmoved mover," the key step is an empirical, undeniable one: "But, indubitably, things do move." The *fact* of movement is the crucial datum. The question it awakens is: "What greater mover put moving things into motion?" What is it that lifts things out of the world of mere concepts, mere possibilities, into the concrete world of perishable existents? Things don't just come into being by themselves. Especially highly intelligible things don't. Some intelligence suffuses them. (Otherwise, detective novels would not grip us.)

For those trained in flatter ways of thinking, this is all ridiculous metaphysical speculation, mere words, unresolvable by empirical tests.

Yet if it is true, it plants an intelligent source of existence at the nerve center of every existing thing in the whole blooming evolutionary panorama. It links each intelligible event to an active intelligence, which understands all the things that exist. This philosophy is wholly compatible with science, even though its mode of arguing is not a subset of scientific arguments. Rather, scientific arguments are a subset of other forms of rational argument.

This philosophy is much more intellectually satisfying than the alternatives. It rests upon and protects the close link between intelligence (greater than our own) and the intelligible existents that come into our ken. It forces us to imagine intelligence "all the way down," and to rule no questions out. It helps to explain the source of our own unrestricted drive to inquire. It suggests that that drive is in harmony with the world as it is. Isomorphic with it.

It would be odd if my friends Hitchens, Dawkins, Dennett, Harris, Mac Donald, and others did not find this way of thinking beneath them. Yet it is the way the common sense of human beings seems to work. It is the way most people for some centuries have thought about the world, although it borrows here from language highly refined over many centuries, by a multitude of philosophers in many different cultures.

This way of coming to God by philosophical reasoning is consistent with, but most emphatically different from, a Christian view that all the world springs from a Creator whose inner life is constituted by *Caritas,* a love proper only to God, a Trinitarian love characterized by Dostoyevsky as the *suffering love* that is the inner secret of the universe. The inner dynamism of this gift from the Trinitarian God transforms human suffering into a thing of beauty and divine blessing, a participation in God's own life.

But all that is another story, which goes far beyond what we can reach by philosophical reasoning alone. The full conversation in Western culture is not simply between atheists and deists (as in the transition of Antony Flew from one to the other). It is not simply "God" who is in question. It is the Jewish and Christian God. It is the Source of all the light of intelligence in all things (the inward insight or *Logos* in all things), the Fountain of all the energy and dynamism that drives the world, that moves the sun, all the stars, and all living things. It is, in brief, the Creator, the would-be Friend of every woman and every man who has ever lived. The God who in giving us life gave us liberty at the same time. And a God who is the inner principle of truth that makes the coming to be of one universal civilization, a civilization of liberty, a distant but practical goal to strive for.

When the one who thirsts for justice says, "That's unjust!" the cynic replies, "That's your opinion." When the honest man says, "That's not true," the cynic asks, "Who says so?" When the brave man says, "You must stop your brutality," the cynic says, "Make me."

The world of humans is in fact scarred by misuses of freedom, by brutality and unbelievable cruelty. Nevertheless, there really is a principle of justice and truth and righteous action in this chaotic world, to which it is a good policy for humans to be faithful, no matter what. Only in that way does a man become a *man*. An image of his Maker.

I once heard Christopher Hitchens read aloud, quite movingly, a poem of Rudyard Kipling's.

> *If you can keep your head when all about you*
> *Are losing theirs and blaming it on you;*
> *If you can trust yourself when all men doubt you,*
> *But make allowance for their doubting too;*
> *If you can wait and not be tired by waiting,*
> *Or being lied about, don't deal in lies,*

Or, being hated, don't give way to hating,
    And yet don't look too good, nor talk too wise:

If you can dream—and not make dreams your master;
    If you can think—and not make thoughts your aim;
If you can meet with Triumph and Disaster
    And treat those two imposters just the same;
If you can bear to hear the truth you've spoken
    Twisted by knaves to make a trap for fools,
Or watch the things you gave your life to, broken,
    And stoop and build 'em up with worn-out tools . . .

If you can fill the unforgiving minute
    With sixty seconds' worth of distance run,
Yours is the Earth and everything that's in it,
    And—which is more—you'll be a Man, my son!

("If," 1910)

This verse seems to engage a fundamental moral law of human nature—about how boys become men (and girls, women)—and how the irrationalities in human life can be transformed by reasoned bravery into a thing of beauty.

WHAT ARE ATHEISTS MISSING THAT EVERYONE ELSE GETS?

In this same vein, one other thought presses upon me. Sometimes I wonder what atheists are missing that everyone else gets. The atheist is inflamed with intelligence that runs right through the middle of his head and out to the farthest speck in the most distant curvature of the universe. What intelligence finds, within and without, mostly makes sense. Everything is potentially intelligible, lawlike, rich with emerging probabilities that run their courses; full of contingencies, chance, improbabilities. All that we find explodes with exultation, with glory: It *is*, it exists. It is heavy not only with intelligence but with the force that drives it, pushes it, into existence—like daffodils and tulips and green grass pushed up through the moist spring soil.

Most of what we experience closest to us is composed of transient things—passing, here today but by no means forever, passing like sand through one's fingers at the beach, or like pink sands through an hourglass. Passing like comets through the night sky, self-incinerating.

Why are atheists not grabbed by the fragility, the passingness of all the bittersweet beauty around them? Why do they not grasp hold of the power and glory of the sheer insight and beauty in all that surrounds them, penetrates them, embraces them?

Why do they not see reflectively that the insight and intelligence that runs through their heads and races through the universe is the first sign of what most common people mean by God? In the wonder that comes over them when they contemplate the turbulent, explosive order of the world. In the sheer mathematics of the thing. Even within chance, mere probability schemes, and what physicists call "chaos," intelligence seeks light, pursues inquiry, draws inferences. Chance is not necessarily proof of the absence of intelligence, but is a pointer to a more sophisticated kind of intelligence: that of an Artist.

After a long and fascinating conversation, Professor Dawkins once asked Michael Heller, the physicist-priest from Poland, who has done brilliant work on the necessary separations and yet connections between science and religion, "What divides us?" Professor Heller answered: "A single letter. You write 'mathematics' with a small 'm,' I write it with a capital 'M.'"

The beautiful intelligence that runs through everything.

In all your life, you see no evidence for the existing God? My God, man, what more do you want?

The fact is, however, that atheists interpret such human experiences one way, and those who know God interpret them in another.

PART FOUR

The New Conversation

I cry out "Injustice!" I am not heard. I cry for help, but there is no redress. He has barred my way and I cannot pass; he has veiled my path in darkness; He has stripped me of my glory, and taken the diadem from my brow.

—Job 19:7–9, NAB

NINE

Secular, but Not "Secularist"

Why did "the new atheism" suddenly arise, and why now?

The barbarism of the simultaneous attacks on the Twin Towers in Manhattan and the Pentagon in Washington on September 11, 2001, ended up bringing a rhetorical bonanza to atheists. Now they had a devastating symbol for "religion." The barbarism of September 11, some said, is typical of all religion. Islamic fundamentalism, Christian fundamentalism—all fundamentalisms are alike. (Except atheist fundamentalism, of course, which is by definition rational and open to inquiry and tolerant.)

Another reason for "why now?" was a broad emotional reaction against the Bush administration in America in 2001. True, the first steps were bipartisan. Education reform (cosponsored with Democratic senator Edward Kennedy) was the first major emphasis, and was strongly bipartisan in nature. But then other items came along that caused huge emotional turmoil among secularists. These issues included "partial-birth abortion" as it is euphemistically known (*infanticide* is the unvarnished term). Later came concerns for and against euthanasia, and voters' sharp divisions over gay marriage, dramatized by public celebrations of multiple outdoor "marriages" by the mayor of San Francisco. Next came the argument over *federal* funding of embryonic stem cell research—not over private money for stem cell research, mind you, only federal funding for it. The president had to choose. He chose to support the principle of protecting the right to life enunciated in the Declaration of Independence—not, as many on the Left now understand it, but as through most of American history it has been understood and by many today is still understood.

In the year 2000—such things change—two-thirds of frequent churchgoers voted for President Bush, while two-thirds of those who go to church seldom or not at all voted for the other party, and over the next six years this division became still more visible. The secularist tendency frequently calls for a politics of principle and for principled voting, but not *then,* not regarding those principles against which, in principle, secularists are opposed. Thus there arose a wail of complaint against religious voters having any real effect on "secular" politics. The idea was that secularist people may have a legitimate impact on legislation, even rescinding laws and practices from the past that were in part religious. But nowadays religious people should not have such impact. A new secularist interpretation of "the separation of church and state" was being enforced.

Thus, in the image of religion cast by the suicide bombers of 2001 as well as in the passions stirred by "the life issues," the term "secular" has come to be contested. Terms such as "religious conservatives" came into use, by contrast with "secular progressives." On the other hand, both atheists and Christians and Jews began to write frequently about Islam's need for a "Reformation" and "Enlightenment." Some extremists argued for supplanting Islamic regimes in the Middle East, Asia, and Africa with "secular" regimes. That is how in our time the term "secular" came to have many meanings and to become much contested.

"Secular": A Term Invented by Christians

Historically, "secular" has been a good word. There are "things of God" that belong to God and "things of Caesar" that belong to Caesar. This distinction is at once a barrier against secular totalitarian governments and a barrier against clerical control over governments and other secular functions. For the churches, plenty of free space is open between clerical control from above, and the quiet working of the yeast of ideas and aspirations in the dough of daily life. (It is legitimate for individuals of all persuasions to carry the influence of their ideas and inspirations into the public square.)

The public space for democratic and pluralistic arguments, ideally expected to be reasoned and civil, should not be naked of religion or of atheism. On the contrary, the public square ought to be alive with the reasoned arguments of all sectors of the Republic. Such is the way a "mixed" society can and does operate—mixed, that is, as between secularist and religious persons.

Some citizens may really wish to secularize everything in the public square, and to keep it religion-free. Other citizens may wish to "sacralize" the public square, leaving no space for unbelief. Both tendencies reject long-standing American traditions. American traditions legitimize a certain Jewish/Christian character to public celebrations and civic holidays. They do so for good reason. The American idea of religious liberty, as worked out first in Pennsylvania and Virginia, depends upon the Jewish/Christian concept of a Creator-Governor-Judge who respects the most inward acts of conscience. This God cannot be deceived; He is Spirit and Truth; and He by willful design made humans to be free to accept the evidence that satisfies the conscience of each. No secular idea of the founding pierces so deep.

A wide chasm, therefore, yawns between the two terms "secular" and "secularism." By contrast with modern terms such as "secularism," "secularization," and "secular humanism," the term "secular" all by itself is actually a Latin Christian word, based upon Christ's rebuke to the Pharisees: "Give to Caesar what is Caesar's, and to God what is God's" (Matthew 22:21, NIV). Not everything belongs to Caesar. Neither the state nor the church is a *total* institution. Neither embraces everything. Each is limited. Each has its own habits, practices, institutions, and realms of discourse.

This teaching is the first great barrier to the totalitarian tendency of states, since not everything belongs to Caesar. It is also a barrier to the church, since not everything comes under the jurisdiction of religious authorities. In secular things, as Saint Thomas writes in *Commentary on the Sentences of Peter Lombard,* it is better to obey the secular authorities than the religious authorities.

John Finnis suggests three different meanings for "secularism," which I will restate in my own words: (1) the belief that there is no God; (2) the belief that there may be a god, but he is utterly indifferent to humans, their destiny, and their actions; (3) the belief that God's concern for humans is easily appeased, so that no demanding reform of human morals is required, because no ultimate divine judgment is to be feared.

In this third version, having liberal opinions on social policy pretty much exhausts the obligations of religion. In even briefer summary, the three variants of secularism are these: (1) an intellectual and willful atheism in the strict sense, (2) a pallid deism, and (3) a practical rather than principled atheism.

Whether or not there is a God, secularists of the third type simply act as if God does not exist.

In this vein, some secularists in America today prefer to call themselves agnostics, rather than atheists, on the grounds that no one can prove, one way or the other, the existence of God. Yet, in practice, no one can *act* agnostically. Action implies choice. Either one acts as if God exists, or one acts as if God does not exist. In practice, agnostics usually act like practical atheists. Sometimes, though, agnostics are quite opposed to atheism and would like to believe in God. They simply have not experienced that insight, that gift, that privileged way of seeing. More than once well-known scholars have asked me—in the first case, Sidney Hook, and in another, Milton Friedman—how to think about belief. Both said they sometimes wanted to believe, but just couldn't find the evidence they sought. I said that all the evidence they need is within them, and they may be looking in the wrong places.

Secularism in all these senses is in one sense an ancient, a medieval, an Elizabethan, and indeed a contemporary choice. Plato was concerned to argue against it, as were philosophers and moralists in every subsequent era.

Interestingly enough, the word "secular" arose in Christian

circles (in contrast to the sacred), as a means of marking off what properly belongs to "this world" as opposed to the Church, that is, the incipient Kingdom of God. The infant Kingdom of God planted in time, the Church, belongs to a larger, surrounding "eternal world," within which time and space and human history are enveloped. To take a pedestrian example, those monks and nuns who give their whole lives to God by some degree of retreat from the hurry and rush of daily life, are called "religious," but those priests who live among the ordinary people in parishes far flung across the world are called "secular" priests. In many senses, however these two "worlds" of the sacred and the secular interpenetrate. For God's presence interpenetrates the world of time and space at every point, not only as its Creator "in the beginning," but as its Sustainer through every staccato moment in time. He is Sovereign over both the sacred *and* the secular, each according to its proper autonomy.

Previous to the modern age, the community of faith saw itself engaged in a cosmic clash between God and Lucifer, launched before the beginning of time (as in Milton's *Paradise Lost*). The Christian view contrasted that eternal order with the present order. In other words, it contrasted the eternal simultaneity of God's love and the eternal war between good and evil (which arose not from God but from a rebellious Lucifer) to a worldly preoccupation with the temporal order. Faith is concerned with the things that belong directly to God. These include the Four Last Things: death, judgment, heaven, hell.

The secular, by contrast, is concerned with building a good city for humans during the span of their temporal lives. In the view of Christian humanism, sacred and the secular are not necessarily adversarial, and they are not mutually exclusive. People of faith also live in this world and contribute to the betterment of this world, bringing into it dimensions of fraternity, liberty and equality, compassion and hope that in Greece and Rome, for instance, were scarcely to be found. They build orphanages, hospitals, and schools for the poor; they build libraries, copy ancient manuscripts for the sake of posterity, found great universities, endow churches to commission immensely talented architects and masons, painters and sculptors, as well as musicians and grammarians.

From the other side, secular thinkers and secular institutions have at times opened up vistas for people of faith—about hygiene, medicine, the overcoming of poverty, democratic governance, the abolition of slavery and torture—that during the earlier centuries of Christian life were either unknown or not achievable. Saint Augustine, for example, wrote that neither slavery nor torture belongs in a Christian civilization, and yet both practices were so universal and so deeply entrenched that he did not foresee how they could be eliminated, but only partially and inadequately tempered by mercy. When Heather Mac Donald observes that many moral improvements flowered in later ages when secularism took hold (see chapter four), she is quite right.

TRACING THE BOUNDARIES

In a way, both Jewish/Christian faith and secular reason have brought fresh energies into human progress, and both have experienced periods of decadence and violence.

The tracing of the boundaries between these two kingdoms, the things of Caesar and the things of God, was perhaps the central project of the entire Christian era in its first two thousand years. This project was carried out by trial and error, and it is a project that continues along today. From Saint Augustine's magisterial account of the interrelations of the two cities, the City of God and the City of Man, right on through centuries of bitter struggle on the part of emperors and kings versus popes in any given period, important historical "markers" were put in place, and under the lashings of experience new institutional forms tried out and sometimes abandoned. To trace out all these changes would take us too far afield—it deserves a book-length summary of its own. (Few have charted the vicissitudes of the last three centuries of this perennial tussle with as much trenchant detail as Professor Russell Hittinger.)

It is worth mentioning one or two dramatic moments. In the year 385 AD, a Roman legion was under orders to surround the cathedral of Milan and enter into it. The bishop of the cathedral, known today as Saint Ambrose, stepped out on the front steps in all his vestments as bishop and, with a great voice, forbade the soldiers to enter, for the reason that this was a place of God, off limits to Caesar. The troops did not enter. Thus were the two realms marked out in the world of practice. The separation of church and state took a first successful step that day. The term "sanctuary" (outside the domain of Caesar) took root.

"Secular" is the realm that is not the primary responsibility of the church or ecclesiastical institutions, but the realm that is tackled chiefly by reason and experience. Reason and experience have a lot to do with the church and its historical development, too, but the main business of the church does not belong to reason alone or to the secular order alone. Rather it belongs (through faith) to those hidden dimensions of reality that are illuminated under the light of eternity (*sub specie aeternitatis*). By contrast, those concerns of human temporal life that draw upon a worldly light, such as the building of the polity, the economy, and a great swathe of cultural artifacts, more properly belong to the "secular" order, which has its own autonomy. This world is also aimed, whether its members are aware of it or not, toward its Creator and self-revealed Friend. Yet it has its own proper autonomy.

In the Christian view, especially since the time of Aquinas and Dante, who were progenitors of a new Christian humanism, faith ought to work in the secular world as yeast in dough. In this respect, Aquinas and Dante were mightily helped by being the first to use the works of the empirical Aristotle to help articulate the Christian faith. They were far better off than their predecessors of the preceding thousand years, who had access only to the works of Plato, in the long tradition of Christian Platonism. The worldview of Plato offered a great, beautiful, and radiantly good framework for stretching out the Christian faith. But Aristotle was even better—more down-to-earth, less utopian, more "incarnational" to borrow from the image of the enfleshed Word. As Christ became flesh within historical time, so also ought his people to keep "enfleshing" his Word in their own time. For that project, Aristotle was far more workaday useful. Although not so poetic as Plato.

Lost Works of Aristotle Suddenly Discovered

Irving Kristol reported in *Commentary* some years ago a common secular view of history. Common, but incomplete: "As any respectable text in European intellectual history relates, 'humanism' in the form of 'Christian humanism,' was born in the Renaissance, as a major shift occurred from an other-worldly to a this-worldly focus, and as the revived interest in Greco-Roman thought shouldered aside the narrow Christian-Aristotelian rationalism endorsed by the Church."

These last two lines in this quote miss a crucial turn. For the first millennium of Christian history, Aristotle was a lost and forgotten aspect of Greco-Roman thought. Only during the last quarter of the twelfth century did some of Aristotle's greatest works see the light of day for the first time in more than a thousand years. These treasures were discovered hidden in old pottery in Toledo, Spain, among them Aristotle's *Politics, Nicomachean Ethics, Metaphysics,* several of his empirical books on botany and geology, and the treatise on Nature. Under the patronage of an unusually farsighted local bishop, Nicodemus of Toledo, a team of Jewish, Christian, and Muslim scholars began translating these works and diffusing them.

The long-lost horizon found in these books dramatically altered the intellectual history of the West. Before that time, the West had relied on studying Aristotle in Arabic translations, done before the time of Mohammed by Christian monks in Syria and other Arab lands. Thus, it was only from the thirteenth century on that Aquinas and Dante, Boccaccio, Bacon, Petrarch, and hundreds of others began putting the new Aristotelian empiricism to work. These novelties were resisted mightily by the dominant stream of Platonists. (Textbooks of the time contrasted "the divine Plato" with "the atheist Aristotle.") The works of Aquinas were burned on the square in Paris not two decades after his death. One fails to grasp the originality and crucial importance of Aquinas to the later history of the West if one overlooks his personal rethinking of the heretofore unknown Aristotle.

Both Aquinas and Dante rejoiced in Aristotle's emphasis on the five senses (*Nihil est in intellectu quod non prius in sensu*: Nothing is in the intellect that was not first in the senses) and on down-to-earth empirical evidence. They found Aristotle more hospitable to the human body, to the concerns of the temporal city of man, and to the world of time, space, and material things, than the more spiritually inclined Plato. In fact, Plato's imbalance on the side of spirit, to the neglect of the body, had actually been a danger to the Christian faith. The creeds of the Church had always affirmed that the human being is both body and soul, not soul alone. Thus, Christian Platonism faced certain intellectual embarrassments in trying to explain how and why Christ would take on human flesh, and why Christianity promised the resurrection of both the body and the soul. For Plato had so demoted the body and uplifted the soul that the Christian message, squeezed through his filters, came out overly spiritualized, off-kilter, out of tune. Plato aimed too high. Aristotle pointed to the lowly earth.

The most frequently painted theme of the early Renaissance was the Annunciation to Mary, the astonishing word from an angel that Mary would become the Mother of God. This scene filled viewers of that time with awe, that God should become man, and through the flesh of one woman, a woman who could be seen and described, a woman of delicate feeling and (much later) excruciating pain. The most touching image of God in Christianity after the Thomistic Renaissance is the infant suckling at his mother's breast in the stable of Bethlehem, breathed upon by farm animals, and visited by humble shepherds. Paintings of this scene were to proliferate among the great painters of the next three centuries. Soaring cathedrals were thrown up to the sky, made of good solid stone, worked with great care, aimed at bringing both sensory and spiritual pleasure. A fitting combination of body and spirit to teach all that God became flesh.

And yet the image of God become man seems like idolatry, even sacrilege, to Jews and Muslims. It seemed so, too, to the Albigensians and many other perennially arising communities clinging to a more "spiritual" (gnostic) understanding of Christianity. The spiritual Plato has great staying power in history.

For Thomas Aquinas all knowledge begins in the senses. What philosophy could be more nourishing to a poet such as Dante? Sense knowledge, images, flesh and blood and bone—these are the stuff that the poet flashes before the imagination while like fireworks his insights into the mysteries of human living, suffering, and aspiring explode in the night. It was the same with Giotto and a great rush of other painters. This early Renaissance did not have to disown Aristotle; Aristotle had liberated them, and taught them to breathe, to smell, to listen, to touch, to celebrate the Lord's creation, and the resurrection of the flesh.

Aristotle had also lit a match to empirical investigations.

The Birth of Modern Science—and the Secular

As Professor Richard Rubenstein explains in his paradigm-shifting book, *Aristotle's Children* (Harcourt, 2003), one of the greatest contributions of Christianity to the West was the enthusiastic welcome the church gave in the early 1300s to the new Aristotelian point of view. Aristotle helped mightily to "ground" the Christian West in the secular, attentively studied. Rubenstein chronicles this Western breakthrough into empirical studies: "Farsighted popes and bishops . . . took the fateful step that Islamic leaders had rejected. By marrying Christian theology to Aristotelian science, they committed the West to an ethic of rational inquiry that would generate a succession of 'scientific revolutions,' as well as unforeseen upheavals in social and religious thought."

The West, which was in 1215 still at a level of civilization below that of the beautiful cities of the Muslim Middle East and Confucian China, thenceforward experienced an enormous leap forward in science, the arts, astronomy, mapmaking, political philosophy, and many new fields of inquiry (not least, new experiments in the brewing of beers, in cultivating wines, and in distilling many new varieties of liqueurs). In some nations, the monasteries led the way in launching many new industries and technologies, taking advantage of the disciplined labor force of the monks and the practicality of a universal system of ecclesiastical law. In some nations lumber, in some wool, in others grains of important sorts were efficiently produced by dedicated monks, who had close organizational ties with their brothers in other lands. Some monasteries became, as it were, the first multinational corporations, selling their goods to far-off nations. These international ties also lent themselves to rapid innovation, each monastery sharing its new technologies with its counterparts in distant lands. Among them originated "the industrial revolution" of the eleventh century.

In due course, heads of secular states attempted to take control over and to domesticate the church—as in every century since the beginning they had always tried to do—that is, to squeeze God out of public life altogether. One can see this process vividly under the French Revolution and again under Napoleon, whose special pleasure it was to stable his army's horses in churches and convents, their religious inhabitants having been slain or driven away in torment.

As Gertrude Himmelfarb taught us in *The Roads to Modernity* (Random House, 2004), there was by the eighteenth century more than one Enlightenment—actually three, in Germany, France, and England. The French and the Germans tended to imagine the Enlightenment as a gigantic effort to reconstruct the world as if God did not exist. They aimed to build a purely secular civilization.

They aimed to generate a religion within the bounds of reason alone. They aimed to establish a universal ethic based upon universal reason. They aimed—by strangling the last king with the entrails of the last pope—to construct a more perfect world that would experience endless progress. The English and the Americans, by contrast, saw no need to choose *between* traditional faith and Enlightenment; both streams watered the same fields of conscience and liberty.

This project entailed compressing biblical religion into the solitary regions of the individual heart. The state, therefore, in dealing with religion no longer faced the church as an equal, but addressed the individual directly. In the empty space formerly occupied by the church, the state waxed ever stronger. Losing the public weight of a church, Christian faith was confined within the solitary individual soul. The Enlightenment could then advance rapidly into regions of the soul formerly occupied by biblical faith. The "tolerance" of one individual for another (so it was thought) would be quite enough.

THE SECULARIZATION THESIS

The secular humanist vision of history may be summarized in this blunt maxim: *Secular enlightenment must grow, biblical faith must diminish.* This is the succinct form of the "secularization thesis" of the social sciences between, say, 1950 and about 1990. As Irving Kristol points out, this set of beliefs is no longer rooted in science; this is ideology.

In this way, the Enlightenment gave rise to a new meaning of the term "secular." From marking a realm of life distinguished from the realm of the sacred, there now was born an ideology: secularism. Earlier, Christians had seen both the sacred and the secular as complementary aspects of virtually everything. To be secularist now meant to drive the sacred out of public and intellectual life. *Écrasez l'Infâme.* In this sense, the tireless work of the American Civil Liberties Union today in driving religion out of public life is exemplary secularist work.

But of course, in the real world, it is not strictly necessary for the secular to exclude the religious, or to set itself up as a direct adversary, in a zero-sum game. That is merely a matter of choice. As Professor Himmelfarb shows, that was neither the British nor the American way.

Yet even in thinking of all three Enlightenments together, it is amazing in retrospect how much this broad new civilizational movement accomplished. The Enlightenment was a noble, even at times a heroic effort, and it has brought much good into the world. Nonetheless, in recent times the secularist movement has begun to bump into rather severe limits in its own capacities. Without wishing in any way to denigrate the huge achievements of the Enlightenment, or to turn back the clock by weakening it, an increasing number of writers, not themselves men of Christian faith, have begun to warn of debilitating tendencies within the secularist Enlightenment. They urge that people of reason pry open the unnecessarily self-enclosed horizons of secularism.

THE EMERGENCE OF THE SECULARIST IDEOLOGY

Let us return to the definition of "secularism" or "secularization," which we broached only provisionally above. Two new features have arisen in modern times to alter the meaning of the term in interesting respects—ever since Darwin, Freud, Comte, and other "moderns." The first is the conviction that the only valid form of human knowing is science, proceeding by way of both mathematical reasoning and empirical research (narrowly considered).

The practical effect of this epistemological choice is to make knowledge of God impossible for humans. For this narrow method confines human knowing to searching for heretofore unidentified bits of furniture in the universe, identified by sensory evidence. But God is not a sense object. God is not an object in space and time like other objects. Such a conception would fall far short of what religious people mean by "God," expect of God, take to be signs of the presence of God. If all God were was another piece of furniture in space and time, or a scientific hypothesis (doomed to be replaced by another), God would be a pitiable thing. Indeed, if God were simply proportioned to human knowing, and not to be found on a far more powerful wavelength, far exceeding our power to grasp, such a god would fall far short of traditional inquiries.

The first feature of modern secularism, then, is that by its very definition of what knowing is, it excludes knowledge of God from the realm of legitimate human knowing.

The second feature is that this new secularism seeks to relieve human conscience of the heavy burdens imposed by any divine judgment at the end of time. It relieves humans of the fear that an undeceivable God sees and knows all things, even those done in secret, even those hidden in the depths of the heart. Modern secularists frequently burst into paeans of praise for the feeling of liberation attained by breaking free from God. One feels free to do whatever one wants, without any supervening judgment from Another. The individual self may then be alone in the universe, yes, but with the consolation of being truly un-mastered and un-judged. Being free from "judgmentalism" is very important to a secularist age. Milton's Lucifer captures this sentiment perfectly: *"Non serviam!"* (I will not serve.) I prefer to be alone.

The Soft Secularist—and the Hard

But here another division within modern secularism starkly appears. Some secularists go on serving the old morality (or most of it) and nourishing in themselves the old virtues—Aristotelian virtues, Stoic virtues, republican virtues, such as a jealous regard for freedom of conscience, fraternity, equality, compassion, justice, honesty, courage, and so forth. Among such secularists, a few have historically been pointed to as "secular saints"—David Hume and

Albert Camus, for instance. We may call this school the soft or "smiling" secularists. There is no God, but the search for truth and fidelity to good morals goes forward, perhaps even better in a secular than in a religious age.

Down quite another route go those who take Nietzsche seriously: "God is dead" means not only the passing of the divine element from the human cosmos, but also the death of truth and the death of morality. Everything is truly relative. There are no values, only your preferences and mine. It is not just that now nothing is white or black, and most decisions fall into "gray areas." There is no gray either. No distinctions are possible.

Add to this a form of natural selection that gives free rein to the powerful and the fit, so as to confer upon them (for the good of the human race) the obligation to triumph over the weak and the unfit. The German General Staff during World War I, a number of whom had been Vernon Kellogg's biology professors (see chapter six), boasted of the moral duties imposed on their superior culture and morality to vanquish weaker Europeans. Add "the additional assumption that the Germans are the chosen race, and German social and political organization the chosen type of human community life, and you have a wall of logic and conviction that you can break your head against but can never shatter—by headwork."

We may call this school the "hard" secularists, the pessimists, the celebrators of the dysfunctionality of human intellect, the champions of a hard and unsentimental will to power.

This may be a vulgar school, but it was in the twentieth century all too powerful under Communism, Fascism, and Nazism. The more reasonable liberal secularists would call this hard school an aberration. But it was all too real, and all too secularist, and its arguments are not easy to refute, as Albert Camus found out before World War II in his exchange of letters with a young friend who became a Nazi.

The Goodness of the Secular: Biblical Humanism

"Secular" (as opposed to "secularist") is therefore a term that marks out its own realm of goodness, purpose, and morality, with its own proper and distinctive autonomy. This secular realm stands face-to-face with the eternal realm within which God dwells. For Christians and Jews, the Creator offers His friendship to women and men in freedom. The latter may reject it, or accept it.

A division by free choice appears from the very beginning. Adam and Eve chose against the one single commandment of God. Cain slew Abel. By the time of Noah, hardly a godly man is to be found. Thus, humans today also choose the "city" to which they give ultimate allegiance. Yet to choose friendship with God does not entail devaluing the goodness and proper autonomy of that other city in nature and time. Exactly the contrary.

The Psalms of David exult in the beauty and majesty of the earth and give God thanks for it. The seven Christian sacraments (Catholic, really) instituted by Christ to give "grace" (which is a way of sharing in God's work, while still in time) are each constituted by physical objects becoming symbols of divine realities: whispering one's sins and asking for forgiveness, bread and wine, holy oils, a ring and a promise, a laying on of hands, a light slap on the cheek, the pouring of water over the head. In these seven physical ways, the things of God—the "sacraments," the sacred acts—interpenetrate the legitimate living secular world. They act as yeast in dough.

Yet the dough retains its own autonomy, and its ability to fall flat. ("I am just not very religious," one hears people say. Or, "I never feel that I am missing anything.")

In sum, prior to the ideological secularism of the last three centuries, there was a Christian humanism, deeply knowledgeable about the ways of this world, often highly sensual, and with a great lust for life. Christian humanism had emphatically a dimension of worldliness. Yet it retained an awareness, as modern secular humanism does not, of participating simultaneously in a far more spacious and dramatic world, that of God's grace forgiving human weakness and fallibility.

In this sense, the secular humanism of today dwells within a far narrower circle of consciousness than Christian humanism did in the past and continues to do in the present. Christian humanism may be more modest in its claims for itself, and properly humble, since the grace it most cherishes among its strengths is an undeserved gift, accepted by and through the dark night of faith.

Of course, there have always been arrogant and haughty churchmen. But it is easily pointed out that such men are living contrary to the example of their Teacher. Christian conversations must be characterized by humility and mutual respect if Christians are to find a new way forward in the coming post-secular age. Our Lord would have Christians converse with all others in an open spirit—and yet not be surprised by the ridicule and contumely thrown their way. These go with the great, rollicking adventure of fidelity to God.

TEN

The End of the Secularist Age

Perhaps the defensiveness in several proclamations of atheism—the odd feeling they give of making one last desperate stand—derives from their timing: here at the end of an age. "We have, in recent years, observed two major events that represent turning points in the history of the twentieth century," Irving Kristol remarked back in 1991. "The first is the death of socialism, both as an ideal and as a political program, a death that has been duly recorded in our consciousness. The second is the collapse of secular humanism . . . as an ideal."

ENTER JÜRGEN HABERMAS

Irving Kristol may have been first in discerning the fall of secular humanism, but since 2001 the prominent European atheist Jürgen Habermas has also been announcing "the post-secular age." He does not hold that atheists are about to give up atheism, or even secularism, but he does believe this much (I summarize in my own words): *Secularism has been pushed into a new position in world history; it now appears to be the persuasion of a fairly small minority in a sea of rising religious commitment.*

Has secularism, he asks, acquired the internal resources to enter into respectful dialogue with religious peoples? Two new facts sowed doubt in his mind. First, the thesis that the human world is becoming increasingly secular—"the secularization thesis"— appears to have been decisively falsified. Second, a powerful religious awakening in the third world, but also in large regions such as the United States and eastern Europe, suggests that secularist Europe is the anomaly, not the norm.

Over the course of Habermas's life work, the key moral concept is "communicative discourse," discourse that arises from the ability of each partner to stand in the other's moccasins and to learn to sympathize with a viewpoint quite contrary to his own. Only in this way do we escape from narrow egotism.

Since the resurgence of religion bids to swamp the atheist portions of the world, can secularists summon up the moral strength not only to tolerate, but also to enter with respect into the viewpoint of believers? Can they do so after so many generations during which they have been teaching cultural contempt for believers in God, the unenlightened, the people of the dark?

Feuerbach taught us that the relation of God and man is a zero-sum game: what is given to one is taken from the other; further, that it is man who creates God out of his own emotional needs, not God who creates man. Karl Marx set out to eradicate religion as an opiate that renders the proletariat passive. Many sociologists thought that the advance of science would shrink religion until it finally disappears. Nietzsche finally uttered the somber verdict "God is dead." He only said what many sophisticated Europeans already believed. A step further on, Sigmund Freud diagnosed religion as a neurotic dependency. It is *The Future of an Illusion.*

Plainly, these great analysts overlooked important sources of vitality in the world around them. By the end of the twentieth century, the burgeoning force of worldwide religion was undeniable. The question may be less whether religion will survive, than in what form secularism will survive. Will it come to seem increasingly isolated, dumbstruck, unable to communicate in the new "tongues"?

In particular, Habermas makes four observations.

The Four Limitations of Secularism

1. MUTUAL RESPECT. Shortly after September 11, 2001, when nineteen Muslims—mostly graduate students and young professionals—flew airliners laden with aviation fuel to burst in orange flame into the Twin Towers of the World Trade Center in New York and into the low-lying Pentagon, Habermas gave a lecture on the occasion of receiving a major prize from the German Publishers and Booksellers Association. He shocked most listeners by presenting an essay called "Faith and Knowledge." His main theme was the need for toleration among secular humanists for religious people, and vice versa—and not just toleration, but mutual respect and open conversation. He believed the future of civilization demanded no less.

A year later, Habermas spoke out forcefully against biological engineering and human cloning, in a brilliant, impassioned essay entitled *The Future of Human Nature*. He wrote of a human right to a unique human identity and expressed revulsion at the prospect of a "human" artifact manufactured by others, a mere object among objects.

In 2004 he accepted a challenge to engage in public debate with Joseph Cardinal Ratzinger, then head of the Congregation for the Doctrine of the Faith, and no "progressive" in theology, although a very learned, modest, and engaging man. (Ratzinger a year later was elected pope.) Again, Habermas shocked the media and many professors in the academy by affirming both the importance of religion for civilization, and the obligation of secularists to engage with religion seriously and honestly. "Sacred scriptures and religious traditions," Habermas argued, "have preserved over millennia, in subtle formulation and hermeneutics, intuitions about error and redemption, about the salvational outcome of a life experienced as hopeless."

An American expert on Habermas explicates: "Religious life keeps intact . . . a number of sensitivities, nuances, and modes of expression for situations that neither his own 'post-metaphysical' approach nor an exclusively rationalist society of professional expertise can deal with in a fully satisfactory manner."

Cardinal Ratzinger, for his part, stressed the indispensable need of Jewish/Christian faith for reason, to diminish the "toxicity" sometimes present in religion. He further emphasized the essential bond between Christianity and the Greek "Insight" (*Logos*): reason and faith are both "summoned to mutual cleansing and healing." This debate with Habermas foreshadowed the sturdy defense of reason that the new pope made some years later at the University of Regensburg, where he had once been vice rector—the famous lecture to which many Muslims reacted, not with reason, but with violent demonstrations.

The next question raised by Habermas in his exploration of uncharted ground between the secular world and the religious world was this: *After so many generations of contempt for religion, did most secularists have either the tools or the moral stamina to carry out an honest, respectful conversation?*

2. HONESTY ABOUT DEBTS. An earlier vein of thought not much noticed in the masterwork of Habermas, *The Theory of Communicative Action* (1981), appeared under a section title in almost untranslatable German, signifying something like "Expressing the Sacred in Words." Honesty, Habermas argued, commands that secular people recognize their linguistic and conceptual debts to Judaism and Christianity. "Ever since the Council of Nicaea and throughout the course of a 'Hellenization of Christianity,' philosophy itself took on board and assimilated many religious motifs . . . Concepts of Greek origin such as 'autonomy' and 'individuality' and Roman concepts such as 'emancipation' and 'solidarity' have long since been shot through with meanings of a Judaeo-Christian origin."

The question is, *Have secularists the honesty to admit these debts openly?* For Habermas, modern notions of equality and fairness are "secular distillations of time-honored Judeo-Christian precepts." Further, the "contract" theories of modern secular philosophy can scarcely be understood apart from the great prestige attached to the "covenants" central to both Jewish and Christian history. For Habermas, secular reason also depends on reverence for themes long maintained in Jewish and Christian life such as moral justice and obligation. Without such teaching, it is doubtful whether modern societies would long be able to sustain their own scientific and political inquiries.

In his remarks to the German Publishers and Booksellers Association, Habermas named a substantial list of moral realities that secular life and thought do not sustain alone:

> For the normative self-understanding of modernity, Christianity has functioned as more than just a precursor or a catalyst. Universalistic egalitarianism, from which spring *the ideals of freedom and a collective life in solidarity, the autonomous conduct of life and emancipation, the individual morality of conscience, human rights, and democracy,* is the direct legacy of the Judaic ethic of justice and the Christian ethic of love.

3. CHALLENGES OF A POST-SECULAR AGE. Habermas asserts that today we live in "post-secular societies"—certainly people in the United States do. This fact has many positive benefits for secularism, he warns, but it also presents the danger that Judaism and Christianity might teach humans to undervalue worldly accomplishment, initiative, and action, in favor of passivity before the will of God. (Habermas is mindful of Nietzsche's impassioned claim that Judaism and Christianity are "slave religions," moved by passive-aggressive *ressentiment*.) He also worries about those Christians who hold that "the fall" of Adam so seriously damages human nature that no intrinsic good can come from it.

Does Habermas, in fact, fully grasp the Christian theologies of the fall? A professor at Calvin College in Michigan has explained that the best way to describe original sin is this: "Anyone who says that man is totally depraved can't be all bad." In that spirit, Max Weber discerned the immense outburst of economic energy in those sectors of Christianity that most feared that they were not among the elect. The Fall, in this view, spurs tremendous energies in a positive direction.

Still, Habermas insisted that, from time to time, the best and highest secular ideals—human rights, solidarity, equality—benefit "from renewed contact with the nimbus of their sacral origins."

4. TWO-WAY TOLERANCE. In 2005, in a lecture at the University of Lodz in Poland on "Religion in the Public Sphere," Habermas posed another question (again I abbreviate): *Are secular men and women ready to admit that toleration is always a two-way street?* Religious persons must be ready to learn toleration not only for each denomination's convictions and commitments, but also for those of atheists, agnostics, and other secularists. In a similar way, nonbelieving secularists must learn to appreciate the creeds, reasoning, and convictions of their fellow human beings who are believers. "For all their ongoing dissent on questions of worldviews and religious doctrines," says Habermas, "citizens are meant to respect one another as free and equal members of their political community." Those on all sides must be ready to stand in the shoes of the other, in order to see the other's point of view "from within."

As Pierre Manent has pointed out, the history of the last six or seven generations seems to show that Christianity has had an easier time identifying with democracy, and done so more successfully, than secular people have done in recognizing the contributions Christians and Jews have made to the intellectual comprehension of rights. The question Habermas poses is succinctly summarized: *Is there sufficient moral energy among secular peoples to overcome this failure to take religion seriously?*

CIVIC DUTIES OF RELIGIOUS PERSONS

On the side of religious people, Habermas also poses a test. Among themselves, they may explain their convictions in the language of faith, and even of the Bible. But in public life, at least those believers who enter into politics or activism have a special obligation to employ a "neutral" secular language. Perhaps Habermas is thinking more of the situation of France or other secular European nations with high proportions of Muslim citizens, where he wants to put pressure on Muslims to become more open to Western views, not to stay closed within their own. Perhaps he believes that the preponderance of peoples in European nations is secular, so that among them secular speech is most readily accessible to the largest number. Whatever his motives, his warning is that language in the public sphere (specifically, governmental offices) should be solely secular, lest religious language invite social divisiveness. Yet Habermas is far more open than John Rawls on these matters.

In his lecture "Religion in the Public Sphere," Habermas writes,

> The citizens of a democratic community owe one another good reasons for their public political interventions. Contrary to the restrictive view of [John] Rawls and [Robert] Audi, this civic duty can be specified in such a tolerant way that contributions are permitted in a *religious as well as in a secular language.* They are not subject to constraints on the mode of expression in the political public sphere, but they rely on joint ventures of translation to have a chance to be taken up in the agendas and negotiations of political bodies. Otherwise they will not "count" in any further political process.

In "Faith and Knowledge," Habermas adds, "The liberal state has so far imposed *only upon the believers* among its citizens the requirement that they split their identity into public and private versions. That is, they must translate their religious convictions into a secular language before their arguments have the prospect of being accepted by a majority" (emphasis added).

For his part, Habermas does not want to put believers at a disadvantage, although he holds that all parties, including believers, must do their best to give reasons understandable to the other parties. So he lays burdens on both believers and unbelievers: "But the search for reasons that aspire to general acceptance need not lead to an unfair exclusion of religion from public life, and secular society, for its part, need not cut itself off from the important resources of spiritual explanations, if only so that the secular side might retain a feeling for the articulative power of religious discourse."

By contrast, the assumption that Rawls and others make is that the secular mode of speech is actually "neutral." In the experience of many believers of various faiths, secular speech is anything but neutral. Speech limited to secular categories has its own totalistic tendencies. It penalizes or even quarantines those with religious points of view, whose insights and public arguments are not given due weight by narrowly secular officials. Curiously, in a set of lectures at the University of Virginia in 1928, Walter Lippmann made a parallel observation about the famous Scopes trial three years earlier. In a lecture framed as a conversation, the "Fundamentalist" says to his counterpart the "Modernist":

> In our public controversies you are fond of arguing that you are open-minded, tolerant and neutral in the face of conflicting opinions. That is not so . . . Because for me an eternal plan of salvation is at stake. For you there is nothing at stake but a few tentative opinions none of which means anything to your happiness. Your request that I should be tolerant and amiable is, therefore, a suggestion that I submit the foundation of my life to the destructive effects of your skepticism, your indifference, and your good nature. You ask me to smile and to commit suicide.

The Modernist does not grasp the total surrender he is asking the person of faith to make by submitting one source of knowledge (faith) to another (reason), when the latter seems to him inferior.

The parallel challenge that Habermas throws down for secular people, then, is an even newer one: that they, now, live in a "post-secular" age and must not be content with understanding social realities in a solely secular way. They, too, must enter into the two-way dialogue by stepping into the shoes, horizon, and viewpoint of those who are believers, just as is expected of the believers vis-à-vis the secularist.

If the tender roots of something like universal democracy are ever to survive and spread around the world, these conceptions—these breakthroughs for a universal ethos of public communication, and mutual reaching out to understand others from within—make an indispensable contribution. But these new rules for public discourse also renegotiate the historical preeminence that "the enlightened" assign themselves, and the language of contempt by which they have taken believers less than seriously. These rules call upon secularists, too, to be learners, and to master the new morality of communicative discourse. It is a morality that calls for mutual respect.

SOME RECENTLY DISCOVERED
INCAPACITIES OF SECULARISM

If one looks back at . . . [the past] century, one sees the rationalist religion of secular humanism gradually losing its credibility even as it marches triumphantly through the institutions of our society—through the schools, the courts, the churches, the media. This loss of credibility flows from two fundamental flaws in secular humanism.

—Irving Kristol

For so many generations, secularists have assumed that the triumph of secularism is fast-approaching. Predictions of the disappearance of religion have been many. So it has been difficult for secularists to absorb their new situation, and more difficult still to learn of significant deficiencies in their own philosophy and moral capacities. Their philosophy is noble, and we are all in its debt. It is quite clear, too, that without religion some can live good and noble lives. But evidence shows that there are also in the secularist worldview clear deficiencies. Irving Kristol mentions two in particular. The first is that "the philosophical rationalism of secular humanism can, at best, provide us with a statement of the necessary assumptions of a moral code, but it cannot deliver any such code itself."

Kristol explains his meaning so: "Moral codes evolve from the moral experience of communities, and can claim authority over behavior only to the degree that individuals are reared to look respectfully, even reverently, on the moral traditions of their forefathers. It is the function of religion to instill such respect and reverence." Then Kristol adds: "One accepts a moral code on faith—not on blind faith but on the faith that one's ancestors, over the generations, were not fools and that we have much to learn from their experience."

The prevailing moral code of the West was, for centuries, informed by the wisdom of our forefathers, but in the new vision of human nature and destiny developed by secular humanism that old code has become attenuated. That biting challenge of Nietzsche still nags at our conscience: If God is really dead, by what authority do we say any particular practice is prohibited or permitted? In the resulting social disarray, the most urgent of all moral questions has also become unsettled: "How shall we raise our children? What kind of moral example should we set? What moral instruction should we convey?"

In the view of Habermas, a society uncertain in its answer to these questions is likely to "breed restless, turbulent generations," some of whom are likely to seek more authoritative answers somewhere else—anywhere. We know this can happen. It happened to that smart and amiable young friend of Albert Camus, who took quite seriously the chatter in the cafés of Paris about the meaninglessness of individual life, and *therefore* gave his all for the triumph of his nation, his greatest good, by joining the Nazi Party.

The second flaw in secular humanism, according to Irving Kristol, is even more fundamental: "If there is one indisputable fact about the human condition it is that no community can survive if it is persuaded—or even suspects—that its members are leading meaningless lives in a meaningless universe."

Secular humanism, Kristol goes on, "encourages individuals," faced with the ultimate meaninglessness of human life, to make something worthwhile of "autonomy" and "creativity." Yet why in a meaningless world is creativity better than passivity, or autonomy better than submission? Thus, even these shining principles are undermined by skeptical nihilists, neopagans, and tormented existentialists such as Nietzsche, Heidegger, and Sartre. Later still, secular humanism has come to be mocked by the new postmodernists, deconstructionists, and structuralists. That is why something has gone out of the self-confidence of secularism. "Secular humanism is brain dead even as its heart continues to pump energy into all of our institutions." These animadversions of Mr. Kristol are only a beginning of the new questions being asked.

Moral Decadence

Ever since the fall of Rome, historians and philosophers have noted *how often civilizations fall by way of moral decadence. What tools does secularism possess to arrest such decadence? How does a secularist society even diagnose moral decadence? By whose standards?* (I do not mean that there are no standards accessible to human reason, only that secularist philosophers in our time seldom challenge the inroads made by relativism and nihilism into the once proud tradition of rationalism.)

In secularist circles, "Awakenings" are treated like matters best generated by religions, not by the human sciences. Further, secularist emphasis on the autonomous and unencumbered individual often leads to an odd theory of the good. For instance, Judith Jarvis Thompson of MIT argues that the good is whatever an autonomous person chooses as a good. Such definitions deprive secularists of any standard by which to *measure* moral decadence, whether in a single person or in an entire culture. Moreover, precisely insofar as any one defines the good as *whatever* a person chooses, such definitions strip human critical faculties of any useful role and are inconsistent with everyday speech.

By contrast, historians teach us that the United States, chiefly because of its Protestant heritage, has historically experienced at least three great "Awakenings." Nobel Prize winner Robert Fogel has written that the country is in the throes of a rolling wave, not yet crested, of a "Fourth Great Awakening." This wave marks a return to tradition and family values, and to serious work and self-discipline. It is not limited to religious people, let alone the Religious Right.

Still, these fairly regular renewals seem to spring from several important Jewish and Christian teachings; for instance,

- a new concentration on high standards
- a turn away from sins against fidelity to God and moral duty
- a call to repentance
- a demand for conversion of life
- a possibility of a fresh beginning (not necessarily by accepting Jesus Christ, but at least by moral seriousness and by a new openness to the transcendent).

Thus even among people fallen into the slough of moral decadence, an inner call to re-awaken to the path of duty, self-governance, and personal dignity can be heard. This inner call (in the biblical view) bears the promise of divine assistance, which imparts inner powers entirely beyond the strength of the autonomous and unencumbered will.

From this promise, many in history have drawn courage. Even those who do not believe in "divine" assistance may well observe changes in behavior among those who do.

In an 1838 address to the Young Men's Lyceum of Springfield, Illinois, Abraham Lincoln explained why such new awakenings are necessary. After reciting some of the ills of his time, he publicly prayed for a successor to "the great Washington," who might awaken this nation. It was from the contemplation of Washington that Lincoln much later conceived the need for "a new birth of freedom." Lincoln had observed that moral life proceeds in cycles of three or more generations, each concluding in a slow but steady decline. Thus, the generation that won the independence of the United States was revered for its courage, because of its amazing steadfastness in the face of defeat, desolation, and lack of popular support. (Almost two-thirds of the people either sided with the British or sat back to watch, uninvolved.) The children of this great generation tried to live up to the high example of their fathers but often failed. In the next generation, the grandchildren were weary even of hearing about their heroic grandparents, and preferred more pleasant paths. Lincoln called the engine of this downward process "the silent artillery of time."

For secularists, a kind of Newtonian law of inertial moral decline presents two problems: By what public moral standard ought decline and progress to be measured? Second, what tools are stored in the secularist arsenal for turning large numbers of citizens from their downward drift back up to the required levels of discipline, self-government, duty, and honor? The classical progressive remedies are "consciousness raising," "education," and "raising public awareness." But such remedies imply publicly available universal standards, and moral exemplars that would constitute a moral avant-garde. The moral relativism of (not all, but far too many) secularists prevents such remedies from getting under way.

A Universal Ethic of Reason?

The secularism stemming from the Enlightenment has been unable to keep its promise of forging a universal consensus on an ethic based on reason alone. Today ethical schools of thought may be more divided than ever. The distinguished philosopher Alasdair

MacIntyre has observed that there is now so little common ground shared by the various schools of thought that rational ethical debate has been reduced to exclamatory cheering sections erupting into "Hurrah!" or "Boo!"

Professors in countless classrooms in many disciplines report that students have already been well taught that, when they are faced with any moral proposition, the proper response is: "That's just your opinion." They are resistant to resolving disagreements by reasoned argument. They aver: "You choose your goods, and I'll choose mine." Reasoned debate is replaced by naked will. I *choose.* Don't ask me to give reasons, I just choose. And don't give me this drill about being responsible for consequences—what will be will be.

This circumstance seems to be what Nietzsche meant when he observed that no man of reason should rejoice in the death of God. Experience will soon show, he was certain, that with the death of God arrives the death of reason. If reason is a compass, it requires a North Star. If it is a tool for getting to the truth, it requires somewhere in its inner makeup a regulative principle of this sort: *Even if no one yet possesses the truth, we must agree that the presentation of evidence through reasoned argument is the most reliable path for coming closer to the truth.* The regulative principle is that, even if no one at present knows what the truth in this or that matter is, there is a truth to come closer to (this principle is discussed in fuller detail in my 2004 book, *The Universal Hunger for Liberty*). Further, mutual conversation about evidence that is available to all parties is the best guide for figuring out how to come closer to the truth of things.

Still, the utility of evidence depends on there being truths to be discovered, or at least to be more closely approximated. Thus, a regulative idea of truth is an essential constituent of any civilization worthy of human reason. Without it, there is no evidence to point to, no mutual acceptance of rules of discourse. No conversation can amount to more than conjoined soliloquies. If God is dead, so is the regulative idea of truth. If all is chance, random, and inherently meaningless, reason has no North Star; its needle spins mindlessly.

At the death of God, therefore, Zarathustra wept.

HUMAN SUFFERING, TRAGEDY, EVIL

As Irving Kristol further pointed out more than ten years ago, *secularism has little to say about human suffering, brokenness, tragedy, remorse, and evil.* Secularism is not very satisfying to those who are in pain at life's extremities, not so much because secular humanism offers little comfort, as because secularism sees so little *meaning* in suffering and self-sacrifice, which are everyday and common requirements of living. Hardly a conversation with a neighbor passes by without one learning of a family member or friend struggling with a horrible cancer; or of a child of ten having to have a leg amputated, because the driver of a van, going too fast on a rain-slick road, lost control and skidded into a group of children at a bus stop. There is abundant suffering in the family worlds of all of us.

Again, secularism offers little in the way of remedy to those who have consciously and deliberately done something evil but now repent of it. Such persons cannot be fooled by "therapy"; they know exactly what they did and that they chose deliberately to do it. They are not seeking "understanding," but rather the removal of real guilt for a real evil that they have deliberately committed.

Secularism is not altogether speechless in the face of death, sin, human suffering, and "meaningless" human tragedy. Yet its voice does sound faint—which leaves it less than comforting to the weak and vulnerable, who under the mad regime of the survival of the fittest do not feel well positioned. And what has secularism to say to the vulnerable that it does not borrow directly from Judaism and Christianity?

Two Upcoming Crises: Islamofascism . . .

What are the long-term prospects of existing secular societies such as those in Europe and the United States? Two difficulties stand out. The first is this: Faced with an extreme ideology such as political Jihadism, conceived in the white-hot passions of resentment and bloodlust, with what can relativism arm itself? Some of the most sensitive members of a secularist community are liable to make excuses for murderous opponents, out of a dread for a principled moral stand—that would be too "absolutist." Some are liable to plead for understanding, tolerance, appeasement. Since such persons have no standard of moral truth that they might appeal to, the danger is that they may drift into preemptive moral surrender. They may unthinkingly give heart to a voracious enemy. (Appeasement, said Churchill, is throwing someone else to the crocodiles in the hopes of being eaten last.)

The totalitarian political threat arising from a minority of Muslims is fired by a new lust to establish a worldwide caliphate under shari'a (Islamic law). It is based on the belief that the West no longer has a serious inner strength on which the will to resist can stand. The methods of this new jihad—explosives, beheadings, torture by driving electrical drills into the body—are organized by unconventional, underground bands of individuals whom we may expect to be armed with ever more deadly means of destruction, capable of being carried in hand luggage. The main cadres of this force, although employing a mishmash of the most cruel and brutal texts from the seventh and eleventh centuries, seem motivated more by a lust for political power than by holiness of life. They are ruthless murderers, even of thousands of their coreligionists. "Pitiless power" seems to be the cry of their hearts. Conquest by migration, segregation, and unsparing indoctrination into hate for rival cultures is their patient, long-term work.

The more secular nations of Europe, and the more secular parts of America (noble exceptions aside, such as Christopher Hitchens), show little will to resist. Few concerted plans for resistance have

been submitted for debate. No strategy for victory. Only a few efforts to mobilize resources and counterstrategies.

"Onward, Secular Soldiers!" has not yet been put to music for
use in wars of self-defense.

. . . And Demography

The second difficulty is a demographic one. Secularism seems to
give few motives to young men and women to have children in
sufficient numbers to reproduce themselves, plus a little more to
allow for future growth. In fact, secularism seems to serve up motives for *not* having children, whether out of perceived moral duties to the environment and fears of overpopulation or simply a
preference for enjoying a relatively carefree life, unencumbered by
the long responsibilities of raising children. (Even in nominally
Christian countries such as France and Italy, churchgoers tend to
be the ones who have more children, while more secular persons
have fewer.)

Possibly, too, the conditions of the social welfare state have the
unintended consequence of discouraging those who want to have
children: high taxes, small apartments, heavily regulated living
arrangements, the weakening of personal responsibilities both to
the older and to the younger generation. Add the unspoken but
demoralizing perception that the welfare state has made far more
promises than it can possibly satisfy. A certain foreshortening of a
bleak future, a certain cultural pessimism, seems to be a natural
concomitant of the social welfare state. Tocqueville predicted a
new soft despotism that would result from an unchecked drift
toward social equality, untempered by a love for individual liberty
and personal responsibility. He feared a dread sameness, an ener-
vation, and a coarsening of life.

It may be good to point out explicitly that child rearing involves enormous sacrifices of worldly benefits. While rational philosophy may be able to motivate great sacrifice in the case of
extraordinary people like Socrates, most ordinary men need some-

thing less pallid than philosophy to move them. What will that be? It could be tribalism or nationalism or political ideology in some form, which have unleashed far greater horrors than religion ever has. For most, it will probably be a religion of heart and concrete tradition that speaks to their senses and memories, universal in its reach, based on the free conscience and universal human brotherhood (inclining them toward international solidarity), and wed to intellectual inquiry. Probably the kind of pluralism I spelled out in my essay "Caritapolis."

ATHEISM OR AGNOSTICISM?

Since secularism means, and intends to mean, the death of God, can it propose an alternative to God? The trouble is that atheism is a leap in the dark; it is not a rational alternative. No person can possibly prove a negative or know enough to be certain that there is no God. Some will lean toward atheism, with some (as they see it) high degree of probability that they are correct. As we noted in chapter two, however, opinion surveys indicate that even most of those who call themselves atheists believe in some deistic substitute for God: a world force, the preeminence of Reason, a kind of pantheism, a firm confidence in a slow spiral upward toward the good, the just, and the true. These are not exactly pure forms of atheism. Like believers, atheists also have their dark night.

That is why agnosticism has come to seem a more modest, skeptically open, and humanistically attractive position. Yet agnosticism, too, has a central flaw. As a spectator sport, agnosticism is at least understandable. Yet every day women and men have to step into the arena of action. They must take action. They must make decisions. There their actions fall under the principles of one theory—or that of another. They cannot go on making decisions *as if God does not exist* without having effectively made a pivotal decision against God. In every big decision they make they will, one way or the other, take sides. They will act in a way cognizant of God's will and respectful of it, as one would act in the presence of a friend. Or else they will act in a way that violates God's will. In the latter case, they act *as if there is no God,* or at least as if there is no way of knowing what God wills. One can, in short, pretend to think as an agnostic, but the pressures of actually choosing how to act oblige one to declare one's relationship to God. In action, there are no agnostics.

Now it may be possible for extraordinary and unusual people to go on *acting as if God does exist,* even if they are atheists or agnostics. But it seems unlikely that whole societies can do that—and highly doubtful that ordinary, commonsense people can do that for long, across more than three generations. To be sure, religious societies are also riven by sin. (Every Catholic Mass opens with the simple public confession that all participants meet as a community of sinners, much as a meeting of Alcoholics· Anonymous opens with a ritual by which one person after another rises to say, "I am an alcoholic." Not one word more, nor one word less. No excuses, no explanations.) And churches, too, have perennial problems with laxity, backsliding, and sheer moral disorder. But the churches also have means and methods for addressing recurrent moral failure.

Where atheism and agnosticism flourish, by contrast, one may expect to find a certain moral carelessness seeping into common life, a certain slacking off, a certain habit of getting away with things. Secularism may be liveable among specially gifted people, but its effects on the general run of humankind seem to be less comforting. One may find, for instance, a coarsening of daily intercourse, as we now seem to be experiencing in America. We remember nostalgically a time when one could leave home with the door unlocked. A number of British writers down the years have recalled with pleasure the old sweetness and courtesy imbued into English culture by Methodism in its early generations.

Further, secular modernity offers few reasons why those who are religious—Muslims, for example—should change their religious commitments. Why should they exchange experience, clarity, and certainty for relativism? And if they do not, what fault in that decision can relativists discern? It is rather late for relativists to be alarmed by the bloody murder of Theo Van Gogh in the Netherlands. To feel that alarm is to discover the reality of evil, and to stand on the verge of resolving to combat it. It is to cease being relativist. Judaism and Christianity, one may think, explain this sequence better than current-day secular humanism does.

Within a culture of relativism one may even find, among the rough-and-tumble sort in any population, a greater sense that there is no price to pay (even in one's own conscience) for the exhibition of brute will and thuggishness.

If humans are just matter—different only in degree from lower animals. If our thoughts are just chemical reactions in our nervous systems. If all human life will end up in nothingness. Then why shouldn't a certain proportion of people just say "eat, drink, and be merry"? Why would a fair number of ordinary people, confronted with a scientific evaluation of the meaninglessness of their own lives, when faced with adversity not just throw in the towel? Why would not a great many just look out for number one and maybe their nearest and dearest? In "a tale by told by an idiot, full of sound and fury, signifying nothing" these seem to be "rational" responses. Maybe not admirable, but highly likely to be rather common.

One hardly ever meets these days the cocky rationalists of the kind that flourished one hundred years ago, secure in their powers of logic and scientific reasoning. Even Dawkins, Dennett, Harris, and Hitchens—outlined against the current resurgence of moral relativism, nihilism, and postmodernism—rise up as ghosts from the graveyard of an earlier rationalism.

Enough on the negative side. There are also some affirmative steps in need of attention.

More Positively, Science Needs Supportive Habits

One reason postmodernism has gone so far is that the sort of reason that lifted up the Enlightenment is not altogether well-suited to justifying itself. Reason, as we are learning again, can be used to undermine reason. Reason has also been used to undermine the morale and moral self-confidence of those whose whole lives have been committed to the Enlightenment, by calling them warmongers or insensitive robots, and the like, in order to impugn their own sense of self-worth. Science depends upon a supportive culture and a measure of social admiration that make worthwhile all the sacrifices of acquiring a scientific education and professional practice. And to stiffen the spine against manifold temptations to cheat.

Science is not just a methodology; it is a set of habits and practices, not supported in all cultures, but emphasized in some. These special cultures form many students in diligence, discipline, and hard work. Young scientists must also be honest and trustworthy in their reports, and cooperative with their colleagues since science these days is seldom for lone rangers. In brief, the life of reason is as much a culture as a method. A great many persons and institutions must be committed to its disciplines, its aims, and its long-term support.

It is not clear that science alone, particularly on the basis of atheism or agnosticism, can long inspire cultural commitments of this sort. If everything is at the end of the day a result of chance, reason seems to be out of harmony with the fundamental nature of reality. What then, exactly, is the point of a commitment to reason? The humanist who in all things seeks reason while insisting that, at bottom, there are no reasons, contradicts himself.

In the face of ultimate pointlessness how long can a culture sustain the experience of the frustration of reason and still continue to attract young people to its necessary disciplines?

AND FAITH NEEDS REASON

The question that most troubled Habermas, however, is, How can a small island of people committed to reason and to science long survive in a great ocean of peoples who see in science and reason engines of demoralization and cultural decadence? It became apparent after September 11, 2001, Habermas writes, that huge portions of the world harbor bitter resistance to the West. The fact that the West is perceived as the culture of modern science and reason does not satisfy the souls of many, many persons. Reason (narrowly considered) and science do not exhaust the world of perception, understanding, and judgment. In such circumstances, what moral resources can science and reason summon to their own defense? And on what grounds?

There may be other questions to ask about the limits of secularism. There may be other reasons for beginning to look over the nearest mountains to a vista of a post-secularist age. It seems that is where we are heading. André Malraux once wrote that "the twenty-first century will be religious, or not at all." But I do not believe that the end of the post-secularist age will necessarily be, or even should be, a religious age. It may be something altogether different.

Habermas seems to talk good sense when he writes that in the world after September 11, 2001, secular and religious people in the West need one another if we are to put together all the elements of a sustainable humanistic culture. The long contest between assured secularism and stubbornly confident religion is still undecided. Religion (true and false) is at the moment assuming more powerful dimensions than secularists had long predicted. The most important imperative is for secularists and people of religion to learn mutual respect, to the advantage of both.

Before he became pope, Cardinal Ratzinger examined this rich potential for common ground in his well-publicized debate with Habermas.

In his comments, Ratzinger made three surprising points. First, he argued that religion will always need to curb and to correct some of its own toxic temptations. Secular progress often prompts progress in religious self-understanding.

Second, he claimed, neither contemporary secular reason nor any individual religion adequately understands other powerful cultural currents on earth. Neither has begun to converse with them intelligently. Intercultural relations at this date remain woefully superficial. Christianity and scientific rationalism must "admit de facto that they are accepted only in parts of mankind and are intelligible only in parts of mankind." If we are ever to attain a planetary consensus on the reasonableness of certain moral principles—such as that to which the Western tradition of natural law and nearly all other cultures once aspired—we will need to interact far more deeply than anyone as yet has done with the Indian tradition of karma, the Chinese tradition of the Rule of Heaven, and the Islamic tradition of the will of Allah.

Third, Ratzinger noted, there are certain creative energies and intuitions that Christianity can bring to secular society. Christianity, after all, is by now found in all nations on earth, and it numbers among its baptized members one-third of all people on earth. It is a fount of practical knowledge about other cultures. Meanwhile, the secular, too, is a legitimate regime, with its own special autonomy, rules, and privileges—but also with its own responsibilities and inherent limitations. There can be, is, and ought to be conversation between the religious and the secular; each must be properly distinguished from the other. But when they are incarnated in particular persons, particular practices, and particular institutions, each typically owes much to the other.

Down through the centuries, the Catholic Church has learned much from successive secular cultures. From the East it learned a sense of the great mystery and transcendence of God—a more mystical and contemplative cast of mind. From the ancient Greeks it learned to love reason, proportion, and beauty. From the Romans it learned stoic virtue, universal administration, and a practical sense of law. From the French it learned the upward thrust of the Gothic cathedrals and the brilliance of *idées claires* and rapid wordplay. From the Germans, metaphysics, formidable historical learning, and metahistorical thinking. And from the Anglo-Americans, a dose of common sense and a passion for the religious liberty of the individual conscience.

There is no point in repeating here the lessons that secularist culture, according to Habermas, has learned from Judaism and Christianity—intuitions; habits of mind, heart, and aspiration; new standards of compassion and conscience; and the like. Even without sharing in Christian faith, secularist persons ought in all fairness to give due recognition to their intellectual indebtedness. In a word, pluralism cannot merely mean mutual toleration. Even to say that pluralism means mutual respect, while far closer to the heart of the matter, is not enough. For the parties committed to it, pluralism must also mean learning from each other.

If there is coming a post-secular age, it is not likely to be an age in which all intelligent people set aside their unbelief in Judaism and Christianity, their atheism, or their deep commitment to science and reason. But it will be, or ought to be, an age in which secularists recognize at last that their own claim to universal superiority—the enlightened looming over those still walking in darkness—was premature. Not by pure secularism alone will the future be more fruitful than the immediate past. The times call for a global conversation among a multitude of human beings, for most of whom a sense of the sacred and the transcendent is as important as science and reason.

To be forced to choose between science and religion, or between the ways of reason and the ways of faith, is not an adequate human choice. Better it is to take part in a prolonged, intelligent, and respectful conversation across those outmoded ways of drawing lines.

Epilogue

Religion therefore is only a particular form of hope, and it is as natural to the human heart as hope itself. Only by a kind of aberration of the intellect and with the aid of a sort of moral violence exercised on their own nature do men stray from religious beliefs; an invincible inclination leads them back to them. Disbelief is an accident; faith alone is the permanent state of humanity.

—Alexis de Tocqueville, *Democracy in America*

The main thesis of this book is that atheists and believers in God can and should open civil, reasoned conversations about questions important to each. Who really are we? What may we hope? How ought we to live?

In the face of such questions, both the atheist and the believer stand in similar darkness. The atheist does not see God—but neither does the believer. If there is a God such as Jews and Christians and many deists have held there to be, such a God cannot be reached by eyes, ears, taste, touch, or scent. Not by imagination or memory either. Not directly even by a clear, distinct concept. The only knowledge of God we have through reason, all the ancient thinkers have taught us, is dark—and by the *via negativa,* that is, by reasoning from what God cannot be. Direct empirical knowledge of God could only be of a false god.

We all stand in darkness concerning our deepest questionings. We all share in some way capacities and hungers for the infinite; in the unlimited *eros* of understanding, for instance, that insistent stirring to keep on questioning. Withal, a certain modesty should descend upon us. Believers in God well know, in the night, that what the atheist holds may be true. At least some atheists seem willing to concede that those who believe in God might be correct. Sheer modesty compels us to listen carefully, in the hopes that we might learn.

Ever since the French Revolution, atheist regimes have slain hundreds of thousands of those who believe in God. All throughout history, believers have also, alas, drenched their hands in the blood of other believers, and sometimes atheists. Certainly in recent times, they have regarded atheists as a great threat to civilization and to morals.

The world of human experience is not all that different for the believer in God versus the atheist. Believers and unbelievers alike compare our longing for justice with the cruel absurdities we encounter in everyday life. Often we stand together in the face of the Absurd. If everything is meaningless, injustices are no anomaly. If everything were just, life's absurdities would be fewer. It is simultaneously holding the thirst for justice together with the actual experience of cruel absurdities that precipitates in all of us the sense of the Absurd.

If it were necessary under fire and smoke for the atheist to rescue the believer, or the reverse, each would gladly do so.

Why not, then, set aside our cultures of mutual mistrust and begin to converse like serious human beings? The question of shared human identity is vital. Even if no one of us reaches conclusions exactly like any other, there is much to be learned, one from another.

I have elsewhere tried to work out a conceptual framework whereby all the different kinds and cultures of humans might, eventually, inch toward a tolerably edgy, if precarious, universal conversation. I call this vision *Caritapolis*. It is at one and the same time a large and generous vision, and also a thin and modest one. It is shallow enough for many to wade safely into for quite some ways out from the shore; yet it is deep enough to float the grandest and most extensive vessels of the human spirit.

In this brief inquiry, however, I have taken up a far more modest piece of work. I would ask atheists to put a halt to the "literature of contempt" with which they have tried to exclude believers in God from any serious two-way conversation. I would ask believers in God to recognize in atheists brothers and sisters who sometimes voice an unexpressed part of our own souls. Neither the atheist nor the believer sees God. Both must live in darkness. Both must try to figure out from many clues, gleaned from here and there, who they really are in this vast cosmos, in this tiny arc of the universe, on this spinning blue-green ball, possibly insignificant among the galaxies, asteroids, cold dead planets, and even deader moons.

Who are we?

It would be good to know. In that way, even the darkness in which we work out our lives is unitive. Let us be kind to one another.

Reflections in Westminster Abbey:
Up from Nihilism

This appendix presents a lightly edited version of my Templeton lecture presented on May 4, 1994, in Westminster Abbey. The theme of that lecture—the way out of nihilism—inspired the scholarly effort that eventually led to *No One Sees God*.

The audience was large and distinguished, the occasion formal. I felt, under the high ribs of the vaulted ceiling, a weighty sense of sacred space, within which the history of English-speaking peoples reached back through many centuries.

"There," the rector told me in the small assembly room at the rear of the nave, "is where Henry V lay in state for three days." He pointed directly to where I was standing. Embarrassed, I shuffled my feet away.

To cover my embarrassment, Lady Thatcher said she had flown all night from the United States just to be there for my lecture. That made my embarrassment keener.

Stateliness, antiquity, history. Memories of London during World War II were also on my mind. Here is how I began.

As we draw near the close of the twentieth century, we owe ourselves a reckoning. This century was history's bloodiest. From the revered and mortally threatened Westminster Abbey some fifty years ago, one could hear the long screech of falling bombs. At a time they didn't choose, and in a way they didn't foresee, more than a hundred million persons in Europe found their lives brutally taken from them. An earlier Templeton laureate, Aleksandr Solzhenitsyn, has computed that beyond the war dead, sixty-six million prisoners perished in the Soviet labor camps. Add scores of millions more that died in Asia, Africa, and the other continents since 1900.

Nor is there any guarantee that the twenty-first century will not be bloodier.

And yet the world has drawn four painful lessons from the ashes of our century. First, even under conditions of nihilism, better than cowardice is fidelity to truth. From fidelity to truth, inner liberty is wrested.

Second, the boast of Stalin, Mussolini, and Hitler that dictatorship is more vigorous than "decadent democracy" was empty. It led to concentration camps.

Third, the claim that socialism is morally superior to capitalism, and better for the poor, was also empty. It paved the road to serfdom.

Fourth, vulgar relativism so undermines the culture of liberty that free institutions may not survive the twenty-first century.

The First Lesson: Truth Matters

For three centuries, modernity has been supremely fruitful in its practical discoveries—in its magnificent institutions of political and economic liberty, for example. But it has been spectacularly wrong in its underlying philosophy of life. An age wrong about God is almost certain to be wrong about man.

History, Hegel once remarked, is a butcher's bench. *Homo homini lupus.* "Solitary, poor, nasty, brutish, and short." Many sober inquirers, who saw how prodigally in this century the bodies of individuals have been thrown around like sacks of bones, understandably asserted that God is dead. Consider this alone: Since this foul century began, how many terrorized children have spent long nights, uncomprehendingly, in tears?

And yet, in this night of a century, a first fundamental lesson was drawn from the bowels of nihilism itself: *Truth matters.* Even for those unsure whether there is a God, a truth is different from a lie.

Torturers can twist your mind, even reduce you to a vegetable, but as long as you retain the ability to say "Yes" or "No" as truth alone commands, they cannot own you.

Further, as the prison literature of the twentieth century testifies abundantly (a very large literature, alas), truth is not simply a pragmatic compromise, although torturers try seductively to present it so. "It is such a little thing," they say. "All you have to do is say 'yes,' sign here, and this will all be over. Then you can forget about it. What harm will come of it? We have been in power for seventy years, we will always be in power. Why can't you be pragmatic? Accept reality. It is such a little thing, like swatting a fly. Who will ever know? Just sign and be done with it."

Yet millions have known in such circumstances that their identity as free women and free men was at stake; more exactly, their salvation. Irina Ratushinskaya, Raoul Wallenberg, Andrei Sakharov, Maximilian Kolbe, Vladimir Bukovsky, Václav Havel, Anatoly Sharansky, Pavel Bratinka, Tomas Halik, Mihailo Mihailov, Armando Valladares—let us summon up the witnesses, the endless scroll of honor of our century.

To obey truth is to be free, and in certain extremities nothing is more clear to the tormented mind, nothing more vital to the survival of self-respect, nothing so important to one's sense of remaining a worthy human being—of being no one's cog, part of no one's machine, and resister to death against the kingdom of lies—nothing is so dear as to hold to truth. In fidelity to truth lies human dignity.

There is nothing recondite in this. Simple people have often seen it more clearly than clerks. This is the plain insight that Aleksandr Solzhenitsyn expressed when he wrote in his Nobel address (1970) that one single truth is more powerful than all the weapons in the world, and that, dark as that hour then seemed in the world, with Communism everywhere advancing, truth would prevail against the lie; and that those who clung to truth would overturn tyranny. (He was correct in his prediction. Truth did prevail over arms—we are witnesses to history; it is our obligation to teach this to our children.)

What those learned who suffered in prison in our time—what Dostoyevsky learned in prison in the tsar's time—is that we human beings do not own the truth. Truth is not "merely subjective," not something we make up, or choose, or cut to today's fashions or the morrow's pragmatism—we *obey* the truth. We do not "have" the truth, truth owns us, truth possesses us. Truth is far larger and deeper than we are. Truth leads us where it will. It is not ours for mastering.

And yet, even in prison, truth is a master before whom a free man stands erect. In obeying the evidence of truth, no human being is humiliated—rather, in that way alone ennobled. In obeying truth, the way of liberty is marked out "as a lamp unto our feet." In obeying truth, a man becomes aware of participating in something greater than himself, which measures his inadequacies and weaknesses.

Truth is the light of God within us. For us its humble mode is inquiry, seeking, restlessness. Innermost at the core of us, even as children, is an irrepressible drive to ask questions. That unlimited drive is God's dynamic presence in us, the seed of our dissatisfaction with everything less than infinite.

The Grand Refusal of the modern age to say "yes" to God is based upon a failure both of intellect and of imagination. Modernity's mistake is to have imagined God as if He were different from truth, alien from ourselves, "out there," like a ghostly object far in space, to serve Whom is to lose our own autonomy. Modernity has imagined God to be a ghostly version of the tyrants we have actually seen in the twentieth century.

It took the real tyrants of our time, jackbooted, oily-haired, self-confident, enjoying the torture of innocents, to shatter that false identity. The tyrants may have thought they were like God; it was idiotic to flatter them that God was like them.

Many who resisted the tyrants of our era turned nihilism inside out. In the nothingness they found inner light. Many came to call the light they found there God. The relation some gradually assumed toward this inner light, whose Source, they knew, was not themselves, was that of wordless conversation or communion. They addressed their God in conversation, under the name of Truth. In the twentieth century, prisons and torture chambers have been better places to encounter God than universities.

THE SECOND LESSON: HONESTY AND COURAGE

Until recently, then, modernity was mistaken in its relation to truth, and thus to God and humankind. But even so modernity has, to its great credit, by grant of Providence, made three great institutional discoveries. Modern thinkers first worked out, as neither the ancients nor the medievals did, the practical principles of the threefold free society: free in its polity, free in its economy, and free in the realm of conscience and inquiry. The great modern achievements in these matters have been supremely practical: how to make free institutions work at least tolerably well, and better in most ways than earlier regimes.

However, despite these happy practical gains, modernity tore down the only philosophical foundations that can sustain the free society. The Age of Enlightenment was supposed to do away with sectarian bickering, but it did not. If you stay within your own school of thought, the foundations of the free society may seem secure. Peek outside, however, and you will hear raucous voices shouting. The Age of Enlightenment has failed to secure an intelligent mode of public moral argument that gets beyond the language of the playpen.

Lest we forget: The twentieth century was not only the bloodiest, it was also the most ideological century. Ideology is the atheist's substitute for faith. Lacking faith, our age did not want for warring ideologies. For nine decades of this century, armies not exactly ignorant clashed by night. Beneath the fearful din, two great practical principles of the free society were mortally contested: first, the *political* principle; second, the *economic* principle.

Despite the books and songs of the 1930s—"The End of an Era," "The Lights Are Going Out All over the World," "The Decline of the West"—despite the boast of dictators that "In three weeks England will have her neck wrung like a chicken" ("Some chicken! Some neck!" Churchill commented)—decadent democracies proved they had the will, the audacity, and the stamina to defeat the principle of dictatorship. They defeated it so decisively that today hardly a dictator anywhere in the world, although many (alas) remain, dares to argue that dictatorship is an ideal form of government. Most are left to argue limply that, in the particular case of their own countries, dictatorship is expedient. They lie.

For poor people, the principles of democracy (the rule of law, limited government, checks and balances) are better than dictatorship. Only thus can people enjoy the zone of civil liberty necessary to ensure their dignity and self-command. Democracy is the world's first great practical lesson of our time, learned at fearful cost.

The second great practical lesson of our century is the futility of social-ism as an *economic* principle. For 150 years, the battle over fundamental eco-nomic principles was conducted asymmetrically. Hundreds of books detailed the wonders of socialism as an ideology, passionately dissected the flaws of capitalist practice, and boastfully mapped out the coming transition from cap-italism to socialism. Not one single book existed—when the time finally came—to map out the one necessary transition, from socialism to capitalism. I doubt whether ever in history so many intellectuals were wrong on a mat-ter to which they themselves assigned highest moment, while thinking of themselves as "scientific." The story of how this happened must one day be recounted.

As Pope John Paul II recently pointed out in his encyclical "The Hun-dredth Year," this story began with the intellectuals' devaluation of the hu-man person. No system that devalues the initiative and creativity of every woman and every man, made in the image of their Creator, is fit for human habitation. On the first day that the flag of Russia snapped against the blue sky over the city hall of St. Petersburg, where for seven decades the Red flag had flown, a Russian artist told me: "The next time you want to try an ex-periment like socialism, try it out on animals first—men it hurts too much."

Indeed, once the Iron Curtain was joyfully torn down, and the Great Lie thoroughly unmasked, it became clear that in the heartland of "real existing socialism" the poor were living in third-world conditions; that a large ma-jority of the population was in misery; that both the will to work and eco-nomic creativity had been suffocated in the crib; that economic intelligence had been blinded by the absurd necessity to set arbitrarily the prices of some 22 million commodities and services; that the omnivorous State had almost wholly swallowed civil society; that the society of "comrades" had in fact driven millions of individuals into the most thoroughly privatized, untrust-ing, and alienated inner isolation on earth; that this Culture of the Lie had been hated by scores of millions; and that the soils of vast stretches of the land and the waters of rivers and lakes had been despoiled.

Three great lessons have been learned from our century, then, even if the cost of learning them was fearful beyond measure. First, *truth matters*. Sec-ond, for all its manifest faults, even absurdities, democracy is better for the protection of individuals and minorities than dictatorship. Third, for all its deficiencies, even gaping inadequacies, capitalism is better for the poor than either of its two great rivals, socialism and the third world traditional state. Just watch in which direction the poor of the world invariably migrate. The poor—of whom my family in living memory was one—know better than the intellectuals. They seek opportunity and liberty. They seek systems that allow them to be economically creative, as God made them to be.

From these three lessons, one might derive reasons for hope: Quite pos-sibly—if along that great plain that runs like an arrow eastward from Ger-many through Poland, Ukraine, Belarus, and the Russian steppes, the new experiments in democracy and capitalism succeed—the twenty-first century could be the most prosperous and free in the history of the world.

Perhaps China, too, if it becomes a democracy under the rule of law as it is already becoming capitalist, will bring to its more than one billion citizens unprecedented liberty.

Throughout Latin America, there is a chance that the fertile soil of liberty will yield new fruits of education, creative energy, and prosperity for all.

The twenty-first century could be the single most creative century in history, bringing virtually all the peoples of the world under the cool and healthful shade of liberty. It could be lovely.

Far likelier, alas, is the prospect that the twenty-first century will be like the twentieth: tormented, sanguinary, barbarous.

For there is still, alas, a fourth lesson.

The Ecology of Liberty

During the twentieth century, the free society was fighting for its life. The urgent need to secure the free polity and the free economy blinded most to the *cultural* peril into which liberty has rapidly been falling.

Many sophisticated people love to say that they are cynical, that ours is a cynical age. They flatter themselves: They do not believe nothing; they believe anything. Ours is not an age of unbelief. It is an age of arrogant gullibility. Think how many actually believed the romance of Fascism. Think how many plighted their troth to socialism. Think how many, now today, believe in global warming; think how many believe in a coming ice age—and think how many believe in both! One thing our intellectual betters never lack is passionate belief.

One principle that many ardent souls of our time most passionately disseminate, for example, is vulgar relativism, "nihilism with a happy face." For them, it is certain that there is no truth, only opinion: *my* opinion, *your* opinion. They abandon the defense of intellect. There being no purchase of intellect upon reality, nothing else is left but preference, and will is everything. They retreat to the romance of will.

But this is to give to Mussolini and Hitler posthumously, and casually, what they could not vindicate by the most willful force of arms. It is to miss the first great lesson rescued from the ashes of World War II: Those who surrender the domain of intellect make straight the road of Fascism. Totalitarianism, as Mussolini defined it, is *la feroce volontá*. It is the will to power, unchecked by any regard for truth. To surrender the claims of truth upon humans is to surrender the earth to thugs. It is to make a mockery of those who endured agonies for truth, at the hands of torturers.

Vulgar relativism is an invisible gas, odorless, deadly, that is now polluting every free society on earth. It is a gas that attacks the central nervous system of moral striving. This most perilous threat to the free society today is neither political nor economic. It is the poisonous, corrupting culture of relativism. The people know this, while the intellectuals do not. If our intellectual betters knew this, they would be sounding the alarm.

Freedom cannot grow—it cannot even survive—in every atmosphere or clime. In the wearying journey of human history, free societies have been astonishingly rare. The ecology of liberty is more fragile than the biosphere of earth. Freedom needs clean and healthful habits, sound families, common decencies, and the unafraid respect of one human for another. Freedom needs entire rain forests of little acts of virtue, tangled loyalties, fierce loves, undying commitments. Freedom needs particular institutions and these, in turn, need peoples of particular habits of the heart.

Consider this. There are two types of liberty: one precritical, emotive, whimsical, proper to children; the other critical, sober, deliberate, responsible, and proper to adults. Alexis de Tocqueville called attention to this alternative early in *Democracy in America,* and at Cambridge Lord Acton put it this way: Liberty is not the freedom to do what you wish; it is the freedom to do what you ought. Human beings are the only creatures on earth that do not blindly obey the laws of their nature, by instinct, but are free to choose to obey them with a loving will. Only humans enjoy the liberty to do what we ought to do—or, alas, not to do it.

It is this second kind of liberty—critical, adult liberty—that lies at the living core of the free society. It is the liberty of self-command, a tolerable mastery over one's own passions, bigotry, ignorance, and self-deceit. It is the liberty of self-government in one's own personal life. For how, James Madison once asked, can a people incapable of self-government in private life prove capable of it in public? If they cannot practice self-government over their private passions, how will they practice it over the institutions of the Republic?

Can there be a free society among citizens who habitually lie, who malinger, who constantly cheat, who do not meet their responsibilities, who cannot be counted on, who shirk difficulties, who flout the law—or among subjects who actually prefer to live as serfs or slaves, content in their dependency, so long as they are fed and entertained?

Freedom requires the exercise of conscience; it requires the practice of those virtues that, as Winston Churchill noted in his wartime speeches to the Commons, have long been practiced in these Isles: dutiful stout arms, ready hearts, courage, courtesy, ingenuity, respect for individual choice, a patient regard for hearing evidence on both sides of the story.

During the past hundred years, the question for those who loved liberty was whether, relying on the virtues of our peoples, we could survive the most powerful assaults from without (as in the Battle of Britain, this city nobly did). During the next hundred years, the question for those who love liberty is whether we can survive the most insidious and duplicitous attacks from within, from those who undermine the virtues of our people, doing in advance the work of the Father of Lies. "There is no such thing as truth," they teach even the little ones. "Truth is bondage. Believe what seems right to you. There are as many truths as there are individuals. Follow your feelings. Do as you please. Get in touch with yourself. Do what feels comfortable."

This is how they speak, those who prepare the jails of the twenty-first century. Those who undermine the idea of truth do the work of tyrants.

No doubt, you have heard objection to this warning. It goes like this: "To accept the idea of moral truth is to accept authoritarian control." Pity those who say this! Between moral relativism and political control, there is a third alternative, well known to the common sense of the English-speaking peoples. It is called self-control. We do not want a government that coerces the free consciences of individuals; on the contrary, we want self-governing individuals to restrain immoral government. We want *self*-government, *self*-command, *self*-control.

If a people composed of one hundred million citizens is guarded by one hundred million inner policemen—that is, by one hundred million self-governing consciences—then the number of policemen on its streets may be few. For a society without inner policemen, on the contrary, there aren't enough policemen in the world to make society civil. Self-control is not authoritarianism; it is the alternative to it.

What Must We Do?

"The Revolution," Charles Péguy once wrote, "is moral; or not at all." This is also the law for the free society. It will deepen its moral culture—or it will die. As human lungs need air, so does liberty need virtue. As does this blue-green Planet Earth, so has liberty its own ecology. The deepest and most vital struggles of the twenty-first century will be cultural arguments over the sorts of habits necessary to the preservation of liberty. What are the habits we must teach our young? Which are the habits we must encourage in ourselves, and which discourage? To allow liberty to survive—and, more than that, to make it worth all the blood and tears expended to achieve it—how do we need to live?

With the ample wealth produced by a free economy, with private liberties bestowed abundantly by free polities, are we not now ashamed of the culture we have wrought, its shocking crimes, its loss of virtue, its loss of courtesy, the decline of common decency?

Can all the sufferings of our ancestors on behalf of liberty have been endured for this—that we might be as we now are?

Nihilism builds no cities. Great cultures are built by vaulting aspiration—by the *eros* of truth and love and justice and realism that flung into the sky such arches as this Abbey's.

We must learn again *how* to teach the virtues of the noble Greeks and Romans; the Commandments God entrusted to the Hebrews; the virtues that Jesus introduced into the world—even into secular consciences—such as gentleness, kindness, compassion, and the equality of all in our Father's love. We must celebrate again the heroes, great and humble, who have for centuries exemplified the virtues proper to our individual peoples. We must learn again how to speak of virtue, character, and nobility of soul.

Liberty itself requires unprecedented virtues, rarely seen in simpler and more simply led societies. Special virtues are needed by self-governing peoples: calm, deliberate, dispassionate *reflection*; careful, responsible, consequence-accepting *choice*. In self-government, citizens are sovereigns, and must learn to exercise the virtues of sovereigns.

The free economy, too, demands more virtues than the socialist or third-world traditional economies: It demands active persons, self-starters, women and men of enterprise and risk. It requires the willingness to sacrifice present pleasures for rewards that will be enjoyed primarily by future generations. It requires vision, discovery, invention. Its dynamism is human creativity endowed in us by our Creator, Who made us in His image.

And so, too, the pluralist society calls for higher levels of civility, tolerance, and reasoned public argument than citizens in simpler times ever needed.

It is a constant struggle to maintain free societies in any of their three parts, economic, political, or cultural. Of these three, the cultural struggle, long neglected, is the one on whose outcome the fate of free societies in the twenty-first century will most depend. We will have to learn, once again, how to think about such matters, and how to argue about them publicly, with civility, and also with the moral seriousness of those who know that the survival of liberty depends upon the outcome. The free society is moral, or not at all.

CONCLUSION

No one ever promised us that free societies will endure forever. Indeed, a cold view of history shows that submission to tyranny is the more frequent condition of the human race, and that free societies have been few in number and not often long-lived. Free societies such as our own, which have arisen rather late in the long evolution of the human race, may pass across the darkness of Time like splendid little comets, burn into ashes, disappear.

Yet nothing in the entire universe, vast as it is, is as beautiful as the human person. The human person alone is shaped to the image of God. This God loves humans with a love most powerful. It is this God who draws us, erect and free, toward Himself, this God Who, in Dante's words, is

> *the Love that moves the sun*
> *and all the stars.*

APPENDIX TWO

Favorite "Dark" Biblical Passages

[Beginners] are, in fact, as we have said, like children who
are not influenced by reason, and who act, not from rational
motives, but from inclination. Such persons expend all their
effort in seeking spiritual pleasure and consolation; they
never tire, therefore, of reading books; and they begin, now
one meditation, now another, in their pursuit of this pleasure
which they desire to experience in the things of God. But
God, very justly, wisely and lovingly, denies it to them, for
otherwise this spiritual gluttony and inordinate appetite
would breed innumerable evils. It is, therefore, very fitting
that they should enter into the dark night, whereof we shall
speak, that they may be purged from this childishness.

—Saint John of the Cross, *Dark Night of the Soul*

FROM THE BIBLE

And ye have forgotten the exhortation which speaketh unto you as unto
children, My son, despise not thou the chastening of the Lord, nor faint
when thou art rebuked of him.

For whom the Lord loveth he chasteneth, and scourgeth every son
whom he receiveth. If ye endure chastening, God dealeth with you as
with sons. (HEBREWS 12:5–7, KJV)

Why, O Lord, do you stand aloof? Why hide in times of distress? Proudly
the wicked harass the afflicted, who are caught in the devices the wicked
have contrived . . . The wicked man boasts, "He will not avenge it";
"there is no God," sums up his thoughts . . . Rise, O Lord! O God, lift up
your hand! Forget not the afflicted! Why should the wicked man despise
God, saying in his heart, "He will not avenge it"? You do see, for you behold misery and sorrow, taking them in your hands. (PSALM 10, NAB, 1970)

But if I go to the east, he is not there; or to the west, I cannot perceive him; Where the north enfolds him, I behold him not; by the south he is veiled, and I see him not. (JOB 23:8–9, NAB, 1970)

How long, O Lord, will you utterly forget me? How long will you hide your face from me? How long shall I harbor sorrow in my soul, grief in my heart day after day? How long will my enemy triumph over me? Look, answer me, O Lord, my God. (PSALM 13, NAB, 1970)

Save me, God, for the waters have reached my neck. I have sunk into the mire of the deep, where there is no foothold. I have gone down to the watery depths; the flood overwhelms me. I am weary with crying out; my throat is parched. My eyes have failed, looking for my God. (PSALM 69, NAB, 1991)

Yet when I looked for good, then evil came; when I expected light, then came darkness. (JOB 30:26, NAB, 1970)

Why do the wicked survive, grow old, become mighty in power? Their progeny is secure in their sight; they see before them their kinsfolk and their offspring. (JOB 21:7–8, NAB, 1970)

For who among men is he that can know the counsel of God? or who can think what the will of God is? For the thoughts of mortal men are fearful, and our counsels uncertain. For the corruptible body is a load upon the soul, and the earthly habitation presseth down the mind that museth upon many things.

And hardly do we guess aright at things that are upon earth: and with labour do we find the things that are before us. But the things that are in heaven, who shall search out? And who shall know thy thought, except thou give wisdom, and send thy Holy Spirit from above: And so the ways of them that are upon earth may be corrected. (WISDOM 9:13–18A, DOUAY–RHEIMS, 1899 AMERICAN EDITION)

Let all the earth fear the Lord; let all who dwell in the world revere him. For he spoke, and it was made; he commanded, and it stood forth. The Lord brings to nought the plans of nations; he foils the designs of peoples. But the plan of the Lord stands forever; the design of his heart, through all generations. (PSALM 33, NAB, 1970)

He is God and he does not relent: the helpers of Rahab bow beneath him. How much less shall I give him any answer, or choose out arguments against him! Even though I were right, I could not answer him, but should rather beg for what was due me. (JOB 9:13–15, NAB, 1970)

For He is not a man like myself, that I should answer Him, that we should come together in judgment. (JOB 9:32, NAB, 1970)

The Lord gave and the Lord has taken away; blessed be the name of the Lord! (JOB 1:22, NAB, 1970)

God has given me over to the impious; into the clutches of the wicked he has cast me. I was in peace, but he dislodged me; he seized me by the neck and dashed me to pieces. (JOB 16:11–12, NAB, 1970)

I cry out "Injustice!" I am not heard. I cry out for help, but there is no redress. He has barred my way and I cannot pass; he has veiled my path in darkness; He has stripped me of my glory, and taken the diadem from my brow. (JOB 19:7–10, NAB, 1970)

Your hands have formed me and fashioned me; will you then turn and destroy me? Oh, remember that you fashioned me from clay! Will you then bring me down to dust again? (JOB 10:8, NAB, 1970)

But I cry out to you, LORD; in the morning my prayer comes before you. Why do you reject me, LORD? Why hide your face from me? I am mortally afflicted since youth; lifeless, I suffer your terrible blows. Your wrath has swept over me; your terrors have reduced me to silence. All the day they surge round like a flood; from every side they close in on me. Because of you companions shun me; my only friend is darkness. (PSALM 88, NAB, 1970)

Then his wife said to him, "Are you still holding to your innocence? Curse God and die." But he said to her . . . "We accept good things from God; and should we not accept evil?" Through all this, Job said nothing sinful. (JOB 2:9–10, NAB, 1970)

Hear, O Lord, a just suit; attend to my outcry; hearken to my prayer from lips without deceit. From you let my judgment come; your eyes behold what is right. Though you test my heart, searching it in the night, though you try me with fire, you shall find no malice in me . . . My ravenous enemies beset me . . . Rise, O Lord, confront them and cast them down. (PSALM 17, NAB, 1970)

Have pity on me, O Lord, for I am in distress; with sorrow my eye is consumed; my soul also, and my body . . . For all my foes I am an object of reproach, a laughingstock to my neighbors, and a dread to my friends . . . But my trust is in you, O Lord; I say, "You are my God." In your hands is

my destiny; rescue me from the clutches of my enemies and my persecu-
tors. (PSALM 31, NAB, 1970)

Do me justice, O God, and fight my fight against a faithless people; from
the deceitful and impious man rescue me. For you, O God, are my strength.
Why do you keep me so far away? Why must I go about in mourning,
with the enemy oppressing me? . . . Why are you so downcast, O my soul?
Why do you sigh within me? Hope in God! For I shall again be thanking
him, in the presence of my savior and my God. (PSALM 43, NAB, 1970)

So Pilate, wishing to satisfy the crowd, released Barabbas to them and, after
he had Jesus scourged, handed him over to be crucified. The soldiers led
him away inside the palace, that is, the praetorium, and assembled the
whole cohort. They clothed him in purple and, weaving a crown of
thorns, placed it on him. They began to salute him with, "Hail, King of
the Jews!" and kept striking his head with a reed and spitting upon him.
They knelt before him in homage. And when they had mocked him, they
stripped him of the purple cloak, dressed him in his own clothes, and led
him out to crucify him. They pressed into service a passer-by, Simon, a
Cyrenian, who was coming in from the country, the father of Alexander
and Rufus, to carry his cross.
    They brought him to the place of Golgotha (which is translated Place
of the Skull). They gave him wine drugged with myrrh, but he did not
take it. Then they crucified him and divided his garments by casting lots
for them to see what each should take. (MARK 15:15–24, NAB, 1991)

My God, my God, why have you forsaken me, far from my prayer, from
the words of my cry? . . . All who see me scoff at me; they mock me with
parted lips, they wag their heads: "He relied on the Lord; let Him deliver
him, let Him rescue him, if He loves him." . . . I am like water poured out;
all my bones are racked. My heart has become like wax, melting away
within my bosom . . . many dogs surround me . . . But you, O Lord, be
not far from me; O my help, hasten to aid me . . . (PSALM 22, NAB, 1970)

He was oppressed, and he was afflicted, yet he opened not his mouth: he
is brought as a lamb to the slaughter, and as a sheep before her shearers is
dumb, so he openeth not his mouth.
    He was taken from prison and from judgment: and who shall declare
his generation? for he was cut off out of the land of the living: for the
transgression of my people was he stricken.
    And he made his grave with the wicked, and with the rich in his death;
because he had done no violence, neither was any deceit in his mouth.
Yet it pleased the LORD to bruise him; he hath put him to grief . . .
(ISAIAH 53:7–10, KJV)

Those who were crucified with him also kept abusing him. At noon darkness came over the whole land until three in the afternoon. And at three o'clock Jesus cried out in a loud voice, "Eloi, Eloi, lama sabachthani?" which is translated, "My God, my God, why have you forsaken me?" (MARK 15:32–34, NAB, 1991)

Acknowledgments

The American Enterprise Institute is, in practice, the happiest and most communitarian scholarly environment in the country. For its many experiences of kindness and friendship, it is a wonderful place to work.

I also acknowledge with full gratitude the splendid work of my assistants, Kyle Vander Meulen and Ashley Morrow, and also of Laura Niver, who preceded Ashley in helping me with research. I don't deserve assistants as devoted as these.

AEI has a reputation of offering the best internships in D.C. It is certainly true that we get the best interns. Three times a year, we have a rotation of terrific interns through our office, from various universities around the country. Of particular help on this project were Bryan Prior, Santiago Ramos, Hunter Watts, Mark Scully, and Brendan Dudley. Every one of them will be able to point to passages at which their own enthusiastic findings have appeared in print. In the final stages of proofreading, Amy Vander Vliet and Joshua Ryden helped finish up the common task.

I have been lucky to have as my literary agent Loretta Barrett, one of the great ones (even in her youth a standout among the founding editors of Anchor Books). She is as good a helpful editor at her writers' side as she is as a promoter of their work among publishers.

I need also to thank the editors of several journals for publishing earlier (usually far briefer) versions of some of the chapters herein: especially *National Review, The American Spectator, First Things,* and *Crisis.* They gave me permission not only to republish these essays, but to rework them into a book, while adding many pages to each.

I am grateful also to my beautiful and accomplished wife, Karen, who although enduring a yearlong health crisis in her usual stoical, calm, and sweet way, encouraged and helped me to keep up this work. Daughter Jana again gave me valuable editorial advice at crucial times.

Last but not least, there was an entire army of friends who read earlier drafts and suggested cuts, clarifications, revisions, and additions. What crucial help they extended to me! Let me list at least some of them here: Meghan Gurdon, Peggy Noonan, Kevin Ryan, Joseph Wood (who at a crucial time suggested the present ordering of chapters), Gordon Green, Father Robert Kruse C.S.C., Father Kurt Pritzl O.P., and with many detailed corrections and fresh suggestions, Stephen Barr, James Bowman, and David Gelernter.

Special thanks go to Heather Mac Donald, whose essays opened up this conversation. She also showed much generosity of spirit in looking over an earlier draft of this work in order to approve of my many borrowings from her writings. My esteem for her grew at each point of contact.

The publishers of Richard Dawkins's *The God Delusion* (Houghton Mifflin), Christopher Hitchens's *God Is Not Great* (Hachette Book Group), and Daniel Dennett's *Breaking the Spell* (Viking) also have my gratitude for allowing me to quote brief passages.

Notes

INTRODUCTION

1   **"neither joy, nor love, nor light . . .":** Mother Teresa and Brian
     Kolodiejchuk, *Come Be My Light* (New York: Doubleday, 2007).

8   **classic song to the *Dark Night of the Soul*:** Saint John of the Cross, *Dark
     Night of the Soul,* trans. E. Allison Peers (New York: Image Books, 1959), 33–34.

11   **"To the place where he (well she knew who!) . . .":** I am grateful to
     Rich Lowry of *National Review* for first inviting me to reflect on Mother
     Teresa's newly published letters.

14   **Asked whether he believed in God, Jung replied:** Vivianne Crowley,
     Jung: A Journey of Transformation: Exploring His Life and Experiencing His Ideas
     (Wheaton, Ill.: Quest Books, 2000).

20   **"At the heart of liberty is the right . . .":** Anthony Kennedy writing for
     the majority in *Planned Parenthood of Southeastern Pennsylvania v. Casey,* 505
     U.S. 833 (1992).

22   **I began reflecting on what goes on *inside* the experience of nothing-
     ness:** Further details are available in *The Experience of Nothingness* (Harper &
     Row, 1970; Transaction, 1998), still moseying along in print after all these years.

CHAPTER 1

31   **Despite the fact that an atheist Zeitgeist dominates university cam-
     puses in America:** The results of a Barna poll released in June 2007 show
     that only 25 percent of college-aged respondents considered themselves to
     have "no faith." The results of a Harris poll of October 2006 were roughly
     similar.

32   **Propagated by pop star and scientist alike:** "Religion Does More Harm
     Than Good—Poll," *The Guardian,* December 23, 2006,
     http://www.guardian.co.uk/uk/2006/dec/23/religion.topstories3.

39   **Nothing about the founding of the Vatican Library:** A few years ago,
     the Library of Congress presented a powerful exhibit entitled "Rome Re-
     born: The Vatican Library and Renaissance Culture" (January 8–April 30,
     1993). The exhibition was stunning for its documentation of the new sciences
     that today trace their beginnings to the collections in the Vatican Library,
     where for the first time immense records of earlier observations and experi-
     ments could be efficiently consulted.

45   **the God of the Absurd:** In 1966, when Fr. Raymond J. Nogar, O.P., spe-
     cialist in the philosophy and theology of evolution, called his book *The Lord
     of the Absurd* (Herder and Herder), the title was for me an illumination.

49   **Since just over two billion persons on our planet today are Chris-**

tians: *Encyclopaedia Britannica* counts 2.13 billion. See "Worldwide Adherents of All Religions, Mid-2005," http://www.britannica.com/eb/article-9432620/Worldwide-Adherents-of-All-Religions-Mid-2005.

51 **Never in history have so many Christians been killed:** Dr. Robert Royal, author of *The Catholic Martyrs of the Twentieth Century* (Crossroad, 2000), estimates that one million Christians died for their faith between 1900 and the turn of the millennium under the atheist regimes of the Soviet Union, Nazi Germany, and Communist China, as well as in persecutions during the Mexican Cristiada of 1926–1929 and the Spanish Civil War of 1936–1939. Another twenty to forty million (authors on the subject have arrived at several different estimates) Christians were not put to the test of dying for their faith, but were wiped out as potential subversives.

52 **For individual atheists "of a peculiar character":** A phrase used by George Washington in his "Farewell Address," taken at the time to be an allusion to Thomas Jefferson.

53 **This extremely practical contribution:** "As for me, I doubt that man can ever support a complete religious independence and an entire political freedom at once; and I am brought to think that if he has no faith, he must serve, and if he is free, he must believe." Alexis de Tocqueville, *Democracy in America*, eds. Harvey C. Mansfield and Delba Winthrop (Chicago: University of Chicago Press, 2000), 418–19.

CHAPTER 2

61 **"In Europe, almost all the disorders . . .":** Alexis de Tocqueville, *Democracy in America,* eds. Harvey C. Mansfield and Delba Winthrop (Chicago: University of Chicago Press, 2000), 297.

62 **Moreover, the many stories:** see Denis de Rougemont, *Love in the Western World* (Princeton, N.J.: Princeton University Press, 1983).

62 **Actually, come to think of it, surveys of sexual behavior:** The National Health and Social Life Survey, in a definitive study of American sexual behavior (University of Chicago, 1994), noted that Catholics and conservative Protestants, both men and women, reported being "extremely physically satisfied" with their partner, and "always having an orgasm" in greater number than survey respondents who claimed "no religious affiliation."

62 **The feminist writer Naomi Wolf published a fascinating essay:** Ms. Wolf writes of the damage that casual sex and overabundant access to sexual images do to many modern relationships: men and women accustomed to promiscuity "are lonely together, even when conjoined." More structured mores, she observes, may actually enhance sex lives: "[T]he power and the charge of sex are maintained when there is some sacredness to it." Wolf further notes the impact of sexual norms on marital fidelity and family stability: "An orgasm is one of the greatest reinforcers imaginable. If you associate orgasm with your wife, a kiss, a scent, a body, that is what, over time, will turn you on; if you open your focus to an endless stream of ever-more-transgressive images . . . that is what it will take to turn you on. . . . Many more traditional cultures . . . know that a powerful erotic bond between parents is a key element of a strong family" *(New York Magazine,* October 20, 2003).

63   **"And here is the point . . .":** Christopher Hitchens, *God Is Not Great: How Religion Poisons Everything* (New York: Hachette Books, 2006), 5.

64   **"Thomas Jefferson in old age . . .":** Ibid., 79.

66   **"For the normative self-understanding of modernity . . .":** "Conversation about God and the World," *Time of Transitions* (Cambridge, UK: Polity Press, 2006), 150–51.

67   **From this conception derives the argument for liberty:** In this book I choose many of my concrete historical examples from the years of the American founding, 1770–1825, when our nation enjoyed a fruitful collaboration of the two wings on which the American eagle took flight: commonsense reason and biblical insight.

69   **"It was, of course, a lie . . .":** Hitchens, 271.

69   **"But throughout his life, Einstein . . .":** Walter Isaacson, *Einstein: His Life and Universe* (New York: Simon & Schuster, 2007), 390.

72   **"For much of her life . . .":** Christopher Hitchens, "Prizing Doris Lessing," *Slate,* October 15, 2007.

73   **Hitchens himself is a public protagonist of compassion:** "Solidarity"— this famous labor union and then Communist and Nazi term—became transformed by Lech Walesa's *Solidarnosc,* a movement inspired by Pope John Paul II's declaration of universal brotherly love, girding the world. Hitchens tends to tint his solidarity in political pink.

78   **The first epistle of Saint John insists that this is the only way:** "Beloved, let us love one another: For love is of God, and everyone that loveth is born of God and knoweth God . . . he that loveth not his brother whom he hath seen, how can he love God whom he hath not seen? And this commandment have we from him, That he who loveth God love his brother also" (1 John 4:7–21, KJV).

78   **But a good self-love, loving yourself as God loves you:** The proper name for the habit of exact truthfulness about oneself is *humility.*

CHAPTER 3

98   **Sometimes so great are these changes of perspective:** "Paradigm shift" is a term first used by Thomas Kuhn in his influential 1962 book *The Structure of Scientific Revolutions* to describe a change in basic assumptions within the ruling theory of science. It is in contrast to his idea of normal science. A scientific revolution occurs, according to Kuhn, when scientists encounter anomalies that cannot be explained by the universally accepted paradigm within which scientific progress has thereto been made. The paradigm, in Kuhn's view, is not simply the current theory, but the entire worldview in which it exists, and all of the implications that come with it. There are anomalies for all paradigms, Kuhn maintained, that are brushed away as acceptable levels of error, or simply ignored and not dealt with (a principal argument Kuhn uses to reject Karl Popper's model of falsifiability as the key force involved in scientific change). Rather, according to Kuhn, anomalies have various levels of significance to the practitioners of science at the time.

CHAPTER 4

103   **In coming to my own views:** Bernard Lonergan, *Insight: A Study of Human Understanding* (New York: Longman's, 1957).

109   **The issue here is how we should think about God:** See chapter seven.

·113   **Simply using straight common sense:** Thomas Jefferson, *The Life and Morals of Jesus of Nazareth* (Washington, D.C.: Washington Government Printing Office, 1904), 15.

116   **"everlasting, blissful, supremely intelligent, and paradigmatically excellent":** Anthony A. Long, "Evolution vs. Intelligent Design in Classical Antiquity," November 2006. Doreen B. Townsend Center for the Humanities, http://townsendcenter.berkeley.edu/highlight9.shtml.

119   **"To be responsible agents means . . .":** Stephen M. Barr, personal correspondence with author, October 9, 2007.

122   **"The really more relevant metaphysical point . . .":** Ibid.

124   **"All we know is that the evil . . .":** David Gelernter, personal correspondence with author, October 9, 2007.

126   **"Why do we thank God . . .":** Professor Barr's point calls to mind the television show *Candid Camera*. The show caught up with three women in a supermarket and told them that they were the one-millionth shopper, the first runner-up, and the second runner-up, respectively. The prizes were announced in reverse order. The third-place shopper was excited to learn that she had won an all-expenses-paid weeklong Hawaii vacation, and the second was delighted by her prize, a two-week, all-expenses-paid trip to the Bahamas. Witnessing the others, the contest winner was beside herself in anticipation. When she was told that her grand prize would be a walking tour of Secaucus, New Jersey, she flew into an indignant rage—how unjust it was to award her the least extravagant of the prizes. But there was, of course, no injustice at all—she had won a free gift; no one owed her anything.

128   **"The thinness of the new atheism . . .":** Theodore Dalrymple, "What the New Atheists Don't See," *City Journal*, vol. 17, no. 4, Autumn 2007.

CHAPTER 6

163   **Dennett's third point begins thus:** Daniel C. Dennett, *Breaking the Spell: Religion as a Natural Phenomenon* (New York: Viking Press, 2006), 59–60.

163   **Dennett finds comfort in heartless fate:** Ibid., 243–45.

164   **"Dennett here makes two claims. . . .":** Barr, personal communication, October 9, 2007. For further ideas on this subject, the reader might consult Stephen M. Barr, *Modern Physics and Ancient Faith* (Notre Dame, Ind.: University of Notre Dame, 2007), 76–93.

167   **"properly refer to scientific ideas . . .":** Barr, personal correspondence, October 9, 2007.

168   **Though many students of the humanities:** Ibid.

171   **"And hence it is . . .":** Adam Smith, *Theory of Moral Sentiments,* ed. Dugald Stewart (London: Henry G. Bohn, 1853), 27, 194.

174   **A duty imposed, no less, by Darwinian natural law:** The biologist Vernon L. Kellogg, a Stanford University professor, was sent to Belgium in 1914 to head up the food-for-peace effort, and was assigned by the Germans to live

at German General Headquarters. Kellogg had done graduate biology studies in Germany, and, in fact, some of his professors were now on the General Staff. He was appalled by their frankness in using "biological laws" to justify their harsh treatment of the Belgians:

> That human group which is in the most advanced evolutionary stage as regards internal organization and form of social relationship is best, and should, for the sake of the species, be preserved at the expense of the less advanced, the less effective. It should win in the struggle for existence, and this struggle should occur precisely that the various types may be tested, and the best not only preserved, but put in position to impose its kind of social organization—its *Kultur*—on the others, or, alternatively, to destroy and replace them.

(Vernon L. Kellogg, *Headquarters Nights: A Record of Conversations and Experiences at the Headquarters of the German Army in France and Belgium* [Boston: The Atlantic Monthly Press, 1917], 29–30.)

177 **Beyond this, the number of believers in the world just keeps growing:** See Philip Jenkins, *The New Christendom: The Coming of Global Christianity* (New York: Oxford University Press, 2007).

CHAPTER 7

180 **What is it, then, that makes atheism so unpersuasive:** Alister McGrath, *The Dawkins Delusion?* (Nottingham, UK: IVP Press, 2007), 42–43.

193 **"A text I always turn to . . .":** Personal communication.

195 **Summarizing the work of many others, Aristotle discovered:** See *Metaphysics* XII.vii, 1072b: "For the final cause is some being for whose good an action is done. . . . The final cause, then, being loved, produces motion."

199 **"I fled Him, down the nights and down the days":** Francis Thompson, "The Hound of Heaven," 1907.

204 **Nothing others do coerces me in my response:** Once again I turn to those Americans whose arguments from reason seem to persuade so many—and yet whose fundamental conceptions spring from explicitly biblical propositions, as in the texts that follow.

206 **"Because we hold it for a fundamental . . .":** James Madison, *Memorial and Remonstrance Against Religious Assessments,* 1785, found in Philip B. Kurland and Ralph Lerner, eds., *The Founders' Constitution,* vol. 5 (Chicago: University of Chicago Press, 1987), 82.

208 **With the second president of the United States, John Adams:** See my *The Universal Hunger for Liberty* (New York: Basic Books, 2004), chapter two.

208 **"I will insist that the Hebrews . . .":** John Adams, letter to F. A. Van der Kemp, February 16, 1808.

CHAPTER 8

213 **"[t]he cosmological argument . . .":** Daniel C. Dennett, *Breaking the Spell: Religion as a Natural Phenomenon* (New York: Viking Press, 2006), 242.

222 **"There is no purpose in the universe":** The first in a series of monthly

online symposia conducted by the John Templeton Foundation on "Life's Big Questions." "Does the Universe Have a Purpose?" September 2007.

CHAPTER 9

234 **In the year 2000—such things change—two-thirds of frequent churchgoers:** The National Election Pool Exit Polls, conducted in 2000 by the Voter News Service and in subsequent years by Edison Media Research and Mitofsky International, are the usual source of such data.

236 **John Finnis suggests three different meanings for "secularism":** For greater detail, see Finnis's "Secularism, Law and Public Policy" (lecture, Princeton University for the James Madison Program in American Ideals and Institutions, typescript, October 11, 2003).

236 **Plato was concerned to argue against it:** As the philosopher Alice von Hildebrand observed in an August 2006 letter to *Crisis* magazine:

> In spite of errors and limitations, Plato has made contributions so profoundly true that they cannot age, which entitle him to be called "the preparer of the way to Christ." Let me mention some of them: "When a man honours [an old parent] the heart of the God rejoices, and he is ready to answer their prayers . . ." (*The Laws*, no. 931). God, being good, is not responsible for evil. Plato tells us that God exercises providence over men. His last work, *The Laws*, is replete with ethical insights that clearly open the way to Christianity.

238 **(Few have charted the vicissitudes . . .):** For a look at the changes and pressures racking Europe as the papacy historically experienced them, see Russell Hittinger, "Pope Leo XIII," in John Witte, Jr., and Frank Alexander, eds., *The Teachings of Modern Roman Catholicism on Law, Politics, and Human Nature* (New York: Columbia University Press, 2007).

239 **The worldview of Plato offered a great, beautiful, and radiantly good framework:** Alice von Hildebrand speaks up for Plato, in criticism of my praise of Aristotle in *Crisis:* "[I]t is worth remarking that the fifth century before Christ—the zenith of Athens's artistic greatness—was under the philosophical aegis of Socrates, Plato's teacher. The role of beauty is prominent in Plato's works ('at the sight of beauty, wings grow on the human soul . . .'), for visible beauty is a faint reflection of Beauty itself" (September 2007).

240 **"As any respectable text in European intellectual history relates . . .":** Irving Kristol, "The Future of American Jewry," *Commentary*, vol. 92, no. 2, August 1991, 25.

242 **"Farsighted popes and bishops . . .":** Richard E. Rubenstein, *Aristotle's Children: How Christians, Muslims, and Jews Rediscovered Ancient Wisdom and Illuminated the Dark Ages* (New York: Harcourt, 2003), 9.

243 **Among them originated "the industrial revolution":** Among many sources, consult Jean Gimpel, *The Medieval Machine* (New York: Barnes and Noble Books, 2003).

247 **But it was all too real, and all too secularist:** Camus recounts a letter from a German friend: "The greatness of my country is beyond price. Any-

thing is good that contributes to its greatness. And in a world where everything has lost its meaning, those who, like us young Germans, are lucky enough to find a meaning in the destiny of our nation must sacrifice everything else." (Albert Camus, "First Letter," in *Resistance, Rebellion, and Death,* trans. Justin O'Brien [New York: Alfred A. Knopf, 1961], 5.)

CHAPTER 10

250 **"We have, in recent years . . .":** Irving Kristol, "The Future of American Jewry," *Commentary,* vol. 92, no. 2, August 1991.

252 **"Sacred scriptures and religious traditions":** Virgil Nemoianu, "The Church and the Secular Establishment: A Philosophical Dialog Between Joseph Ratzinger and Jürgen Habermas," *Logos,* vol. 9, no. 2, Spring 2006, 26.

252 **An American expert on Habermas explicates:** Ibid.

253 **This debate with Habermas foreshadowed:** James V. Schall, *The Regensburg Lecture* (South Bend, Ind.: St. Augustine's Press, 2007).

253 **"Ever since the Council of Nicaea . . .":** Jürgen Habermas, "Religion in the Public Sphere," lecture for the Holberg Prize Seminar, November 29, 2005.

254 **"For the normative self-understanding . . .":** Jürgen Habermas, "Conversations About God and the World," *Time of Transitions* (Cambridge, UK: Polity Press, 2006), 150–51. Emphasis added.

255 **The Fall, in this view:** Michael Novak, "Beyond Weber," in Victor Nee and John Swedberg, eds., *On Capitalism* (Palo Alto, Calif.: Stanford University Press, 2007).

255 **Habermas posed another question:** Habermas, "Religion in the Public Sphere."

255 **As Pierre Manent has pointed out:** Pierre Manent, "Christianity and Democracy (Part I)," *A Free Society Reader* (Lanham, Md.: Lexington Books, 2000), 109–15.

257 **"In our public controversies . . .":** Walter Lippmann, *The American Inquisitors: A Commentary on Dayton and Chicago* (New York: Macmillan, 1928), 62–66.

258 **"Some Recently Discovered Incapacities of Secularism":** For all Kristol quotes in this section, see Irving Kristol, "The Future of American Jewry," *Commentary,* August 1991.

259 **It happened to that smart and amiable young friend:** Albert Camus, "First Letter," *Resistance, Rebellion, and Death,* trans. Justin O'Brien (New York: Alfred A. Knopf, 1961), 5.

267 **What will that be?:** For a fuller discussion of this vision, see "Caritapolis" in *The Universal Hunger for Liberty* (New York: Basic Books, 2004), 23–47.

271 **In his comments, Ratzinger:** Nemoianu, "The Church and the Secular Establishment, 30.

EPILOGUE

275   **I call this vision** *Caritapolis:* For a fuller discussion of this vision, see "Cari-tapolis" in *The Universal Hunger for Liberty* (New York: Basic Books, 2004), 23–47.

APPENDIX 2

286   **[Beginners] are, in fact, as we have said:** Saint John of the Cross, *Dark Night of the Soul,* trans. E. Allison Peers (New York: Image Books, 1959).

Index

Lucretius, 157
Lunn, Arnold, 86

Mac Donald, Heather, 31, 80, 129, 160,
    238
  challenges to religion by, 83–84,
    101–2, 113–27
  signals of the divine in, 132–34
MacIntyre, Alasdair, 144, 262–63
Madison, James, 47, 67, 114, 204, 206,
    283
Maimonides, 37, 54
Malraux, André, 271
Man, Paul de, 53
Manent, Pierre, 255
Mansfield, Harvey, 117–18
Marcus Aurelius, 157
Maritain, Jacques, 200
Marx, Karl, 180, 251
Mary, Mother of God, 241–42
Mason, George, 67
Mass, sacrifice of the, 55
Materialistic fallacy, 158–60
Maxwell, James Clerk, 164
McGrath, Alister, 180
Meaninglessness, secularism's inability to
    address, 260
*Memorial and Remonstrance Against Reli-
    gious Assessments* (Madison), 47, 67,
    204
Metaphysics, 104
Metaphysics (Aristotle), 186–87, 240
Michelangelo, 40
Mihailov, Mihailo, 24, 278
Milton, John, 93, 130, 237, 246
Monod, Jacques, 223
Moral decline, 133
Morality
  atheism and, 52–54, 146–47, 161–62
  Darwinism and, 174–75, 296–97n
  evolutionary biology and, 161–62
  God and, 263–64
  Jewish/Christian faith and, 76–77,
    113–14, 261–62
  religion as source of, 132–33
  secularism and, 259–63
  survival of the fittest and, 169–70

Moravia, Alberto, 49
Moroni (angel), 107
Moses, 2, 193
Movement (change) in the universe, ar-
    gument from, 187–90, 226–27
Mozart, W. A., 200
Multiverse v. universe, 164–65, 223
Mussolini, Benito, 51, 282
Myth of Sisyphus, The (Camus), 20, 23

Napoleon, 243
Natural law, 113
Natural reason, 113
Natural selection, 71, 152, 167–69
  as boon to atheism, 152–53
  See also Darwinism; Evolution
Natural theology, 87
Natural things, contingency of, 218–19
Nazism, xix, 51, 52, 247
Nelson, Lord, 60
Newman, John Henry, 35, 43, 86, 145
Newton, Isaac, 59, 67, 164
Nicodemus of Toledo, 240
Nicomachean Ethics (Aristotle), 30, 240
Niebuhr, Reinhold, 86
Nietzsche, Friedrich, xxii, 18, 21, 22,
    88, 164, 247, 251, 254, 259, 260,
    263
Nihilism, xxi, 16, 21–24
  Nietzsche's definition of, 18
  path out of, 277–85
Nogar, Fr. Raymond J., 293n
Nonfalsifiability of theological claims,
    139–40
Nothingness, experience of, 18–25, 218
Novak, C.S.C., Fr. Richard, murder of,
    2–3

Ockham's razor, 138, 148–49, 168–69
O'Connor, Flannery, 35
Origen, 30
Original sin, 254–55
Origins of man and the cosmos, 59–60
Otto, Rudolf, 17

compatibility of sacred and secular, 236–38

meanings of terms "secular" and "secularism," xxiv, 235–36

term invented by Christians, xxiv, 237

Secularism, xxiii–xxiv, 236, 245

agnosticism and, 236

culture of relativism and, 267–69

debts to Jewish/Christian faith, 253–54

demographic problem faced by, 266–67

Enlightenment and, 243–45

evil and, 264

as ideology, 244–46

Islamofascist threat and, 265–66

limitations of, 252–55

meaninglessness and, 260

morality and, 259, 260–61, 262–63

mutual respect between believers and secularists, 37, 55–56, 252–53, 255, 271–73

"neutrality" of secular speech, 257

politics of, 234

science and, 242–43, 245–46

soft and hard versions of, 246–47

"Secularists, What Happened to the Open Mind?" (Krattenmaker), 27

Secularization thesis, 244–45

Self-love, 78

Seneca, 49, 106, 157

Sexuality, 60–63, 79, 294n

Shakespeare, William, 60, 61, 93

Sharansky, Anatoly/Natan, 24, 32–35, 41, 134, 278

Shaw, George Bernard, 69

Silone, Ignazio, 49

Sin, 46–47, 254–55

Slavery, 238

Smith, Adam, 54, 171–72, 203

Smith, Joseph, 107

Socrates, 58–59, 67, 99, 185, 195, 198, 266

Solidarity, 295n

Soloveitchik, Rav Joseph, 60

Solzhenitsyn, Aleksandr, 277, 279

Spinoza, Benedict, 164

Stalin, Joseph, 51

Stark, Rodney, 148

Stoics, 67, 71

Stove, David, 170, 172

Suffering, human, 45, 88–90, 95, 111–16, 123–34, 149–50, 160–61, 165–66, 227–29, 264

of children, 123–25, 278

Suicide, 20

Supreme Court, U.S., 20

Survival of the fittest, 169–70

Sympathy, 171–72

Teresa of Avila, St., 4, 8–9, 10

Teresa of Calcutta, Mother (Agnes Bojaxhiu), 1–2, 4, 10–11, 14, 15, 56, 74

Terrorist attacks of September 2001, xxiii, 233, 252

Thatcher, Margaret, 277

"Theology and Falsification" (Flew), 139–40

Theory of Communicative Action, The (Habermas), 253

Thérèse of Lisieux, St., 3, 4, 9, 10, 13

Thomas Aquinas, St., 30, 50, 54, 86, 94, 106, 235–36, 239, 241, 242

God, concept of, 213–17, 226

Thompson, Judith Jarvis, 260–61

Tillich, Paul, 86

Tocqueville, Alexis de, 53, 61, 266, 274, 283, 294n

Torture, 238

Totalitarianism, 51–52, 179–80, 203–4, 235, 282

Transcendent, sense of the, 129

Trinity, the, 197–98, 227–28

Truth, 262–64, 208, 278–80

reason and, 88, 107–8, 262–64

regulative ideal of, 208–9, 263–64

Truth and falsity of religions, 107–9

Turgenev, Ivan, 21

Tyson, Neil deGrasse, 222

Understanding, 40, 69, 100, 154–55, 160–61, 186, 219–22

drive for, 154–55, 219–20

MICHAEL NOVAK received the Templeton Prize for Progress in Religion (a million-dollar purse awarded at Buckingham Palace) in 1994, and delivered the Templeton Address (see Appendix I) in Westminster Abbey. With Milton Friedman and Vaclav Klaus, he was awarded one year's International Prize by the Institution for World Capitalism. He has also received the Antony Fisher Prize for *The Spirit of Democratic Capitalism,* presented by Margaret Thatcher; the Weber Award for contributions to Catholic Social Thought in Essen, Germany; the Cézanne Medal from the City of Provence; the City of Bratislava (Slovakia) Award; and the Catholic Culture Medal of Bassano del Grappa in Italy (including a case of Grappa labeled in his name). He was presented with the highest civilian award from the Slovak Republic in 1996; and the Masaryk Medal, the highest Czech award, presented by Vaclav Havel of the Czech Republic, in 2000.

Here at home, he received the Boyer Award of the American Enterprise Institute in 1999; and in December 2001 the Gold Medal of The Pennsylvania Society, part of a 100-year line extending from Andrew Carnegie and Andrew Mellon through President Eisenhower, various senators and governors, James Michener, and other Pennsylvanians; and also many other awards.

His writings have appeared in every major Western language, and in Bengali, Korean, and Japanese. His masterpiece, *The Spirit of Democratic Capitalism,* was published underground in Poland in 1984 and in Czechoslovakia in 1990, in Germany, China, and Hungary, and in many editions in Latin America. One reviewer called it "one of those rare books that actually changed the world."

Ambassador Novak also served, with Senate approval, as a member of the Board for International Broadcasting (the private corporation that governed Radio Free Europe/Radio Liberty) from 1984 to 1994. He has served in public roles for every U.S. president (of both parties) since Gerald Ford, and twice as the ambassador of Ronald Reagan to the UN Human Rights Commission (1981, 1982), and to the Bern round of the Helsinki Process (1986).

His teaching career began as a Teaching Fellow at Harvard. From 1965 to 1968 he was Assistant Professor of Humanities at Stanford, where in two out of his three years the senior class voted him one of the two "most influential professors." He later held a tenured chair at Syracuse University, and a visitor's chair at the University of Notre Dame.

His earlier books, *Belief and Unbelief* (1965) and *The Experience of Nothingness* (1970), indicate the centrality in all his work of the question of God.

He is the recipient of twenty-four honorary degrees, at home and abroad.

His website is www.michaelnovak.net.